Other books by David Mas Masumoto

Distant Voices: A Sansei's Journey to Gila River Relocation Center 1982, Inaka Countryside Publications, 1982.

Silent Strength, New Currents International, Tokyo, Japan, 1985.

Home Bound, with Art Cuelho, Seven Buffaloes Press, 1989.

Country Voices

The Oral History of a Japanese American Family Farm Community

by David Mas Masumoto

with illustrations by Tom Uyemaruko

Inaka Countryside Publications
9336 E. Lincoln
Del Rey, Calif 93616

Partially funded by Japanese American
organizations and individuals.

Published by Inaka Countryside Publications
9336 E. Lincoln, Del Rey, California 93616

Illustrations by Tom Uyemaruko
Composition by Glenn Hamamoto
Cover Art by Tom Uyemaruko
Cover camera work by Glenn Nakamichi
First Edition, 1987
Second Printing, 1989
Third Printing, 1995
ISBN 0-9614541-0-5

Library of Congress Cataloging-in-Publication Data

Masumoto, David Mas.
    Country voices.

    Includes index.
    1. Japanese Americans-California-Del Rey-Social life and customs.
2. Del Rey (Calif.)-Social life and customs. 3. Farm life-California-Del
Rey-History-20th century. I. Title.
F869.D29M37 1987   979.4'82   87-3126
ISBN 0-9614541-0-5

Country Voices was supported by community organizations and individuals. We are grateful to the following for their contributions and belief in this book and project:

Bowles Buddhist Church
Christ United Methodist Church of Fresno
Del Rey Japanese Reunion Committee, 1985
Fresno Betsuin Buddhist Temple
Francis Fujihara
George Fujihara
Manabu Fukuda
Kimie Ishimoto
Gary Iwai
Yoshiki Kagawa
Max Kawano
Fonda Kubota
Mr & Mrs Tak Masumoto
Richard Miura
Rev. Roger Morimoto
Aiko & Mary Mukai
Nakamichi Photography
Grace Parker
Sanger Howakai
Selma JACL (Japanese American Citizens League)
Selma Japanese Mission Church
Mr & Mrs H. Taniwa
Mr & Mrs Noboru Togioka
Mae Tsushima
Tulare County JACL
Visalia Buddhist Church
Yoshiharu Yamagiwa
Mrs. T.J. Fujita Yamasaki
George Yokota
Ken Yokota
Also thanks to Tom Uyemaruko and Glenn Hamamoto who believed in this work enough to give the gift of their time and talents.
And a very special thanks to the Fresno JACL (Japanese American Citizens League) whose support provided the impetus to keep this project alive.

Grateful acknowledgement is extended for permission to reprint articles by David Mas Masumoto that originally appeared in the following:
"Brown Rice Sushi", from <u>Western Folklore, Journal of the California Folklore Society</u>, volume XLII, Number 3, April, 1983.
"Cultural Delivery", from Holiday Edition, Pacific Citizen, December, 1985.
"Empty Harvests" (original title "A Farmer's Empty Obsolenscence: Nothing More to Dream") from Los Angeles Times, Editorial Section, August 5, 1985.
"Prisoners of War, The Evacuation of Japanese Americans From Fresno County", from <u>Fresno County In The 20th Century</u>, edited by Charles Clough, Panorama West Books in cooperation with Fresno City and County Historical Society, 1986.
"Snapshot, 1944", from Holiday Supplement, Rafu Shimpo, December, 1979.

Dedicated to my wife
who allows me
to live for my writing
and my family
for their blind faith,
and friends
who cling to a vision
of the world where
values remain important,
and the community
that supports my writing and
believes we can learn and grow
from a sense of history
and shared story.

A special thanks to individuals in the community
who donated their time for interviews
and provided photographs for use.
Their names are numerous
and stories priceless.
Some humbly requested
their names not be mentioned
and a partial listing would not do justice
to the gifts they have given
in the form of memories and stories.

To the members, past and present,
of the Del Rey Japanese American community,
I humbly give thanks.

TABLE OF CONTENTS

Table of Contents

Table of Contents

Table of Contents

Table of Contents

"Hito-
person"

"Farmers, we're like that
Japanese character hito,
you know hito,
written in two strokes,
a long one with the
other hold'n it up.
A farmer can't stand alone,
has to lean against someone.
Today that's the way it is."

A Nisei farmer.

CHAPTER ONE

THE JOURNEY BEGINS: INTRODUCTION

The journey begins here, a journey into the everyday life of a farm community and the ordinary experiences of families that have worked the land for generations.

This is a story of the family during raisin harvest, hauling in their raisin crop each year. Imagine a small, wagon pulled by an old, Ford 8N tractor, a child slowly steers it down the vineyard rows, wooden blocks attached to the tractor clutch so that short legs and little feet could reach the pedals. Along side, brushing the vines, the father stoops over to lift each roll of raisins and toss them to the mother who squats atop the wagon. There, she carefully stacks each roll and gradually builds a pyramid of raisins, two hundred rolls per load, without one falling: each wagon a sculptured work of art, each harvest a family operation.

This is a journey into the voices that populate a farm community, the stories of common folk who speak simple truths about their work and play. Three generations are heard, changing voices from the *Issei*, first generation Japanese to America at the turn of the 19th century, to the *Kibei*, American born Japanese who were sent to Japan for education, to the *Nisei*, second generation and today the *Sansei*, third generation. Each resounds clear and distinct with their own particular rhythms, from the immigrant voices in broken English where actions were louder than words, to the bilingual *Nisei* who live in two worlds with two languages, to the *Sansei* professionals with college education. Yet stories are born when these voices meet, like during the summer of 1942 and an *Nisei* trying to explain relocation and evacuation to perplexed *Issei* parents or the *Sansei* doctor who journeyed home at the request of a *Kibei* parent to help with the drive to a distant Japanese folk medicine healer.

These stories merge into a common history of family and community. Traditions have survived with a resiliency and retained by a people with a

SAN FRANCISCO

• FRESNO

●DEL REY

LOS ANGELES

A *Nisei* once described, "Del Rey is about 20 miles south of Fresno, 200 miles from San Francisco or Los Angeles and 100 years from Japan."

bond to the past, and yet continual change reshapes and redefines actions and meanings.

This is a journey into one family farm community called Del Rey, a small, unincorporated town 15 miles southeast of Fresno, California. The story of Del Rey and her Japanese parallels that of hundreds of other small farm communities, rural outposts that once served as home for thousands of Japanese Americans at one time or another. Most Japanese Americans have the *inaka* (country) in their history, at some time families once worked with the land or were impacted by a spring frost or collapsing produce prices. The farm community remains a vital part of the Japanese American experience, alive with stories of change and struggle and a history that continues to evolve and grow.

This history explores the experiences and emotions of farm families, it is a story of men and women and children with dirt on their hands and mud on their boots and shoes. These stories do not revolve around national politics or events, personal voices carry special meanings unique to these families and their communities. For example, while other histories may document the poverty of the Great Depression, these Japanese weren't phased by it much. As one *Nisei* explained: "We didn't know what the depression was all about, it wasn't anything different than we were living anyway. When you're already poor, there's always depression living with you."

A sense of history lives in these farms, each with private histories, buried memories, and families married to their lands. A farm carries an inherited legacy, the ghosts of the past daily walk through every vineyard and orchard.

In this oral history, the story is told by the people themselves as individual experiences take center stage and history becomes a type of collective drama. In this community of farm families, national affairs had little to do with an early spring frost on delicate vine buds, and university research on weed control was staunchly ignored by some who would always believe the only way to control Johnson grass was by the shovel and lots of sweat. A type of equality is born when private and personal histories are elevated to an importance no less vital than national or international developments. What people perceived as important became the historical reality told here, the daily life of a community is what mattered.

Throughout the generations historical forces have pulled on everyone, families balanced between conservative forces pulling for stability and dynamic forces that pushed for change. Old traditions from Japan were practiced and maintained while at the same time slightly altered and reshaped by new, American ways. A summer *Obon* festival continues throughout the generations, never mind the fact that the *hachimaki* (headbands) with *kanji* (Japanese characters) written on them and worn by little boys is upside down, and a proud but illiterate (in Japanese) *Sansei* mother standing nearby. Tradition is still celebrated.

Del Rey and her Japanese are a case study, symbolically representing a rural people's developments. Tradition becomes a unifying theme, a tradition anchored in Japanese American culture and in a sense of the family and community. Traditions carry a meaning that lies at the heart of the human spirit in this farm community.

Research for this book consisted of dozens of interviews conducted in the last three years in addition to hundreds of conversations heard and noted over a lifetime while I grew up as a member of this community. The majority of conversations did not take place at formal interviews, they often occurred at a community pot luck or picnic, or during a visit with a family friend in between gulps of tea and talk about raisin prices, or at a wedding or funeral and overheard conversations and stories.

Folks here don't say much, they spoke to me partially because my family was part of this community and I too have "come home" to this farm valley. Most of the names have been changed in this book, these are a private people who simply aren't used to nor do they want public exposure. (Once a local farmer was disturbed by the local paper who printed his name in the "police beat" column about his tractor being vandalized. "It wasn't anyone else's damn business" he felt).

This is not a community of storytellers. There is though a silence that, when understood, can clearly convey emotions and feelings. It's a pause, a passing moment in a conversation that is full of meaning. Like the story of a farmer working with his wife, together lifting 120 pound sweat boxes full with raisins, arms moving in tandem and when asked about this physical work, he answers with "I don't know how we managed..." Then a silence follows like a speechless gratitude though the couple's eyes wander but never meet.

The stories I retell and relate convey these spirits and emotions. They combine into a journey into the lives and souls of a people, a journey into a rural past many of our families have at one time or another been a part of, a journey into the human spirit and the webs of our traditions.

SECTION I

COMMUNITY HISTORY

No one knows who were the first Japanese in this valley or even in Del Rey, nor is it important. The history of a community doesn't lie in names and events but rather in processes: the rise and decline of the J-town (Japanese town); the everyday life of surviving through the depression; the evacuation during World War II; and the organizations that were so much a part of the rebuilding of the community following the war.

Through these stories, the history of a community is told, felt and understood. The first pioneer Japanese in the valley wouldn't forgive us if we didn't talk about their "bootlegging of *sake* (Japanese rice whiskey)" because that's what was important. Or the creation of the "U and I Club" for *Sansei*, organized so that these children would "run around with each other and hang around the right kind of kids." These were the important things.

And the pioneer *Issei* wouldn't have minded for they enjoyed their *sake* (whiskey) and would have wanted their grandchildren to associate with the "right type" of kids. They too knew what was important.

CHAPTER 2

SETTLING AND BOOM YEARS

SETTLING

They came for the rich farm lands and work in the fields, and created a Japanese outpost in the American West. They brought with them Japanese culture, not of the elite class but one with the folk ways of their country villages and crowded homes of Japan. They were different yet no different than the Swedes, Germans and Armenians who also collected on this rich patch of farmland and railroad stop. They were the *Issei*, first generation Japanese Americans who came at the end of the 19th century and the beginning of the 20th century to settle and found new homes, families, and communities.

They were exclusively men at first, seeking work and attracted by the stories they had heard. Word had spread that in places like Del Rey you could find good work.

Mr. R. Matsui, an *Issei:* "Japanese, those days... mostly bachelor you know, where they find work, they move to another part of the state. Move all over, not just Fresno, come back summer time to grape picking, fall fruit picking, then they go to asparagus... oh, lots a workers go to Imperial Valley for melon picking.

"Bachelors live in boarding house, some of them too live on ranches and work out there. A few had cars, people stay in boarding house until work begin, then they move to labor camp. Then work kind'a slow down and they move back to boarding house."

Mr. N. Hiramoto, a *Nisei:* "Back in 1906, my dad heard about the railroad, you know, Chinese working the railroad. He thought they might need a maintenance man. So he had enough money to buy fare to San Francisco... he told me he had a $20 gold piece left. He landed at Oakland.

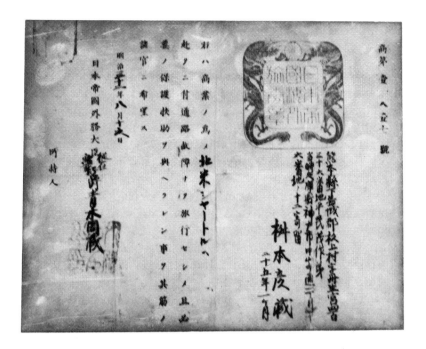

Passport document for Hikazo Masumoto, 1899. He was the second son of a large family from a small farm village outside of Kumamoto, Japan. He came to America in search of a better life and rich future. Along with thousands of other *Issei,* he found a demand for his strong back and quick hands in exchange for low wages.

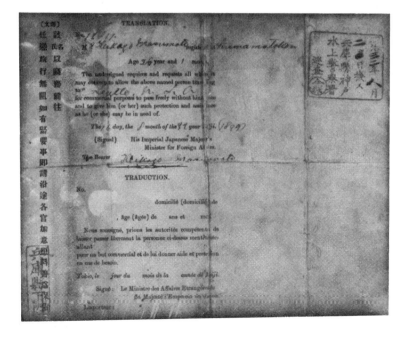

"He had a few relatives in Fowler and he came there and worked there for a year or so, then he bought a boarding house and they keep all the bachelor there. And then this land was for sale, about 40 acres, for sale for a couple thousand...was it $5,000 *kana?* Back in 1913. So he came out and bought that ranch. And then a caucasian came riding around, looking for a job. He stopped and saw my dad working out in the fields and asked, if there were an place with a job.

"My dad said yea, he had heard of a neighbor place. So they both went over there and both of them got a job. Dad was working night time his own place and daytime over there."

Mrs. V. Ishikawa, a *Nisei:* "My parents went from Japan to Hawaii and then first came to Sacramento. I don't know just where, they didn't stay there very long. They heard the valley was good, the San Joaquin Valley and they heard there was this Japanese man and that he had like a labor camp and so they came to the big Del Rey Ranch.

"A Japanese man was the foreman of the camp, he had this labor camp... he had a lot of Japanese people there, young men, lots. Dad worked from there out in the fields.

"Then, I don't know whether he heard it or wherever, or the Japanese foreman told him, but they said that a ranch wanted a Japanese workman and that's how they went to this ranch where we were born and raised."

Mr. Y. Hashimoto, a *Nisei:* "My dad wasn't sure about coming over. He came from a large family, had about 4 boys and 2 sisters in Japan. So there were 6 in the family and he didn't want to go back to Japan. Of course he had a little land, a little wood lot he had bought... in case it's *haiseki* [rejection] in America... the environment of this country got bad and we have to go back. But we never came to that point so I don't know what ever happened to the land..."

But not only was there abundant work in this area, according to an *Issei*, Del Rey also had Tanaka-*san.*

Mr. H. Tanaka was from Kumamoto-*ken*, a southern state in Japan and homeland of many *Issei* immigrants. Like many other regions in Japan, Kumamoto natives strongly identified with each other, even their language and dialect marked them different, separate.

According to the *Issei*, Mr. S. Sakamoto: "Kumamoto people help each other. Kumamoto-*kenjin* [natives of Kumamoto]... they one of your own kind, you trusted them.

"Like a Del Rey, around 1910... Del Rey all Kumamoto people you know. Tanaka-*san*, he have store and it do pretty good, so Kumamoto people hear about it and come. They get good advise from Tanaka-*san*. These people don't know nothing you know, they ask who doing pretty good, someone from Kumamoto-*ken*... and they ask Tanaka-*san* what to do, where to go and where's best farm to work.

"Tanaka-*san* help lot of Kumamoto people. Del Rey, all Kumamoto then, one of the few places all Kumamoto."

A *Nisei*, Mr. P. Hatakeda theorized about Japanese immigration: "You can take all the theories and ideas about immigration and the *Issei* and they'll all neglect one thing: the Japanese immigrants were damn lucky that California agriculture in 1900 was just beginning to take off when they arrived. Not only was there good work but opportunity. You won't read about this luck, it's just too simple of an answer."

Call it luck or part of the economic expansion and exploitation of land owners in the early 20th century, Japanese found that their quick hands and strong backs were in demand. And at the same time Japanese were hungry for work, the rich earth of California appeared ripe for ambition.

Crew bosses. The words seems to carry an evil ring with them but where ever you found farm workers, you found crew bosses. Energetic, driving, both exploiting and enterprising individuals, usually from the same ethnic group or class as the workers, they handled crews of laborers as an intermediary between the farmer and worker. These bosses were miniature godfathers, they took care of the workers and their families, located housing and employment, advised and educated naive immigrants about the ways of California agriculture.

Del Rey had its share of crew bosses, they were the first leaders in the community and managed the labor camps which served as shelter for migrant workers and newly arrived immigrants. Despite meager surroundings and low pay, these camps were the first homes for thousands, their beginnings in America.

Mrs. V. Ishikawa, a *Nisei:* "Not everyone was migrant workers. My dad, he got a job on this ranch, there was this big ranch and they had housing, a building in back. They had this camp and a Japanese man, Mr. Yoshioka, he was the head man. That's how my dad heard there were a lot of Japanese in the valley and Del Rey, because of this camp.

"This Mr. Yoshioka, he was more than a crew boss. He ran the camp, he was famous for this. Those days there were a lot of young people, bachelors. My dad used to tell us some of the women, there they would work on the ranch... to cook and help with the camp, whatever that meant.

"But this one camp, the wife of Mr. Yoshioka, she never had to work, my dad told us. She didn't even have to cook, they even had a cook hired. They were big time, they had so many ranch hands.

"You know, even later, after the war when we came back, there was a lot of this labor camp thing because people who didn't have a ranch or some place to go back to... they landed in different places and these camps. You know, everyone didn't open their arms to Japanese... certain people did and this one farmer, he had a camp and he took in a lot of Japanese families into his labor camp. It was like the Japanese had to start all over."

Mr. M. Awakawa, an *Issei:* "My story's a little different. I was born in Japan and arrived in Seattle with my mother in 1906 and my father came to meet us, he was here five years prior to our arrival. We lived in different places, my mother cooked sometimes. We went up to Redding or down to Fresno to pick grapes and when we finished picking we went back to Sacramento. We followed the crops, just like the Mexicans do today. Many were doing the same thing, but we went as a family. Certain seasonal work was already known so we followed the pattern. Places like Del Rey, 400-500 Japanese came to pick grapes during the season. Some stayed on for the pruning season.

"One man, Mr. Yoshioka, he had a pretty good sized Japanese settlement. During the summer, farmers from Sanger, Parlier, Fowler, Reedley and Selma, all used to come to Del Rey to recruit Japanese laborers."

Land, money, hope, these ingredients combined for the next phase of growth: the sending for wives and the beginning of family.

The Alien Land Laws of 1913 (and later 1924) prevented *Issei* from ownership of property since they were classified as aliens and not allowed to become US citizens. Instead, many *Issei* rented land either on a cash rent or percentage of the crop basis. Some managed to purchase land in the names of others, friends who were US citizens, or by forming a corporation which purchased the land. But the land offered new hope.

As workers saved money and business prospered, women from Japan came to California. Some *Issei* men had returned to Japan and marriages were arranged; others sent for wives via photographs, "picture brides" with

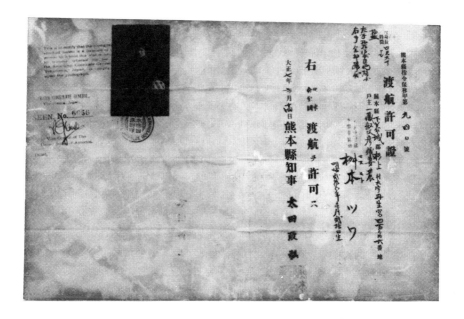

Passport for Tsuwa Masumoto, 1918. Issei women became a second wave of Japanese immigration. Together with their husbands, they began families and communities and founded homes in this new land.

marriages arranged by family. But with the combination of land, wives, and family, new homes were formed.

Mr. R. Matsui, an *Issei:* "Most Japanese, first bachelors mainly, it a big doing when you got a wife. Those days, it cost lots a money to go back to Japan and get a wife you know. That's why a picture bride, save money.

"Oh, some *Issei* women shocked. Some men send somebody else's picture to Japan or a young guy in their picture when he isn't young... those kind of pictures... or the man he working for a *hakujin* [Caucasian] man and take the picture of farmer's big house in the background, pretend a rich, big shot or something.

"Then the wife come along and find just nothing you know. Living in small shack. Some women didn't stay. Oh yea, most women complained... she think he a good looking young man in picture and rich... and just an old man...ah, a mess...."

Mr. G. Sato, a *Nisei:* "I understand my dad used to be a pretty good pool player. This is what I hear from friends. When my mother came over from Japan, they had to land in San Francisco, they had to be quarantined there. My father's friend, the go-between who helped arrange the marriage, they went to meet her and my dad had nothing to do with it. He was playing pool when my mother came in.

"When you think about it, my god, those girls were only 18 or 19. Came across and that open to meet somebody they didn't even know. They had guts."

"Japanese had no way of communicating. *Issei* weren't fluent in their English and they couldn't speak it that well and so they wanted to expand like with their own fruit packing plants or raisin companies... but they couldn't communicate and were being taken by those American packers and that's as far as they got," Mr. A. Inouye, *Nisei.*

English and communication became one of the ingredients for success in America and one of the major barriers. Most Americans who have never lived in a foreign country don't understand the feeling of being without language, stripped of your ability to even ask the simplest question, a loss of identity as you remain isolated and alone. You become dependent, at the mercy of others, trusting and accepting. Removed by two or three generations, *Sansei* have no conception of the silent world the *Issei* endured.

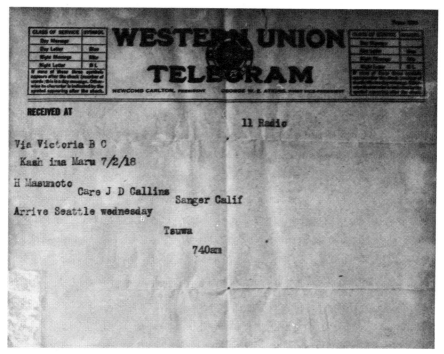

A Western Union Telegram, July 2, 1918 from Tsuwa to Hikazo Masumoto. This was found folded in an old, white handkerchief, tucked away in a corner of a dresser. Tsuwa had sent this telegram from the Kashima Maru, her ship traveling from Yokohama to Seattle. She notified her husband (who was working at the J.D. Callins farm) of her arrival in America on Wednesday. It was unclear which Wednesday she would arrive though, since many Wednesdays would pass before she would be admitted on August 5, 1918.

Mr. G. Sato, a *Nisei:* "Just a few *Issei* people, only a few learned English, not too many talk with *hakujin* [Caucasian] people. Yea, on the farm you got to know your neighbors, be friends, but not talk too much, never know English.

"The Armenians, they like the Japanese I think, not speak lots a English either and they didn't treat us badly. Lots speak only Armenian just like *Issei*, they came about the same time too. But I think they learned a little bit more English than Japanese did and they looked more American and I think it helped them a lot."

Mrs. H. Morimoto, a *Nisei:* "My dad could talk and understand a little bit, my dad did all the talking, he had gradually learned the English language and he could speak, write and read the paper. But my mother couldn't. So my father taught her to write our family name.

"I asked her once, 'How could you learn to write when you can't speak at all?'

"She said, 'I count the hills.' Our name had m's in it and she'd count 1, 2, 3 hills and the m's would turn out OK.

"So she learned to write her name, and she wrote it real nice, it looks like a 1st or 2nd grade handwriting, real clear, legible. By golly, my dad had terrible writing but he showed her how to write and she could sign our report cards and he taught her to sign that much because he said that's shame to just do 'x' for your name when you go to the bank. So he taught her how to write her name."

BOOM YEARS

A "boom town", that's what they called Del Rey in the early 1900's. From a collection of scattered houses and a railroad stop emerged a bustling Japanese town, a gathering of *Issei* and their shops and services. A few boarding houses had opened followed by a few stores, which attracted more Japanese and more building and more stores. *Issei* entrepreneurs cashed in on the swelling population and *Issei* laborers felt comfortable in a place where they could buy some Japanese goods and eat their Japanese food and share company with other Japanese.

Just as California in the early 1900's prospered with expansion and an era of optimism, this one Japanese community, like dozens of other Japanese communities scattered across the rich farmlands of the West, swelled in size and activity. A "boom town" accurately described the settlement, a frenzy of expansion and opportunity, with rising expectations buttressed by an optimism that seemed to have no end.

Mr. K. Sasahara, a *Nisei:* "One time Del Rey became very populated with Japanese. We had about four or five boarding houses; we had three pool halls; two or three chop suey houses. We had a *tofuya* [*tofu* shop] and a *sakanaya* [fish store]. One man came in 1922 I think and even started an auto repair shop.

"One man, a Mr. Matsuda, he was a tiny fellow but aggressive, and he had a lot of people come to town and encouraged people to start businesses like that. He had a store himself.

"We owned a boarding house and a store. My mother used to cook and board people, about 10 or 15 people and at times as many as 25. My mother was a hard worker.

"I delivered for the store, groceries, down to Sanger. I went to Sanger to Kirkman Hill, to Centerville, down to Uchiyama's in the river bottom area was my last stop. One week we took orders and the next week we delivered. I started to do this in 1917, then credit got so bad that we quit delivery service about 1934.

"Father had bought a Ford from Fresno in 1915. We made a box at the back end and delivered out of it. I remember he paid $515 and I had to crank it to get it started. Since Henry Ford had made a commitment in the newspaper that if he sold a million Fords he would give a rebate and we got a check for $50. The price of the car sounds cheap today but wages were 15 cents to 20 cents an hour, 10 cents for a quart of milk and 10 cents for a loaf of bread.

"I took over the business from my dad in 1926 and by then we didn't have the boarding house. You know, my father had bought the property through another man and had built the store himself in 1912. He was quite a capable man. It was a two story frame building and was lighted by kerosene lamps which were suspended from the ceiling. The boarding house had no electricity either until 1913.

"In 1919 a new store made of bricks was built by contractors and I did the electrical wiring myself. The original store was later condemned and demolished. The new store of course still stands.

"Del Rey was noted for its beautiful girls. Some men would ride their bikes from Fresno and Bowles at the end of their work day just to see these beautiful women. There was one woman, she was just like a cover girl on Japanese magazines. She was really very beautiful. Some people even came from San Francisco purposely to see her."

Mr. R. Matsubara, a *Kibei:* "Oh yea, Del Rey was a real big time. Had big Japanese population, all kinds of merchandise can buy, lots of Japanese food. Expensive? Can't say if expensive or not, you know, it was good food.

"They had all kinds of Japanese food, *miso, shoyu, kombu..* had general merchandise too, American clothes, work clothes, *zori* [slippers] too. And lots fish, most from San Pedro I guess.

"The boarding houses nice places, better than labor camps on farms. At boarding house had Japanese food there... like *misoshiru, nishime, musubi...*

"And barber shops, they began later, after people there. Those days, bachelors there, good for business.

"Some bachelors saved money, send to Japanese bank, Saiwa, Shokuginko, Sumitomo *ginko* [bank]. Lots just gambled. It was like being in Japan, you know."

Mrs. T. Masuyama, an *Issei:* "Del Rey was a thriving town in those days with many Japanese stores and Chinese gambling houses. Groups of men, we called them *buranketto* boys - workers who carried blankets with them and went from place to place to work - they'd walk into Del Rey on weekends, cutting across fields instead of waiting for horse and buggy just to come to Del Rey. Oh, Del Rey was famous."

Mr. G. Sato, a *Nisei:* "It was like family, we had a boarding house, my dad took care of a lot of these workers, the *Kibei's.* The young men who came over to work in the summer, out on the farms. In the winter there's no work so they came into town and worked out, pruning and things like that. They go out from our place. So we had a lot of young fellows. And you know how these people are, no wives, no girlfriends, so all they had was that liquor and pool tables.

"We, my dad ran that boarding house. It was pretty good size, we had a big basement, first level and upstairs. A good 20- 25 people would stay there during the winter. Practically all the young fellows. In fact, as I know them then, they were all my brothers you know. I actually called them *Niisan* [brother]. They treated me like one of the family. I knew practically everybody there.

"All the boarding houses had just about the same people every year. The first just came in, just any place to stay during the winter when there wasn't too much work you know. They didn't want to stay out in the farm camps so they came into town. Our place had a bath house in back and a great big dining room where everyone ate. My mom cooked all Japanese food. Just like an old time Japanese hotel."

They called it simply "the Hall", the centerpiece of the Japan Town, a monument to the sense of community held by the *Issei.* They built it in 1919 to house community activities, cultural events, meetings, shows, it served as the heart of a community. The building of the Hall marked the beginning of a new phase: these immigrants were no longer sojourners with simple hopes of quickly earning money and returning to Japan. The Hall symbolized the establishing of a life for these Japanese here in America.

Mr. G. Fujita, a *Nisei:* "My dad helped built the Hall. He had someone design it, and he took the work of contracting it. Things were very reasonable in those days, so the whole thing cost about $2500, for lumber and labor... and it's still there.

"It was used as a Japanese language school. Of course, the Hall was also used for community gatherings. And it was also used for Fresno Japanese Congregational Church Sunday School on Sunday and the Buddhist services every other Sunday."

If the Hall became a symbol of a community, then the tennis courts built adjacent to the Hall a few years later symbolized the outlook on life at that time: a boom town economy and era of good feelings, of new found leisure and recreation, American style.

Today it looks like a huge parking area, weeds growing between the cracks in the cement slab, the surface weathered and chipped over the years. To *Sansei* it was a basketball court, no memory of the tennis net but rather wooden basketball poles and backboards. Few recall it began as a tennis court, the image of the *Issei* playing the game in their whites seemed to contradict the history of the farm workers in the fields and the immigrant's saga of struggle.

Mr. N. Hiramoto, a *Nisei:* "These old timers, they want to play tennis so they built that tennis court. The *Kibei's*, they liked to play a lot too. When I was a kid then, they'd play tennis, every Sunday...oh yea, they were very dressy, in their white outfits, yea, they were pretty good at it.

"I played a couple of times, ahh, who in the heck wants to bounce that ball and chase it. But the *Kibei* played, not just the businessmen but the farm workers too.. oh, they kept playing...just before the split, that argument started about the Christians and Buddhists, they quit playing about then."

Mrs. V. Ishikawa, a *Nisei*: "When we were going to Japanese school, some people who used to know how to play tennis, the teacher's daughter and a few others knew... we used to fool about out there and watch them play. There was a net and kind'a like a wood post on each side. I don't know what happened to them. There was a fence too, completely around it. And there was a pump house where there was a water faucet, it was a little shed and we used to sit in the shade and people played tennis and we watched them play."

"Del Rey [in the 1930's] had 46
families, about 217 people...ranch
owners 12, they owned about 650 acres.
About 320 acres leased... Organizations,
Kyowaikai, Fujinkai, Young Bussei,
Kumamoto Kenjinkai, two Japanese
Schools (Kyowa-gakuen and Del Rey
gakuen). Kyowaikai founded 1917...
main produce of farmers grapes and
peaches..." (From Japanese in America
by S. Murata, published 1940, courtesy
George Shoji)

デ・ル レ ー

概　観

フレスノ市を東に十哩、在留同胞戸数は四十六戸で人員二一七名、土地所有者が十二名で六百五十英畝を有す。歩合耕作三百八十英畝。協和會、婦人會、佛男女青、熊本海外協會布哇支部の四團と協和學園、デルレー學園の二個を有す。協和會は一九一七年創立を凡、當時の會長は平岡篤次郎、幹事は小塚三郎君で、記錄が紛失したので他の幹部員不明。現在は會長間野丹、副幹事近敬瓊、會計村井米大、同監査中川爲八、立及芳太郎、幹事篠原龜吾の八氏で厚園生徒は兩校を合し八十名である。主要農作物は葡萄、桃等である。バイオニアは平岡篤次郎、間野丹、松尾平六。

CHAPTER THREE

GAMBLING, BOOTLEGGING AND THE FIRE

Gambling and Bootlegging

Shiko, bakape, chiha. In these games and others the *Issei* gambled with their wages from hours of work and days of toil in the fields. Why? Possibly for the same reasons folks gamble today, hoping to win, daring to dream, breaking the monotony of a life of poverty or a destiny of impotence.

Mr. T. Morita, a *Nisei:* "Oh, the *Issei* gambled lots, and lost lots a money, even the married ones with family. It was tragic but what the hell, you work so hard, so hard and only wanted a chance to win the big time."

Mr. N. Hiramoto, a *Nisei:* "Them days, a lot of *Issei* were good gamblers, like to gamble. They go pick grapes out there and begin playing *hana* [Japanese card game] at their breaks. They were bachelors and had no initiative. These *Issei* were real drinkers too, boy I tell you. Then they go get into fights and boy they really fought, yelling at each other in Japanese.

"The second and third generations calm, don't fight but the *Issei*... why they fight? No other recreation, that's why, only work, come to the Hall once and a while, talk and gamble... that's about all. Those *Issei* were adventurous. The *Issei* I tell you, couldn't read but knew their cards."

Mr. R. Matsubara, a *Kibei:* "The Chinese dominated the gambling scene, already established with their gambling houses, they opened their doors to the *Issei*.

"Japanese don't own gambling places, they start later. Why Chinese first? They smart people I guess. Games? Mostly Japanese *hanafude* [card games] and the Chinese gambling... saaa... all kinds of games, card game and *bakape, shiko*... The Chinese experts at those games, some even speak *Nihongo* [Japanese]."

Mr. G. Sato, a *Nisei:* "Chinese had those opium dens and *shiko* and all that stuff. You could go in there and I can still remember how it smelled in there, that sweet smell going in there. Later on I found out, 'oh yea, that's opium.'

"Chinese were smart, house always won. My father's friend gambled his whole ranch away, that's why his wife left him and he's all by himself. His whole place... high stakes but he like it. Why the gamble? Nothing else to do. Not many other Japanese around, so Chinese knew just where to get the money. Ohhhh, they were smart."

Mr. H. Kato, a *Kibei* from Los Angeles was a migrant worker in his youth. He easily recalled the memories of gambling, not just any gambling house but the Chinese house.

"Chinese ran those houses in every small town, they'd have some type of store or laundry that became also a gambling house.

"Chinese had a pattern in every town. The first night you go in with your money you'll win 20 dollars. Then the next night you might again win 20 dollars. But then the last night you go in and loose it all, everything they take from you.

"They had all kinds of games, *shiko, bakape, chiha.*

"*Shiko* was a game that began with a pile of beans or small, objects to count, and a pot or container, and a stick. The object was to guess how many beans would remain in the last pile, one to four beans possible.

"The dealer would take a handful of beans, plunk them in the center of the table and cover them with the pot. Bets were made and the counting began. The dealer would take four beans away from the pile in a small handful or push them with his stick. Then he'd take another four and then another four. You won by the number of beans left, one to four. But the dealer was quick and his hands blurred, lots of cheating like taking five beans in one set near the end so that the count made fewer winning bets, the house pocketing the rest.

"Two other games were like American keno, numbers or points were taken out of a larger pool and you won by the winning numbers you had chosen. One was called *bakape* and used a Chinese poem with characters instead of keno numbers. There were about 60 characters in this poem and after a certain amount were crossed out, the one with the most matching ones won.

"Another game was *chiha*, but instead of numbers or characters, they used a chart with the human body... and with pressure points like an

Del Rey Japanese town, 1920's. A backside view of Del Rey's Japanese town showing the housing for families behind their businesses. The wooden buildings were tightly packed together as if they, like the early Japanese immigrants themselves, huddled together for security and comfort. A backside view reveals a sense of community. (Courtesy Ken Swanson)

acupuncture chart. When these points were crossed out, just like in keno, you won the with most matching points you had chosen.

"There were other games...I don't remember them too well, one was like giant dominoes and others were the games like Japanese *hana*. Of course now, don't get me wrong, I didn't gamble much but just heard about all of this..."

About half way between the Hall and Bert Mori's grocery store stood a stately two story brick building. I remember walking by the structure, the ground level store fronts long ago boarded up with plywood and Mexican graffiti spray can painted in distinct lettering of Del Rey Chicanos.

Upstairs a few windows were open and the rooms appeared occupied, a dingy, yellow curtain blew outwards in a spring breeze, dancing in the air and waving to me, beckoning like a siren. Lively Mexican music flooded out of the corner window and I could have sworn I heard the soft, low laugh of a woman, the haunting, erotic one adolescent boys overhear and it stays with them for days.

Years later at a New Year's community pot luck dinner, I discovered the history of that brick building. An old *Kibei* man told me that it used to be the Tokyo Club, the centerpiece of J- town in Del Rey, the local mecca for gambling and prostitution along with some stores and restaurants that served the community, sort of like an *Issei* cultural center of those days.

I tried to imagine the soft giggle of a Japanese prostitute coming out of those upstairs windows or escaping through an ajar door on the ground level, and the lively jeers, laughter and yells of *Issei* farm workers gambling away a week's wages. I could almost smell the hot steam of *udon* [noodles] cooking in the corner restaurant or the pleasant welcome *"irashai"* as I stepped into the corner store for some candy or treat. This was the life of Del Rey's J-town.

Later that evening at the pot luck dinner, a *Nisei* woman told me she used to spend a lot of time upstairs in the Tokyo Club. My eyes widened in shock, her children were my best friends from Sunday School days and I refused to believe her words. Then another woman, a doctor, told me the same. And they both exchanged stories of the dancing and music and their *sensei* [teacher] from San Francisco.

"Sensei?" I gulped.

"Yes, *sensei*," they repeated and asked each other if they remembered any of the dances. "Oh no," they both agreed, "we were too young."

"Young?" I asked.

Young dancers. That's what they were. Upstairs for a few weeks a year, a dance instructor from San Francisco came and brought some Japanese culture to this rural outpost called Del Rey. A group of young country girls would go upstairs and take a few lessons in a large room on one side of the building, the same side that some of the Tokyo Club and other store owners lived with their families. The "ladies quarters" were on the other side of the building, far enough away that a question of morality was never raised. It was all part of the *Issei* pioneer culture.

"The Tokyo Club was... built by four or five Japanese investors, but before the depression," the *Kibei* man explained. "Let's see.. they had another club in Visalia too." But the Del Rey club didn't last too long, raisin prices dropped, bachelor laborers moved away and they lost business. "They just close up after three or four years, things going bad."

Eventually I learned the building got sold and along with the rest of the the Japanese boom town of Del Rey, businesses folded. Yet for a while, the Tokyo Club was the cultural and community center for the local Japanese.

It's hard for us today to think of prohibition and bootlegging. Alcohol permeates our world and it's difficult to imagine one without it. From advertising to mothers against drunk drivers, booze is in the news.

It's even harder to think of the *Issei*, the hard working *Issei*, even affected by prohibition, our image of them purified by time and an inherited legacy.

But prohibition was real and alcohol illegal but that didn't stop a nation nor the *Issei* from drinking their favorite booze. And of course, for the *Issei* that drink had to be *sake*.

Mr. R. Matsubara, a *Kibei*: "No, my store didn't make much money, the *mizumise*... but... ah... I don't know if I should tell you this or not... Ahhh... *kinshin ga atta na* [those dry years]. Bootleggin' you know na.

"My uncle, he help Murata Chop Suey, he the main character you know. They make it in the country someplace and bring it in town and sell. That's how we really make a money those days."

Mr. G. Sato, a *Nisei*: "My parents ran a boarding house and bootleggin' operation. They made *sake*... many a time I went to sleep with a gallon jug in my baby crib.

"Oh everyone knew what was going on, more of a matter of who got found and who didn't get found. My dad got caught plenty of times but he knew the judge. Dad was one of the fellows that was educated. He went to school here and learned to speak fairly fluent English. He'd tell the Judge, 'OK, put me in jail but you watch out for my family.'

"So the Judge says, 'OK... then you just go home and stay out of trouble.'

"And my Dad would go home and get the *sake* working again. Practically all the Japanese had their own still."

THE FIRE

There comes a time when it seems all the forces of history come together and explode, forever altering the course of development of a community. No one remembers the exact date or year, sometime in the mid 1920's. They just call it "the fire" that swept through Del Rey's J-town, destroying half of the businesses and boarding houses and marking a turning point in history for this community. It had to be spectacular as a city block was consumed in a glorious blaze, an inferno that engulfed people's dreams and left only charred remains the next morning.

Mr. N. Hiramoto, a *Nisei:* "The whole block was burnt, the year was nineteen twenty..uh...three *kana?* Sort of around there. It started around midnight, eleven o'clock. The railroad track engineer, he saw that fire coming up, he blew the whistle and woke up everybody. It was around April or May *kana?* Nobody died but all wiped out."

Mr. R. Matsubara, a *Kibei:* "Yea, about 1927 maybe? That day a windy day you know, fire at nighttime. Everybody sleeping, some men usually play cards too late, so fire had to be late, maybe early morning, everybody sleeping.

"Where started? You know all town have boardwalk, you know, like sidewalk. All wood... like front of boarding house. Maybe there kana? There fire started, in front of boarding house. Some one set fire, against the building I guess. Some *hakujin* [Caucasian]... that's what we figure, but nobody saw it. You know, there were other little fires before this big one, year or two before. First fires started but firemen put water and stop it. Arson you know...

"Some problem, *hakujin* and Japanese didn't get along too well. No fights but Japanese were lot of people but they don't go to *hakujin* stores. Lot of Japanese bachelors knew Japanese but they can't speak English you know. Business all here in Japan town. Those days Japanese town boom town you know and *hakujin* town just dead. Yea, not much business you know."

Mr. G. Sato, a *Nisei:* "My folk's boarding house went completely, they lost everything. We were on vacation when it happened, down in L.A. We came back and there was nothing left... the only thing left was dad had a great big safe. That's all I remember, I was 9 years old. My folks didn't say anything. Nothing, just one of those things. Typical Japanese... nothing you can do about it."

Half of J-town was destroyed, most of the boarding houses gone. With no places to live, these laborers left Del Rey, some went to other towns, others left to find shelter on the farms where they worked. With the loss of some businesses to draw customers, the rest of J-town gradually declined and closed its doors. The height of business development had been reached, the fire a turning point forever.

There always seems to be an eternal opportunist that stands out amid disaster, something that appears to be good that emerges out of the bad, a simple, innocent action following a calamity.

Mr. G. Fujita, a *Nisei*, explained how the great fire provided him and lots of other kids with a new adventure and opportunity: "That fire must have been in spring, there wasn't no rain. When we went there it was still smoldering. Not a cloud, a bright day.

"Del Rey was a gambling joint, the whole place had underground trenches all the way through. If they had a raid on this gambling house, they'd move to another house through these tunnels. You could never catch them, those Chinese smart.

"I knew about these tunnels because right after the fire we were in there trying to scrape up the pennies and nickels and dimes. We were picking them up. We went there every day to look for money, burnt money too, all in there. We found quite a bit.

"They didn't bury those tunnels for a long time, they had it open. My kids even remember it when we'd pass by."

CHAPTER 4

THE DEPRESSION AND EVERYDAY
LIFE CONTINUES

"Trying To Stand On Our Own Feet"

They called it hard times, the Great Depression, or to some the time when the rest of America "came down to our level and began to know hunger," as one *Nisei* farmer described.

For the farmer, the stubborn and hard working individual, the Depression was a time you simply "tried to stand on your own two feet,- yet the world seemed to keep knocking you down." Bad weather, poor market prices, no future hope, you gave up trying to get ahead and simply hoped to just keep standing.

But despite the hardship and struggle, life continued, families grew and community became even more important. "Family and community, it was about all folks had," a veteran of that era explained.

The era had begun with a blaze, depressed raisin prices and ended with World War II and evacuation. And in between was simply more "hard times."

Mr. R. Matsubara, a *Kibei:* "After the fire we just folded up, closed the store. The town started to die out you know. They left, no, not right away but most everybody left...some to farm, some to other towns... others back to Japan. Whole town went away."

Mr. N. Hiramoto, a *Nisei:* "Dad said about the depression... if we were in Japan we'd have this everyday, so don't worry about it. So they don't worry about it. We poor to begin with so when we came to it, just don't worry about it."

Mrs. V. Ishikawa, a *Nisei:* "We grew up in the depression, it was sad, especially too because we didn't have family around. Like Thanksgiving, those families would have, you know how Thanksgiving is, everyone come to grandma's for dinner. And here my mother would roast two little chickens, we didn't have turkey, it was just my sister, my brother and folks. We had no aunts or uncles or nothing at that time.

"But my folks never complained, they tried to be cheerful and naturally we did too. Supposedly we had a Thanksgiving... and we always had Christmas tree too...I don't know why we had a tree, we were always Buddhist, maybe my folks just wanted us to have something at Christmas."

Mr. G. Fujita, a *Nisei:* "My father had to borrow money to keep going. It was hard for us... even to get shoes to go to school. I remember that.

"I don't remember dad telling us this was the Depression. But I remember picking trays for raisins and it was only one cent each. We pick a hundred trays and get only one dollar, can you imagine? It was really rough in those days. But dad still made us go to school no matter what."

Food became a symbol of the Depression. Not that the Japanese Americans of Del Rey didn't have good food, being a farmer during such lean times had its advantages- you always had a garden and some chickens or animals. But food became a true metaphor of "hard times."

Japanese tradition reveres food almost as a sacred element, and it's not just the food but how it's presented too, as if something more is being expressed and said. The *Issei* had a language barrier with their children but not when it came to food. That's how many found out about the Depression, via food.

Mrs. V. Ishikawa, a *Nisei:* "My mother sat us down, before we used to get a lot of bologna and salami sandwiches and all of a sudden my mother sat us down and said, 'No more meat sandwiches.'

"I remember asking her, 'Why?'

"She just said, 'You're going to have peanut butter and jelly sandwiches. There's just no money. We just can't buy any meat.'

"And that was all that was said to me, that's all I remember about the beginning of the Depression. But I didn't feel it any other way, my folks didn't seem to deprive us, you know, they got us our food, they didn't seem to skimp otherwise. We didn't eat like these days, it's not meat and steak and chops, it wasn't like that. It was always *okazu* [stir fried vegetables] with rice... without meat of course."

Mrs. D. Murashima, a *Nisei:* "We always seemed to have peanut butter everyday. We couldn't understand... that was all we had. My folks talked a little about the Depression, but when you're a kid, you don't know what Depression is. We just didn't know why we have to eat peanut butter bread everyday. And no waxed paper and instead, wrapped up in newspaper, so naturally it gets hard.

"Those were hard days. Except we didn't know it was hard, nothing else phased us much. The only thing that was hard were those peanut butter sandwiches... wrapped in old newspaper."

The headline read "Japanese Woman Takes Own Life."

The Depression had just begun and hard times crushed many souls. Suicides were common and with bleak news from other parts of the nation and world or from other family members, the future turned dark and hope clouded. According to the paper, this *Issei* woman had just received two letters from Japan relaying tragic news. The story read: "Woman's mind was unbalanced by the news of the death in Japan of her father and two sisters."

The husband and nephew of the *Issei* woman had worried about her melancholy state and watched her closely. But "on Friday morning she arose with her husband at 5:00 and shortly after left the house. When she failed to return her husband and nephew went in search of her and found her dead in an outbuilding.

"She had taken a short piece of cord, doubled it over a projecting piece of timber, about four feet from the floor, to form a loop and sat down, allowing the cord to strangle her to death. Her feet were apparently on the floor at the time and a slight effort on her part would have released the pressure of the cord.

"So great was the Japanese woman's desire for death that she chose to endure the agony of slow strangulation rather than make the slight effort which would have meant life to her even after she had embarked on her suicide venture.

"Funeral services were conducted at the Japanese hall, Del Rey."

EVERYDAY LIFE CONTINUES

We tend to think about the Depression in a depressed way. It has to do with time, memories begin to lie a little, the hard times become harder, the good times sweeter, and they all fit into nice stories for families to pass them down to the next generation or to anyone who wants to be reminded or is willing to listen. Part of an ancestor worship we tend to perpetuate.

But if you manage to make it through the first five minutes of truly depressing stories of hardship, the conversations about the everyday life begins to slip out and a different type of spiritual strength is unveiled. People coped only as they could and Japanese Americans "still had to have their rice" or "came into town for an occasional *samurai* movie" or splurged for that once-in-a-lifetime trip to the hot springs of Porterville that "turned out to be so good and reminded everyone of Japan so much it became an annual vacation" no matter how tough life was. Besides Porterville was within reach and a return to Japan was not.

Mrs. V. Ishikawa, a *Nisei:* "Rice and Japanese food was not hard to get. Where there was a demand the businessmen stepped in to fill the need and make a few dollars or cents in those hard times.

"We always still had Japanese food, no matter how rough things got. There used to be a grocery peddler, a Japanese store in Fresno, it was called Arata and Co. and they would have a truck go around to all the country. I can't remember if they came once a month or once a week... but they used to come around... And I remember the truck and everything and he'd open it up and they had all these dried stuff and they had *tsukemono* [pickled foods] and they had the rice and maybe *kamaboko* [processed fish].

"We used to sometimes go to town and the store... but my mother and father always worked on the ranch so I guess they liked it, the peddler coming. They welcomed that truck coming around, save time going shopping and they could buy most food that way."

Mrs. D. Murashima, a *Nisei:* "My folks would go to town and buy their rice for the whole year, buy the new crop when it comes out. The crop comes out in the fall, and you buy rice for the whole year, then you wouldn't have to buy any for the rest of the year. We used to get six or seven hundred pounds, when you have the money in the fall after harvests you buy it. The rice was there and of course the money is there too."

The couple sat at the kitchen table, talking about the Great Depression and food. "Food was all we had," the 60 year old *Nisei* husband began. "But there's something else we remember a lot, something that went with the food. See... we had a box, made out of screen and gunny sack..."

"Ah yes... the coolers. That's what we called them, the refrigerator of the Depression," she injected.

"And they," he continued, "had water dripping down from the top on the outside."

"That's right," she added in the background, nodding her head.

"Just like the swamp cooler but no motor or fan."

"No, nothing like that," she added.

"It just came from the top and dripped down."

"It kept the gunny sack all wet," she began. "The framework was all gunnysack and they made a door and they had a hinge and they had shelves in there and they could keep stuff in there."

"Yea, so it was pretty cool in there," he added.

The wife quickly turned to her husband and said, "And the weather was cooler those days, it was." He looked at her and his face contorted into a frown. "It was," she asserted.

"Awwww," he said, "it was hotter in those days."

"But how could food keep?" she asked, "just because a gunny sack?"

"No, no," he said, "used to have a ice box too you know."

"Oh, people had both?"

"Not everyone," he answered.

"Now I remember, the Yanagi's, just had the cooler," she said and then grinned with a new realization. "So that's why that man used to go to town everyday. He used to go shopping everyday. I could never understand... see he was renting and could do that... but I really marveled at it because he used to go everyday to town and my dad was just a laborer and had to work and could never go to the grocery store in the middle of the day. And I used to think how great because when Mr. Yanagi would come back he'd bring us Popsicle or something and I'd be waiting for him."

"The cooler was just a wooden frame," the husband said, "with a screen and gunny sack around that."

"Yea, I forgot about those coolers. Well..." she said and then pointed a finger to her husband, "well, he's a year older and would remember those things."

"But the fancier ones were made out of cement," he continued. "They were round, circular and still dripped water. They were nice."

She kept nodding her head, lost in memories of coolers and ice boxes.

An economic depression never did nor never will stop romance and courting or matchmaking. *Baishakunin* is the Japanese term for matchmaker, the go-between, that traditional, crucial link between a young man and young woman and their courting and possible marriage. There didn't seem to be a lot of rules about what exactly the *baishakunin* did, the role they played. It was more like a tradition and they provided some advice if needed. Despite the Depression, courting and marriages still flourished.

Mrs. F. Matsubara, a *Nisei:* "We already knew each other before. But in those days, everyone had a *baishakunin.* For my husband, it was Mr. and Mrs. Yoneda and for me we had Mr. and Mrs. Masuda.

"We already knew each other so they just put their names in... and if there was going to be any trouble, they would talk it over and talk with us. That's what the *baishakunin* is for."

Mrs. F. Suzuki, a *Nisei:* "*Baishakunin?* They used a lot before the war. Like my sister, she was going around already with George, and they decided to get married but wanted to do it properly, Japanese style. They told dad and he said, 'Oh, we better get a *baishakunin.*' And see, they had already decided it.

"So they asked someone, a family friend, to stand by them. They were really cute people, the *baishakunin.* The man said to my sister, 'My gosh, you got everything planned and all cut and dry. You don't need *baishakunin.*

"They sort of laughed, it really wasn't *baishakunin* but things were changing fast. Just a few years before another couple, they were married with the traditional *baishakunin* who got them together. But after the war, I don't know anyone... the only ones were those who got their wife from Japan, prearranged. Those are the only ones now."

Mr. H. Maruyama, a *Nisei:* "I knew her parents and went to talk with them. There some trouble because my parent's didn't want any religion, you know. She Buddhist and I like to do Buddhist ceremony but my parents against it so we cut it out and went to the judge.

"The *baishakunin* went with us, make it official as witness you know, when we get the license. We got married there in the judge's office but we did in Japanese style with *san, san, ku* [the drinking of *sake*].

"Later on we have reception, the next day, like ordinary reception with people help prepare food and some Japanese singing, same like now. She had same wedding clothes like American, stay quiet at reception you know, act really shy."

Mrs. D. Murashima, a *Nisei:* "When I got married the folks invited who they wanted. We were married in Fresno *Betsuin* and family friends came, mostly only men that were invited, that's how obedient we were.

"We had a traditional ceremony, I wore white with bridesmaids and groomsmen and 'Here Comes the Bride' song.

"I remember the reception, we all went out to eat, Chinese place I think. And I remember the *baishakunin* telling me, 'don't eat the food, just sit quietly and smile.'

"The fathers and friends gave speeches but I tried to keep quiet and not hungry. After the reception we finally got to go out and eat something."

If you talk to a lot of Japanese Americans, many don't have a lot to say about their neighbors, the non-Japanese community. It's not as if the Japanese of Del Rey lived in a vacuum, but neither did they "melt" into the greater Del Rey community. "The Japanese? They like to keep to themselves" is the description overheard.

But there's the story about Mrs. Young, the old lady who owned 40 acres of grapes and hired the Saito family to take care of the place. She must have been 60 or 70 and came by to visit the Saito family every once and a while, which created a peculiar situation since the *Issei* Saito couple spoke very little English and Mrs. Young spoke no Japanese and the only ones who could translate were trained to be quiet and respectful. So the children just watched and whispered between themselves.

The story goes that old Mrs. Young would knock on the back door of the Saito's little shack and be invited in to sit at the kitchen table. Of course Mrs. Saito would offer something to eat and drink and about the third or fourth time a little homemade wine was offered and finally accepted.

From then on a lot more was understood and with each periodic visit, Mrs. Young sat at the kitchen table, sipped the homemade wine and sighed, 'hmmmmm.' Then she'd tip her glass to slurp the last drop, smack her lips and quickly rise and proclaim 'nice day' to the staring Saito family.

They'd all stand too, sort of bow (by the tenth visit, they realized Mrs. Young didn't understand how to bow but they couldn't help but do a little bow anyway, a reflex) and open the door for her to leave. After all, she was the owner and boss.

On another ranch, the Misawa family rented a farm from "farmer Jones" or "Jones-eee" as they called him. The Jones', a retired older couple lived with an unmarried daughter, a school teacher. Their house was next to the Misawa's tenant house. The school teacher, Miss Jones "treated everyone real well, she had what they called a good heart," as the Misawa family described.

One summer she invited the Misawa kids to dinner and was shocked to discover how awkward they were at etiquette and had a lot of trouble with their forks and knives. Her school teacher ways got the better of her and she set out to educate these children. An intensive short course on manners and use of eating utensils began and she taught these children how to be polite.

Apparently it worked well and they remained renters all the way up to the war. Of course about all the children recall about their "etiquette lessons" were the good meals they got "in the big house."

Del Rey had one incident that stood out, kidnappers had abducted two boys on their way to school sometime in the mid 1930's. A scare swept through the community and at the grammar school an assembly was held and warnings given and parents were urged to pick-up their children from the school grounds.

Most Japanese parents though didn't hear about it until their kids walked home as usual but it didn't matter much since few Japanese had cars and the majority always were out in the fields anyway.

It turned out that only one boy was nabbed, the other who was a *Nisei* kid wouldn't get in the car with the stranger. The kidnapped boy eventually escaped a few miles down the road when his abductors stopped for gas. Since the child felt this was a good excuse to play hooky, he decided not to go to school and played for the rest of the day.

For many, the community-wide event of the year in Del Rey was the Legion Fair. A little like a small country fair, the annual event was held in September at the American Legion Hall in Del Rey. They had a small merry-go-round of their own which attracted hundreds of excited, frenzied children. And there were baking contests and produce displays.

Many of the *Nisei* children knew of this grand event and since this was held during the raisin harvest, they would "pick like hell in order to finish early enough to go to the fair."

But the Del Rey Japanese left their mark on this event, year after year they won awards in the produce display contest and were the odds-on favorite to win the *"azuki"* bean category, in that they had a monopoly.

The Depression had affected every aspect of life. When money was scarce, all anyone could afford were a few social outings a year and the memories of them had to last. People relived the excitement and entertainment over and over, stretching it out over months, truly getting their money's worth. The Del Rey Hall soon established itself as a cultural and social center for the community, home to plays and movies and recreation.

The Shibai, circa 1920's-30's. The Shibai was a Japanese play or skit. Actors performed for large audiences in the Del Rey Japanese Hall. The costumes and props were elaborate and detailed, often imported from Japan, creating an interesting contrast with President Washington's and Lincoln's portraits. (Courtesy Virginia Ichihana)

Mrs. F. Fujita, a *Nisei:* "We always had parties at the Hall, not many families could get together on their own. We always celebrated the emperor's birthday, we had a saluting the Japanese flag and all that, all before the war. At the Hall they'd have a big program, all get together, wear suits and tuxedo and big get together.

"There at the Hall we had like a god... Japan god not like the Christian God, a different god. They'd have... it's not exactly like a shrine but similar... built and we pay homage to the god and they have the emperor too... all like a *Shinto* [Japanese belief] type. After the war it all went away. I remember they had a big one in Fresno too, a party for the emperor... was it at the old memorial hall?"

Mr. G. Matsubara, a *Kibei:* "Singers came around too, from San Francisco, to give a show at the Hall, called *Naniwa Bushi*, I don't know what you call that in English. They sing, not just folk songs but older time songs. Sometimes lots people, sometimes not too many. See Del Rey was the biggest hall around here, people from Sanger, Parlier, Selma and Fowler, they used to all come to Del Rey whenever there was anything."

The Shibai brought entertainment and culture to the rural community. During the Depression, social outings were few... people relived the excitement of the Shibai over and over, the Hall becoming a social and cultural center for the community.

Mr. G. Sato, a *Nisei:* "Oh they had shows at the Hall. The *Byakudokai* club put on these shows, sort of like plays. I remember Henry Hiramoto, I can still remember, he was up there in a *samurai* armor and standing there, I can picture him right now. They really put on some show."

Mr. R. Matsui, an *Issei:* "Movies, at the Hall... yea, used to come around. They not talkie but like a man doing all the talking... an announcer. He read what going on, explain. No change his voice for women but doing all the talking. He came around, like a tour, one town to another, same movie. He sponsor himself and make money that way."

Mrs. V. Ishikawa, a *Nisei:* "We never went to the theater, other than the Japanese sword thing which we didn't understand because no subtitle or nothing in those days. Was there voice? There must have been but I never understood.

"I sat with my friends, I had Japanese school friends so we usually sat together, just socialize. We just went, sometimes the film cut, you know the ribbon break and I loved it because the lights go on and they sold stuff to eat. That's when they'd break and we could visit. But otherwise the old folks kept going, 'shhhh, shhhhh' to us."

Mrs. F. Suzuki, a *Nisei:* "There wasn't a lot of doing those times, just used to have movies at the Hall. There was a Japanese bachelor, he fooled around with a camera and movies, he was kind'a hep on that kind of stuff. He ran the projection machine.

"Later on a traveling man, go town to town and show these *samurai* movies on weekends. That was his business. He gave himself a name too. Folks sponsor the movie too, sort of like a benefit.

"Everybody gave donation to see the movie and they write it all on a piece of paper, big paper with our name and how much we donate in Japanese. They would double it those days, to make the others dish out more. If you donate ten dollars they'd put up twenty, that's what everybody would do.

"I remember the signs going up with the names and donation numbers and a man sitting there with his *fude* [Japanese brush] writing. And they write beautiful and hang it up and I could always identify my own name naturally.

"The Hall was packed, it was always a full house. The whole family would go, babies and all. It was their only outlet, it was a big to do..."

Mr. J. Hata, a *Nisei:* "They hang those banners, with the names and donations from the movies. They want to increase donations and out beat the next family or something, that's the idea. They always list family names, for everybody to see... like advertising. They want you to donate more, trying to out-beat the next one, trying to save face."

The *Onsen*

Onsen, that's what the *Obaasan* called it.

Onsen meant hot springs and also meant a pause away from the vineyards and sweat and labor and a stolen moment for relaxation and one's self. The *onsen* had etched itself in the *Obaasan's* memory, a sparkling moment from her past and as she aged she spoke of it more and more often and her vision of the *onsen* grew clearer and clearer.

The *onsen* she spoke of at first was the California Hot Springs of Porterville. A popular place with the *Issei*, the Hot Springs had become a mecca, an indulgence they gave into, a reward for their struggles and escape from the poverty of the Depression and bleak futures. Some journeyed annually, others, like the *Obaasan*, had made only one or two trips in their lifetime yet relived the memory a thousand time

"*Nihonjin* [Japanese] didn't know how to vacation in other ways," an *Issei* once explained. "Ah, but the *onsen*. Ah... that something they understood."

A lot of the Del Rey Japanese understood because of the famous hot springs of Kyuushu Island and their homelands in Japan. Perhaps the *Obaasan* had visited one of these *onsen* in Japan as a child, adding a special memory and fondness. But as she aged the one thing she distinctly remembered was the *onsen* and she spoke of it often.

"*Onsen?*" she'd say. "Ah, *onsen*. With the hot *genki* [healthy] water? It's good for people, very healthy."

Over the years, the *onsen* became a dream for her, she merged the Kyuushu and Porterville Hot Springs together into a single, magical memory, one of the few moments of joy in her life. And in her last years, she began to ask to be taken to the *onsen*. Not just any *onsen* like the one in Porterville or Kyuushu, but the *onsen* with her family and the Japan she knew in her youth.

She'd pack her bags often, announcing she was ready and wondered if anyone would take her.

"Do you want to go back to Kumamoto?" her family asked.

"Oh no, why go back there? Del Rey is my home. But take me to the *onsen* for a *chotto* [quick] visit," she'd answer.

The Porterville Hot Springs, 1930's. This was the onsen, hot springs... a pause away from the sweat and labor and a stolen moment for relaxation. For many Japanese it was a sparkling moment from their past and as they spoke of it the vision of the onsen grew clearer and clearer.

A Nisei explained: "The Hotel Del Venado was part of the Hot Springs but only the rich and lucky stayed there. We always stayed up the road a ways, in the cabins. That's where all the Japanese were anyways." (Courtesy Viginia Ichihana)

"The *onsen* in Porterville?"

"Oh no, the *onsen* I always go to," she said.

"In Japan?"

"No, no. The one I went to, with my *kaasan* and *toosan* [mom and dad]."

Further discussion only created more confusion. The family would finally grow impatient and answered with a "No, we can't take you there anymore, *Obaasan.*"

Once she asked her grandson, "Why don't you come with me?"

He was about to tell her, "I can't" but paused and could only answer with silence.

Later he realized only if she went by herself could she reach her true *onsen*. When *Obaasan* died, he did believe her pilgrimage was accomplished.

It was the end of the Depression and right before the war that a new fad swept through the Del Rey community, especially with the *Nisei*. Families were slowly working their way out of poverty and the young were filled with new energy. The YMA, the Young Men's Association of the Buddhist Church swelled in numbers and activities, and the sound of ping-pong echoed in the Hall, the new rage amongst the Japanese Americans.

Del Rey had gained a reputation for its ping pong players, and tournaments were routinely held pitting the best from Del Rey against the surrounding communities, Fowler, Selma, Sanger, Reedley and Parlier. Even within the Del Rey club, competition grew fierce with ladders and players ranked. As soon as a club meeting was over, the important stuff began with the little white ball bouncing back and forth, from paddle to paddle, players locked in concentration, oblivious to the times and the world outside.

Perhaps it was only fitting that a fierce and hard decade drew to a close with the soft, delicate sounds of a ball pinging off a paddle or ponging on a table. The innocent sounds of a game sandwiched between an era of poverty and the terror and confusion of a war and it's hysterical racism against Japanese Americans.

CHAPTER 5

THE EXILE: PRISONERS OF WAR
AND SNAPSHOT, 1944

Prisoners of War, The Japanese American Evacuation of Fresno County

Death accompanied war and with death, the grieving began. Immediately following Dec. 7, 1941 and the bombing of Pearl Harbor, a nation grieved, not only with sorrow but also with an anger and a cry for action concerning the "Japanese problem." 120,000 people of Japanese ancestry, the majority who were American citizens by birth, lived on the West Coast and overnight had become threats to national security. Over the course of the next nine months, hysterical fears spread and paralleled the unfolding stages of grief that progressed from shock to anger, fear and a final clamor for action. In those nine months, a nation witnessed the erosion of a people's civil rights until the ultimate solution was reached: a total, en masse evacuation of Japanese Americans from the West Coast.

Thousands of Japanese had immigrated to Fresno County at the turn of the century, attracted by agriculture and the need for labor. They had settled and established homes in Biola, Caruthers, Del Rey, Fowler, Kingsburg, Parlier, Reedley, Sanger, Selma and other rural regions of the county. Yet after Pearl Harbor, these quiet, rural communities were thrust into a national debate as America wrestled with the grief and anger of war. Between December, 1941 and August, 1942, these communities grappled with their own "Japanese problem" and unknowingly residents participated in the creation of an unprecedented type of American "prisoner of war."

Soon after Pearl Harbor, local newspapers reported on their community shock. The Fowler Ensign cautioned against "irrational thought" concerning not only their Japanese residents but also those of

German and Italian Heritage. "Responsibility fell upon all Americans that no discrimination nor unjust treatment" occurred and that Fowler citizens maintain a "level-headedness." The Kingsburg Recorder reported that "race prejudice must be guarded against." The Selma Enterprise commented: "Selma people are aware of several hundred persons of Japanese ancestry as well as many Japanese nationals living in or near this community and it is to the credit of this group that no doubts have been raised as to their loyalty to the land in which they are living."

Likewise, the Sanger Herald described the situation as: "Shameful... people have forgotten the bitter lessons of the last war in regard to unfairness and viciousness of the whispered rumors stated regarding good Americans of foreign descent. Thousands falsely accused and terribly hurt by these campaigns and time had proven nearly every accusation false and unjustified. Persons of Japanese, Italian and German descent are beginning to feel the effect of idle rumor... The FBI is doing a magnificent job in rounding up and imprisoning traitors or even suspected traitors to this country. Let that agency do the job it is so capable of doing and let everyone else tend to his own knitting."

The Japanese American reaction to Pearl Harbor was also immediate, they too shared in the shock and disbelief of the killing. In Kingsburg, a headline read: "US is Our Home, Local Japanese Say," and an article quoted in the local president of the Japanese language school affirming his and his people's loyal.

In Reedley, the Japanese American Citizens League issued a statement calling for "100% for defense and sacrifice of our personal interests for the downfall of the militaristic regime in Japan."

However, after the initial shock of Pearl Harbor, public sentiment quickly turned to anger. All aliens were warned to stay away from military bases and power plants and the FBI conducted searches of Japanese homes and businesses, confiscating guns and ammunition and arresting "suspected aliens." Locally, the Selma Community Club singled out Japanese aliens and favored moving all of them from California as a "precaution against fifth column activities." The Japanese problem, according to a club speaker, was that there were "300,000 persons of Japanese birth or ancestry in California and every one of them constitutes a problem socially if not from a military standpoint." Even Koreans living in the Reedley area, fearing prejudice due to their similar physical appearance to Japanese, adopted badges to show their nationality, a button adorned with the American and with the American and Korean flags and the slogan "Korea for Victory with the US."

As questions of loyalty arose, many Japanese Americans sought to prove themselves in the eyes of the public. In Fowler during Dec. 1941, 75 Japanese Americans signed up for the Civilian Defense Committee. Japanese women in Selma contributed money to the newly established war relief fund. In Reedley, the Red Cross held three classes for women of Japanese ancestry who sought to assist the war effort by volunteering to do "defense sewing work." Despite such efforts, public anger remained and the tide of racial prejudice was swelling.

Historically Japanese had faced prejudice since first arriving in the United States. They were confronted by discrimination and laws that barred "exclusively aliens of oriental descent" from owning land in California and immigration restrictions that halted the influx of Japanese to America in the 1920's. Portrayed as the yellow peril and menace, labor unions had attacked orientals, especially in recessionary periods of California's economy. Yet by 1941, Japanese were entrenched in many areas such as Fresno County and considered this land their home.

Two editorials in local newspapers were written on Dec. 25, 1941 and commented on the growing tension against Japanese Americans. "Be American" was written in the Reedley paper, "in hysteria of war crisis, misdirected feelings of patriotism are all too often vented against loyal Americans of foreign origins or upon innocent aliens... misguided zeal had even affected our school yards with fights (between) one time playmates."

The Selma paper proclaimed: "...those of us who live in communities with Japanese have an added responsibility. We must assume that the vast majority of these Japanese Americans will be loyal to this country. Those who were born here are citizens of the US and entitled to the rights and privileges. We do not believe they will be less willing to serve their county than those whose ancestors may have come on the Mayflower."

"Evacuation of Japanese was to be the last resort," General DeWitt claimed in early Jan. 1942. Lieutenant General DeWitt had been appointed the commander of the Western Defense Command and of the Fourth Army, he was in charge of insuring the security of the West Coast and claimed authority over the "Japanese problem." He had stated the "evacuation will not be undertaken except under conditions where frequent and continuous bombing (of the West Coast) can be expected." But many Californians did expect bombing and a Japanese invasion, civilian defense squads were created to "watch the skies for enemy aircraft." Local newspapers ran

VEGETABLE HOT CAPS,
TAGGED AND NUMBERED CITIZENS
TRAINS FOR UNKNOWN OUTPOSTS
FOR AMERICANS.

articles and illustrations on "identifying aircraft and distinguishing between allied and axis plane markings."

In early January 1942, as fears of enemy spying and subversion grew, Japanese aliens were required to turn in all guns, radios and cameras. The anger had translated into fear as aliens including not only Japanese but Germans and Italians were also soon required to register with the government, carry identification cards and get permits to travel outside of city limits where they resided. "Axis aliens must be registered" headlines read, "to further insure the nation's safety of all Italian, German and Japanese nationals." Interestingly, the orders were obeyed mainly by the Japanese. "The order affected all aliens," wrote the Fowler Ensign and Sanger Herald, "no Italians or Germans have as yet reported."

Local incidents during February and March 1942 aroused suspicion as the public sentiment against the Japanese grew. The FBI arrested numerous local Japanese, "part of the statewide roundup of enemy aliens," reported the Fowler Ensign. In Kingsburg a Japanese was held by police for FBI questioning, suspicion had been raised, "when he had been questioning employees on matters which were none of his concern at the Kingsburg Cotton Oil Co."

In early March, the Sanger Herald wrote about a public forum concerning the war. "The invasion of California was predicted by one speaker. Questions were posed by audience members on the subject of Japanese settlements in the San Joaquin Valley. Several Sangerites, all for putting the Japanese in their places, were advised by the speaker to leave the matter in the hands of the army."

The Selma Enterprise was one of the few papers to challenge the growing prejudice and on February 19, 1942, an editorial stated: "Responsibility (lies with) the general public to prevent any outbreak of racial hatred that does not discriminate between those who are guilty and those who are innocent of conspiracy or treason against this country. The situation is delicate with so many Japanese aliens. No where can self appointed guardians of public safety function without endangering the peace of the community. Loyalty left to properly constituted authorities is only more complicated if private individuals or groups attempt to execute their own ideas."

However, there was never much of a debate. The angry demands many had felt were answered by Executive Order 9066 signed by President Franklin D. Roosevelt on February 19, 1942. This order granted authority to the military to designate "military zones" from which "any or all persons may be excluded." A bargain had been made, the "Japanese problem" was taken out of the hands of civilians and the military was empowered to remedy the situation.

As if the plot of a tragic novel were unfolding, the evacuation of Japanese from the West Coast commenced. In the following months, a step by step process unfolded, each act seemed a rational and military necessity at the time, each order further eroded the civil rights of a people and yet appeared acceptable to a nation still in shock with the war.

The first orders for evacuation were made in early March. It designated the western halves of Washington, Oregon and California as military areas where Japanese Americans were to vacate. They would either be evacuated by the military or could voluntarily move inland. The military dividing line in California was Highway 99, Japanese were allowed to live and remain east of this line. Many towns including Kingsburg, Selma and Fowler were divided, often the Japanese quarter literally laid on the wrong side of the highway and people were forced to move. A new curfew was also ordered covering all "enemy aliens of Japanese ancestry" including American born Japanese.

Despite the impending orders to evacuate, Japanese farmers were still urged by the military to produce their crops and continue their farming practices in order to show their loyalty. The Sanger Herald reported: "alien farmers facing possible evacuation from coastal and border areas should continue to till their land and demonstrate their loyalty. Defense command and the fourth army officials have heard of reports of some Japanese (who) have plowed under crops..."

Many Japanese Americans felt that the added restrictions would be their sacrifice to the war and an opportunity to display loyalty. Most hoped the February evacuation order and the Highway 99 demarcation would be the extent of military demands upon them.

Many residents in Fresno County supported the evacuation order, it appeared to be the best option. The Kingsburg Recorder reported that the local Defense Council initiated a resolution which was later passed by the city council. The resolution "supported the restrictions upon Japanese Americans for the protection of the Japanese people themselves. We think there can be no objection to abridging the rights of a few citizens for the general good. All Japanese and all aliens should be moved from west of the Sierra Nevada Mountains."

The Sanger Herald editors wrote: "Wrong, that it can't happen here - enemy submarines have dropped shells on the California coast and enemy planes flew over the West's largest city... While there will undoubtedly be many injustices in this mass evacuation, it is felt that the move is best for the nation's welfare and temporary sacrifice of those moved is no more than that of the family whose sons have been taken away by the army. The order is for the safety of all and those effected seem to be accepting it with good grace."

On the other hand, the Selma Enterprise did not support the military order. Editor Lowell Pratt commented: "It is a constitutional provision that protects all persons born or naturalized. Citizens cannot be deprived of liberty. To accuse of wholesale disloyalty is contrary to the letter and spirit of the American constitution. Let us not descend to the level of unreasoning and unreasonable race prejudice. Let us not wipe out in one brief moment that which has taken years of tolerant effort to build up. We are Americans."

During the month of March, many Japanese began voluntarily moving inland, out of the restricted zones west of Highway 99. Soon, many communities became alarmed with this influx of Japanese and requested the authorities to deal with this new problem. The Kingsburg Recorder editors wrote: "Japanese have been told to move from vital defense areas, to voluntarily move... they have settled in Lindsay but that community is protesting, likewise other communities faced with heavy influx of Japanese will protest. But as yet no one has said where else they can go. Some authority must decide, the whole situation is being handled in a haphazard manner..." The Sanger Herald reported of "Japanese Invading Sanger" and a wave of new families entering schools and opening new bank accounts.

In Reedley, already with a large Japanese American population, many Japanese had migrated to live with relatives and friends. The Reedley Chamber of Commerce, in response to this influx, adopted a resolution: "In the best interest of the community and the Japanese... realtors and property owners having property for rent or sale should give careful consideration to the cause and effect of such rentation or sale to a Japanese would have on the adjoining property and upon the attitude of the people in that community and that sales of property to Japanese should be discouraged wherever possible."

For the Japanese Americans, the inland movement was their only option other than military incarceration. However, as Japanese moved east, the cry from the inland areas prompted the authorities to restrict all even out of the military zone west of Highway 99. Confusion reined within the Japanese community, rumors of "death camps" circulated along with stories of forthcoming plans to send all Japanese Americans to Japan. Unlike the coastal regions where the status of Japanese Americans had been decided, the inland pockets still lay in limbo.

Some members of the non-Japanese community took advantage of the confusion and tried to profit from the situation. In the Selma Enterprise, an editorial was written about "reputable businessmen trying to purchase property owned by local residents of Japanese ancestry." These businessmen would "use pressure to buy property at less than real value." Japanese owners were told that evacuation would be forthcoming and "better to sell out rather than be forced to abandon." In another incident, the Enterprise reported: "supposedly honest concerns have told Japanese they must pay at once all the unpaid balance of loans." The article continued, "attempts to cheat the Japanese discredits the principals of American democracy for which we are fighting axis powers..."

In Del Rey, one incident broke out that incited a near riot. Headlines in the Sanger Herald read, "Jap Evacuees Apprehended in Beating." In Del Rey an officer had been questioning four young Japanese for reckless driving. After an argument, one Japanese was handcuffed and apparently the others overcame the officer and beat him. This brought an angry crowd together and emotions grew heated. "All four Japanese were from Southern California" the article pointed out. Following this incident, members of the local Japanese community cautioned against all contact with the outside community and emphasized that these youths were not from the valley but were imports from Los Angeles. They urged continued display of loyalty and citizenship.

In early May, new restrictions were placed on Japanese living east of Highway 99, travel and all movement was halted outside one's city limits. This was viewed by many as "the next step in army evacuation," the protests of the inland communities had been heard: no one wanted the Japanese.

Beginning in April and continuing into May, coastal Japanese were moved into assembly centers, holding facilities prior to their departure to the inland camps. Two of these centers were located in Fresno County, one in Pinedale and another at the Fresno Fair Grounds and its horse stable which together held over 10,000 Japanese Americans (other centers included Tanforan Racetrack and Santa Anita Racetrack, where evacuees lived for months in the horse stalls). In mid May, 1942, many of the relocation camps had been completed and the incarcerated Japanese began to leave for these facilities. A few weeks later, all Japanese in the state fell under a new order: complete, en masse evacuation was ordered. Any hope that the Japanese east of Highway 99 would be spared further hardship was lost; the ultimate solution had been decided.

Throughout Fresno County, service centers were established by the government to meet "practically every possible situation as the Japanese prepare for evacuation." These centers were to "make it possible for evacuees to close their businesses, farming operations and personal affairs without undue loss and to prepare for evacuation in an orderly manner." In addition, any unfair disposal of property was to be reported at these centers: "all efforts to force the sale of property, equipment or other assets hurriedly and at a sacrifice should be reported. No Japanese is compelled under law to dispose any property or take any action in connection with personal or business affairs." Japanese Americans were not forced to sell property yet no one knew when and if they were to return and even their destination, the relocation camp location, was not known at the time.

A Wartime Civil Control Authority (WCCA) was also established to assist the evacuation process. A WCCA office opened in the Reedley area where all Japanese farmers were required to register immediately. Because of the war, all farm products and future harvests were important, Japanese farmers had to register and provide information about their crops in order that "substitute farm operators could be found." Earlier, when Japanese American farmers had been evacuated from the coastal areas, the government had problems finding farmers to take over these operations despite offering an attractive deal. In early April, a promotional campaign had been launched hoping to attract responsible replacements: "Farms Vacated by Japanese Available" the headline read. "Wanted: good farmers to take over on-going operations to keep war production on the move. Heavy investment not necessarily required, full credit available for experience. Thousands of fertile acres, most already planted and on the way to harvest. Vacated soon by Japanese tenants under evacuation orders."

By the arrival of summer, 1942, the Japanese American community was rampant with confusion and uncertainty. A few families had escaped to the East before the final travel restrictions took effect on June 2, 1942. Others refused to believe that as American citizens and American veterans of World War I, they could ever be evacuated. Most, though, hoped for

The Pinedale Assembly Center, 1942. In Fresno, two emergency camps were built to hold relocated Japanese Americans prior to their departure to inland camps. The Pinedale and Fresno Fair Grounds held over 10,000 Japanese Americans in the summer, 1942. The horse stalls at the fairground were used as housing. (Fresno Bee collections)

the best and had no idea what to expect. Rumors continued to be circulated, many stories of camps in cold, desolate mountain regions were told.

Accepting their fate, Japanese rushed to purchase certain merchandise before departure, especially travel suitcases and heavy clothes for colder climates. This sudden surge in buying was happily greeted by local merchants whose sales had slumped with the wartime economy and migration of people to military manufacturing centers. The Kingsburg Recorder wrote: "shopkeepers have been enjoying mild prosperity as Japanese are making heavy purchases in preparation for their evacuation, possibly to colder localities. Stocks of some items have been completely cleaned out by the Japanese."

Also a story in the Sanger Herald read: "Japanese Boom Business, Preparing for Evacuation With Big Buying Spree. It's an ill wind that blows no body good... to merchants of Sanger and other communities, ill wind blew good. Japanese are buying freely and in large quantities. Suitcases, overcoats, drugs, food... all necessities if they are removed to a relocation point in a colder climate. Businesses enjoyed a record month of June, it has taken up the slack of the other months caused by the war and the slack that will be caused by the elimination of ordinary purchases of Japanese once they are gone. It's a regular Saturday nite rush everyday. The jingle of the cash register is soothing music for many a merchant who has been torn with anguish over the effects of war on his business."

Some Japanese had anticipated the final en masse evacuation order because of the pattern that had been established, the gradual erosion of rights beginning with registration, curfews and the coastal removal of Japanese Americans. Yet within the local Japanese American community, grief over the impending uprooting spread. Suicides and illnesses occurred, such as the Selma Japanese woman who hung herself, "despondent over evacuation." Some individuals in the non-Japanese community too expressed sympathy and stories were heard of a neighboring farmer vowing to care for his friend's, his Japanese friend's land and crops amid the slurs of being called a "Jap lover." Reporting yet another viewpoint, the Kingsburg Recorder wrote: "many of the prospective evacuees, most of whom have never been out of the state, are cheerful about their new adventure and are looking forward to their new homes for the duration with a spirit of optimism." By mid July, the final order was given that by August 11, 1942, all Japanese were to be removed from the entire West Coast and placed within relocation camps.

In order to help their Japanese American friends, the local religious community met and organized assistance groups. Earlier in Oakland, a Committee on Fair Play had been organized to help with evacuation and now that Japanese Americans in Fresno County were suffering similar fates, numerous Fair Play Committees were formed in Reedley, Sanger, Kingsburg, Parlier, Fowler, Del Rey, Dinuba as well as Fresno. "Respectable groups of citizens will help Japanese," newspapers reported. Ministerial associations and church organizations will "attempt to assist Japanese families in preparation for evacuation and assist in getting ready, packing and finding place to store or sell belongings."

The various Fair Play Committees quickly attempted to deal with two ironic circumstances. First, even though orders were made for Japanese to report to various departure train stations for evacuation, no arrangements were made for transportation of them and their personal suitcases to these stations. The committees had to ask for "help to transport Japanese to their points of entrainment." Second, refreshment committees were formed to provide some food on the day of departure. In Reedley,the committee made tea and sandwiches on the belief that the least their community could do would be to send off their Japanese with a nourishing final meal and full stomachs.

As the reality of evacuation neared, the agricultural community soon realized that an acute labor shortage would arise. In the early part of summer, 1942, there seemed plenty of labor for the harvests, especially

WESTERN DEFENSE COMMAND AND FOURTH ARMY
WARTIME CIVIL CONTROL ADMINISTRATION
Presidio of San Francisco, California
May 11, 1942

INSTRUCTIONS
TO ALL PERSONS OF
JAPANESE
ANCESTRY
Living in the Following Area:

All of the City of Fresno, State of California.

Pursuant to the provisions of Civilian Exclusion Order No. 64, this Headquarters, dated May 11, 1942, all persons of Japanese ancestry, both alien and non-alien, will be evacuated from the above area by 12 o'clock noon, P. W. T., Sunday, May 17, 1942.

No Japanese person will be permitted to move into, or out of, the above area after 12 o'clock noon, P. W. T., Monday, May 11, 1942, without obtaining special permission from the representative of the Commanding General, Northern California Sector, at the Civil Control Station located at:

2107 Inyo Street,

Fresno, California.

Such permits will only be granted for the purpose of uniting members of a family, or in cases of grave emergency. The Civil Control Station is equipped to assist the Japanese population affected by this evacuation in the following ways:

1. Give advice and instructions on the evacuation.
2. Provide services with respect to the management, leasing, sale, storage or other disposition of most kinds of property, such as real estate, business and professional equipment, household goods, boats, automobiles and livestock.
3. Provide temporary residence elsewhere for all Japanese in family groups.
4. Transport persons and a limited amount of clothing and equipment to their new residence.

The Following Instructions Must Be Observed:

1. A responsible member of each family, preferably the head of the family, or the person in whose name most of the property is held, and each individual living alone, will report to the Civil Control Station to receive further instructions. This must be done between 8:00 A. M. and 5:00 P. M. on Tuesday, May 12, 1942, or between 8:00 A. M. and 5:00 P. M. on Wednesday, May 13, 1942.

2. Evacuees must carry with them on departure for the Assembly Center, the following property:
   (a) Bedding and linens (no mattress) for each member of the family;
   (b) Toilet articles for each member of the family;
   (c) Extra clothing for each member of the family;
   (d) Essential personal effects for each member of the family.

   All items carried will be securely packaged, tied and plainly marked with the name of the owner and numbered in accordance with instructions obtained at the Civil Control Station. The size and number of packages is limited to that which can be carried by the individual or family group.

3. No pets of any kind will be permitted.

4. No personal items and no household goods will be shipped to the Assembly Center.

5. The United States Government through its agencies will provide for the storage, at the sole risk of the owner, of the more substantial household items, such as iceboxes, washing machines, pianos and other heavy furniture. Cooking utensils and other small items will be accepted for storage if crated, packed and plainly marked with the name and address of the owner. Only one name and address will be used by a given family.

6. Each family, and individual living alone, will be furnished transportation to the Assembly Center or will be authorized to travel by private automobile in a supervised group. All instructions pertaining to the movement will be obtained at the Civil Control Station.

Go to the Civil Control Station between the hours of 8:00 A. M. and 5:00 P. M., Tuesday, May 12, 1942, or between the hours of 8:00 A. M. and 5:00 P. M., Wednesday, May 13, 1942, to receive further instructions.

J. L. DeWITT
Lieutenant General, U. S. Army
Commanding

The War Relocation Authority bulletin ordering all Japanese Americans (of Fresno) to report for evacuation, May, 1942. (Courtesy Fresno County Library) with the new influx of Japanese that had occurred. However in every farm community discussions were held about a new "Jap problem."

The Sanger Herald head lines read: "Jap Problem Studied at Mass Meeting. Labor Shortage and Shippers Interest in Jap Crops Hold Attention of Ranchers." The article continued: "The Farm Bureau has reported an unprecedented labor shortage. The ranks of agricultural labor will be thinning to 2,000 when 6,000 Japanese are evacuated. The power of attorney was given to shippers to operate ranches and market crops of Japanese once they have departed. Shippers were to get a percentage of the market price. The Farm Bureau (feels) a discrimination would result against individual ranchers since shippers (handling Japanese farms) would scour the district for Mexican help and pay an increased wage scale. Individual ranchers would get their crops picked and shipped after the Japanese. This would give the Japanese farmers preferential treatment even after they have been evacuated. (Discussion centered on) the need to establish a standard wage scale. It was passed that an order also be made for the retention of Japanese labor in the district."

Farmers were assured of help from the Fresno County Board of Supervisors and together they submitted a petition to the military requesting that the Japanese be retained at the Fresno Fair Grounds and Pinedale Assembly Centers until harvests were over. Farmers sought to keep Japanese in Fresno County a few months longer to "help in the war effort and harvest needed crops." When the petition was rejected, farmers scrambled for extra labor: the Japanese would be immediately missed.

On August 11, 1942, thousands of Japanese Americans loaded trains and departed Fresno County. In many ways this final departure seemed almost anticlimactic. The debate had been resolved, grief had run its course and now Japanese Americans began a new cycle: the shock of their bleak environment and barrack "homes."

Some of the departing Japanese bought space in local papers and wrote a community farewell letter. In the Fowler Ensign was written: "Dear Friends- After 40 years in Fowler I am closing my store to co-operate with the national defense program. I regret that such an unexpected and unfortunate event has occurred to cause everyone much inconvenience. We are happy to have had this opportunity to live in Fowler and were able to lead a most happy and peaceful life. The pleasant associations I had in this city will be carried in my heart.. with this parting word, I bid you good-bye."

Written in the Kingsburg Recorder was: "Our departure is necessary to the future peace we all look forwards to and in temporarily establishing our homes elsewhere we do so in the spirit expressed by words and deeds of the people of the Kingsburg community."

Only two papers commented on the final evacuation. In the Sanger Herald was written: "Farewell. With somewhat a tinge of regret that many people will bid farewell to Japanese friends and neighbors of long standing. No argument but that the evacuation orders are best both for the good of the Japanese themselves and the nation as a whole. War brings many stern orders though and this is one. To the credit of the Japanese of Sanger, they proved highly co-operative and helpful during the entire evacuation. The locals seemed to make the move in good spirits. Only in America would such an orderly and generous movement of people and possessions of an enemy nationality group be allowed. That's one of the things that makes America great in the eyes of the world and worth fighting for."

The Kingsburg Recorder also published an editorial: "After tomorrow you will see no more Japanese, that is going to seem rather peculiar. Parts of our towns are like ghost towns, the Japanese sections deserted. Arguments remain between radical pros and radical cons with most persons in between. In the next few years California is going to find out if she is better off without the Japanese. The answer is going to surprise many."

Today, a final effort has been launched by some in the Japanese American community to redress the wrongs of this wartime experience. Among the requests are an apology from the US government, a monetary settlement for the losses of property, and the creation of an educational trust fund to further document the history of Japanese American evacuation. Two camps have surfaced in this debate within the Japanese American community itself. One claims that the past should be accepted and people must continue to move onwards, the other voice claims that the violation of civil rights must never be forgotten and only by proper redress can the tragic experience be acknowledged.

A product of this debate has been new inquiry into evacuation and a public discussion of this chapter in American history. Fresno County, with its large Japanese American population, witnessed the entire episode and this has provided an unique vantage point. For Fresno County residents, both Japanese American and non-Japanese, the grief and anger of Pearl Harbor was not quickly settled and over a span of nine months, communities struggled with this issue as the drama unfolded. More than witnesses, Fresno County residents were participants in this traumatic moment in American history.

SNAPSHOT, 1944

I stare at the silent and still faces, expressions frozen in a snapshot. My family stands to the right, *Jiichan* holds a flag, *Baachan* lifts a photograph of her dead son. The Aunts and Uncles gather to the side; they look uncomfortable, cramped next to each other, unsure about their hands. Dad remains in the back, his face blurred in the shadows almost unrecognizable. It was my Uncle's funeral in 1944 at someplace called Gila River Relocation Center, Arizona.

Jiichan stood erect, his chin out, body stiff. He did not press the American flag to his chest. His hands were loosely folded around the flag. His son lay in the US Army uniform and casket behind him.

I never met *Jiichan*. He died before I was born. All I know are the stories my dad told.

"I remember the hot, summer nights and Pop's wooden platform. Fresno's hundred degree days would beat down on the place we lived. That shack had a tin roof, the inside took hours to cool after sunset. We didn't have a cooler or fan but it didn't matter, out in the country we didn't have electricity," said Dad.

"Pop made a low, wooden platform from old barn wood. It rose about two feet off the ground with a top area big enough for all us kids. In the evening Pop led everyone outside, the whole family would lie on the platform, side by side, almost touching. After a day's work and a hot dinner and *ofuro* (Japanese bath), we gathered, talking, relaxing, gazing upwards at the night sky. The dirt yard was beneath us, the vineyards began a few feet away. If a little breeze came we could hear the grape leaves shifting and rustling. It seemed to make you feel cooler.

"Every summer we'd do that until it was time to go inside and sleep. Sometimes us boys would sleep all night on the platform. Quiet, sort of peaceful."

The platform is gone but some of *Jiichan's* works survive. In the back of our house stands a wooden bench. Simply made, the wood was never painted or sanded yet it has become smooth from wear. Dad and I use it to take off our shoes after work. It felt good to relax for a moment, the afternoon heat dissipating, the dust and sweat drying on our backs. In

"I stare at the silent and still faces, expressions frozen in a snapshot. It was my Uncle's funeral in 1944 at someplace called Gila River Relocation Center, Arizona." (War Relocation Authority)

black letter Hikazo Masumoto is painted on one leg. "After the camps, Pop was getting too old for work on the farms," explained Dad, "but he loved to sit and stare into the fields. He made himself this bench and he'd sit silently for hours."

In the corner of our living room, in a special compartment recessed in the wall, is the *butsudan* (Buddhist altar). "Pop made it during camp, from scraps of wood," said Dad. It measures about two and a half by two feet. The outside is painted black, the inside a flat gold, neither varnished nor finished. A series of hinged doors fold open, three small altars with pillars, railing, and steps fill the interior. Most of the joints are notched, only a few nails used. The hinges are wooden slots and pegs fitted together.

Every so often, Mom opened the *butsudan*, lit the candles and incense, and offered fresh rice or food. The *butsudan* seemed to stare out at us, the incense dancing in the air and the candle flickering with any movement.

A photograph of *Jiichan* is kept before the *butsudan*. He was standing in front of a peach orchard when they took the picture, his arms hang to his sides and body slightly slouched. He wore a black suit and a clean,

pressed white shirt with a tie. Yet peaking beneath *Jiichan's* pants cuffs
were his old work shoes.

I'd study the picture, wondering about the old man I had never met.
I'd look up at the *butsudan* and watch the incense drift through the air.

Baachan clutches the photograph of her dead son. She stands next to
Jiichan who is on her right and on her left is Fumiko, now the oldest child.
Baachan lifts the gold framed picture, her dark hands curled around the
edges as she elevates it slightly, trying to hold it steady between herself and
Jiichan.

Baachan lives with us, usually trying to keep out of the way, almost
hiding, melting into the furniture. She does a little gardening, but forgets
about the running water and often floods the backyard, or she doesn't
remember where she planted the tomatoes and begins digging a new area
for more plants.

I try to talk to her but the Japanese I learned isn't the same. With
Baachan, jitensha (bicycle) becomes *bai-ku*; *hon* (book) is *buu-ku*; digging
weeds around vine stumps becomes *sha-bu-rin*; and most weeds are *warui
kusa* (bad grass), while Johnson grass is *abunai kusa* (dangerous grass).

Jiichan died over 25 years ago. *Baachan* says she's just waiting to die
and join him. We tell her not to talk like that, at 85 she should be happy to
be healthy. She doesn't answer and only nods her head.

When the photo exhibit of Executive Order 9066 was displayed in San
Francisco, my aunt took *Baachan*. My aunt had to explain to *Baachan* that
they were in the Gila River photograph of the funeral for three families with
dead sons. "*Baachan* cried," said my aunt. When they returned to Fresno,
we asked *Baachan* about the exhibit. She couldn't remember much and said
only a little, mainly about the drive there.

Sometimes *Baachan* just sits and stares, talking to herself. The same
thoughts keep turning over and over in her mind. If I'm with her, she'd
ask me five or six times in an afternoon, "Are you going to school? What
kind of work you going to do?" The same questions, over and over.

She does remember the years of work, *shaburin* the vines, picking
grapes next to *Jiichan*. But *Jiichan* and her never got a farm. After the
camps, Dad worked and brought a farm but for some reason, *Baachan*
insists the farm belongs to her and *Jiichan*.

She argues, demanding for her farm. Her face changes, the deep
wrinkles shift their pattern and muscles tense. Her hands, the rough
callused hands that used to *momo* (massage) my back, become clenched

into fists. Her talking grows louder, the Japanese spliced with some English, "No!" pierces her phrases. Her fist hits the table, she stands and begins raving about the land. She worked hard all her life, in the fields, next to *Jiichan*. Something belongs to her. The years, clearing the *abunai kusa* (dangerous grass), her and *Jiichan*. She threatens Mom, "you kicked me out of my home, I have no home." Then silence. *Baachan* cries, no sounds, only tears. Dad gets her a tissue and they sit together. No one talks.

You can barely see Dad, the blurred figure standing at the edge of the snapshot. Between Dad and *Baachan* were Aunt Fumiko, Uncle Kenji who left for Chicago as soon as they let Japanese out of the camps; and Aunt Kimiko, the little sister in bobby sox. Dad doesn't say much about the snapshot. "Yea, I remember it," is about all he'll give.

Following the camps and the army, Dad returned to the valley and farming. He found the family living in an abandoned grocery store. He hired himself out in the fields and hunted up jobs for an aging *Jiichan* and *Baachan*. The family tried to stay and work together; if Dad pruned vines he'd have the old folks *nakagiri* (cut the center wood of the vines off the trellis wire), or when Dad picked grapes they'd spread them out on the wooden trays. Eventually he told Aunt Kimiko to get some job in the city, housecleaning, anything so she could support herself and get out of the fields.

Dad continued to hustle for more work and money, learning to farm by renting some land and then gambled on a place of his own. A gamble *Baachan* never approved of because it was too risky, too many things they did not know about, and she never approved of it even after the land was paid for and a farm established.

Dad's over 60 now, he still retained a farmer's tan: a dark face and branded "v" on his chest where the work shirt opens, with hands and arms browned until just above the elbows and rolled shirt sleeves. In the last few years he has begun to slow down. On winter mornings he stays inside an extra hour or two before going out to prune. We talk more about farming and economics and politics or football and baseball.

But once, a thought about the snapshot did escape, a slip, a momentary flash of emotions. It happened on a cold winter morning, a chilling fog hovered outside, the type of fog that seems to penetrate your body down to the bones. Dad stared outside and began whispering to himself, he was lost in his thoughts, a trance overcame his face.

"What was I supposed to say?" he mumbled. Then came a story about the funeral when Uncle died. Dad fell into the role of being the eldest son. Suddenly he had to take charge, he had the responsibility for the family, he had to have all the answers.

"And what could I say to pop? And mom had all those questions, what was going to happen? Questions... and what was I supposed to say?"

He sat and stared outside, the fog hugged the ground and enveloped the vineyards. You can barely make out their silhouette.

Silent expressions locked in a snapshot. *Jiichan* and *Baachan* clutch the remains of their dead son. Dad stands in the blurred background.

I do not and cannot know what they felt. I was born ten years later in a different time and place. But a silence penetrates such gaps, linking me with my past: a silence felt by my family and carried through the years; a silence that teaches yet I do not fully understand; a silence captured for a moment in a snapshot, 1944.

CHAPTER 6

BUILDING COMMUNITY
AND COMMUNITY ORGANIZATIONS

Building Community

They didn't have much to say about their return to Del Rey from the camps. "Wasn't much to come home to," said a quiet *Nisei* farmer.

I asked again, "What was it like, tell me what you really felt coming home?" And the same response, a blank stare and silence, then only broken with a mumble, "Not much." This was followed with a long pause and then a burst, "What more do you want me to say?" I had not listened to his silence.

The *Issei* came home to this valley, to Del Rey. For some it was like an elephant's final trek to a land to die in, lives had ended with the 1942 train rides to the camps and the leaving behind of a lifetime of memories and lost dreams. They had no place to go so they returned to Del Rey, accompanied by children obligated to try and take care of their folks. A generation that had grown too old to care for themselves and a new generation that had to follow.

They trickled back, families drawn with a driving instinct to return home and start again. It has to do with a place on a map, a land you feel at ease in, weather that made you feel comfortable and a place you and a handful of neighbors considered as home, your community.

Del Rey J-town had all but evaporated, a few Japanese stores reopened, Bert Mori's Market, Sakai's Pay Less Department Store and for a while Suzie's Noodles. Only the old community hall remained standing, a monument to the past, a new center for a *Nisei* community rebuilding itself.

The Del Rey Japanese community was now composed of people scattered over a countryside of vineyards and orchards, with undefined physical borders yet with a community boundary clear in the minds and souls of the residents. They had come home again.

Mrs. Y. Iwamura, a *Nisei:* "When we came back in January, 1945, we hoped to come back to one *hakujin* [caucasian] farmer where dad had worked for years before the war and where we had left all of our things. By then the old grandmother was gone and her son, a bachelor 'wino' was farming, so we moved in temporarily with him. When he didn't drink he was nice, there was nothing wrong with him, just that he drank...

"My dad expected to go back to work, he was forty at the time. When we came back the *hakujin* said that he was very sorry, that he could temporarily stay there, in their house because we had no where to go but he would not let dad go back to work for him. There was this... I shouldn't say this... but there was this Okie who did all the tractoring and all the work and he said that he would quit on the farmer if dad came to work, something about if the farmer put a Jap on the place...

"The *hakujin* farmer was such a nice man but he was kind'a a softy... He's a good man and I think he really felt bad for us but he just said he was sorry but the work had to be done and since my dad then didn't know how to drive a tractor...

"So we were welcomed to stay, they felt bad I guess, to stay in the house as long as we wanted and they didn't charge us either so they were kind'a nice about it. They felt sorry for us but they had to look out for themselves I guess.

"So then in the meantime my dad, he never did this before, but he got started, because he could understand English and Japanese... all the old folks came back but they were all in their 40's and 50's and they had to find work so my dad became a crew boss and ran a crew. He began getting workers and began taking people to work and then one place he went to work, dad had taken a crew there and the farmer said, 'I'll fix a house for our boys if you'll come and stay at our place and work for me.' My dad said OK and went to work for this farmer."

Mr. H. Hiramoto, a *Nisei:* "After the war they formed a club in Del Rey, a type of community club. Two guys said, 'We don't want any Jap in this organization.'

"When they start calling you names like that to hell with it. The older generation still had a grudge against us, so I didn't go around and try and make friends out of those guys.

"This one *Nisei*, he tried to make friends and he agitated those guys and made matters worse. He tried to integrate with them, you know, the war was over and the past is the past... but that *hakujin* caucasian generation, the old timers have to die off before we could do anything. Better to keep separated until then.

Mr. K. Sasahara, a *Nisei:* "November, 1945. We drove back to California, back to Del Rey. We unboarded the windows and reopened the store. It had not been broken into and nothing had been taken. We had a home in the back of the store, across the alley, which we had rented out. And everything was all right.

"Well, business wasn't too good. Some came in to say we like you to come back here. Some said they wanted to trade with us, but were afraid people would talk. There were some Mexican people and they gave us quite a bit of business.

"Right after the war I needed a part for my Ford truck and I went to a Ford garage in town. And I waited at the counter 10 or 15 minutes, they bypassed me. So I said, 'When are you going to wait on me?'

"He said, 'What do you want? We don't have it.'

"I said, 'You didn't even go back in the stockroom to look.'

"We don't have it."

"That's the only incident I remember... on the whole, the *hakujins* were very nice.

"There was segregation in the movie theaters. I'd go in there and they would say, 'This way please.' Yes, it was segregated. The *hakujins* were seated in the center section and I would be with the Chinese and Mexicans on the side section. That was before the war and segregation continued until about 1950."

He had been discharged from the service and journeyed home only to find his parents hungry and desperate, living in the back of a grocery store. He had to find some work and a more permanent shelter to live in.

He heard GI's could get a loan, a program for veterans. He learned he was eligible, he had served his country but because he was Japanese they wouldn't give him the loan unless he had an "American" co-sign with him. "American" meant *hakujin*.

Enraged, insulted, he stormed out of the office, "I risk my life in the army to get this by my own country?"

But his folks were hungry, out of work, and he had no choice. He talked with a *hakujin* friend and they both went in, signed the papers, and he got the money.

TENTH ANNUAL CENTRAL CALIFOR...

Community Organizations

While growing up, most of the *Sansei* out in the country had three sets of friends. One was from school, another were cousins, and still another were a set of Japanese friends from the community. Most saw and played with all three sets in mutually exclusive times, school friends at school, family cousins at family gatherings, and Japanese at community functions that seemed to fill a calendar because there were a lot of organizations and clubs in each community, Del Rey was no exception.

In Del Rey four or five different organizations overlapped each other, most families belonging to all of them. Yet each organization functioned differently, subtle differences that only the adults understood and even today many can't figure out why nor how the activities and traditions got divided up.

Some divisions made sense, like the *Kyowakai* (community club) handled all the funerals, making arrangements for the services and helping the families with the business matters of a funeral and assisting with support and condolence. And since the community had both Buddhists and

The YBA (Young Buddhist Association) conference, Oct. 1940, hosted by the Del Rey club. Held at the Del Rey Elementary School, this conference brought together hundreds of young *Nisei*. It would be a little more than a year later, December 7, 1941 that would forever change the lives of these *Nisei*. For many, this would mark the end of youth and following the war, they would return as adults. (Courtesy of Virginia Ichihana).

Christians, utilizing the *Kyowakai* made sense. But why did the Sunday School and later the ABA, Adult Buddhist Association, begin the tradition of celebrating 25th wedding anniversaries? After all, didn't the Christians also have anniversaries?

The answer was revealed only after discovering the story of the baby showers. The Sunday school, which was run mostly by women, had once decided to throw a party for a member who was expecting a baby. This sounded like a good idea but once you start that kind of thing you have to do it for all the expectant mothers and their babies. They did limit it though to the first child in each family. The women thoroughly enjoyed their gatherings, a chance for a women's afternoon out, away from the fields and home life.

But then something happened, they began running out of babies. Sad times appeared on the horizon as the child-bearing years slipped by, the biological clock doomed a generation of women to life on the farm. Then one woman got a bright idea, how about celebrating 25th wedding anniversaries? And that's how the tradition was born in the Buddhist Sunday School Club and that's why it became property of the Sunday School.

Of course there's more to the story. Seems that these women were merrily going along, celebrating anniversaries and the women's night out, with the husbands staying at home and taking care of the kids for once. Then at one restaurant during their dinner celebration, a waitress asked, "What were the ladies celebrating?"

"A 25th wedding anniversary of course."

"And where's the husbands?"

The women thought about it and debated amongst themselves, "Why not include the boys? Besides, the majority of the children were now old enough to take care of themselves, so why not let the boys join them?"

Sexual equality took a leap in the Del Rey Japanese community, and the ABA soon assumed ownership of anniversary party planning, the gathering had outgrown the small circle of women involved with only the Sunday School.

Community clubs provided social life for Japanese Americans. While businesses struggled, the spirit of community thrived at the pot lucks and picnics and dinners and gatherings. And for a generation of Japanese American kids, friendships grew and strengthened at each activity and each meeting.

The following are a description of some of these community clubs. Other communities may have different organizations that overlap with the Japanese of Del Rey. For example Christians may not have their own club in Del Rey yet they may belong to a Fresno Church group and be part of that community, or active JACL'ers (Japanese American Citizen League members) in Del Rey joined organizations in other communities like Sanger or Selma. And also other communities may have different organizations with different activities and functions.

The point is that community organizations played a vital role in the lives of most Japanese Americans, Del Rey just like Sanger, Selma, Fowler or Reedley and the Buddhists just like the Christians: community organizations instilled a people with life and meaning.

The *Kyowakai*, The Community Club

One of the first organizations renewed by Japanese Americans following the war was the *Kyowakai*, the community club. The *Kyowakai* had a long history, beginning with *Issei* settlers who banded together to erect the hall in 1919 and regularly met to "iron out problems the community faced."

The *Kyowakai* helped root a people to a place. For the *Issei*, it substituted for a type of sense of place that they had in Japan with the village structure. In California most farmers lived on their land, separate from each other instead of in a village or hamlet as often found in Japan. Physically people were separated, part of the individualism of America and the New West.

Mr. R. Matsubara, a *Kibei:* "*Kyowakai* gets the community together, all the people helped each other. Farmers help each other, like when someone gets hurt, they pitch in and help with the work. Everybody that's Japanese in Del Rey area, they have to join *Kyowakai*, an automatic member. Christians, Buddhists, doesn't matter."

Mr. N. Hiramoto, a *Nisei:* "Oh after the war, Japanese had to work together, no one else to turn to. The community worked so well together, during our period we had so much racial prejudice against the Japanese, this is where we always stood together. We had to whether we liked it or not.

"*Kyowakai* was the main, took care of picnic and funerals and some shows. The club put people together and we should get together. It's no use we wandering and be loner, that's the worst thing to do in your life. And that's what the Kyowakai does, keeps us together."

The *Kyowakai* was a community organization, boundaries vaguely extended to where that sense of place extended to. For example Del Rey had many labor camps in the area, temporary homes for migrant Japanese laborers. The *Kyowakai* included these camps in their activities, the camps and any residents were part of the community. "That was part of what made Del Rey attractive to those boys, they'd come and find a home here," explained one *Kibei*.

The activities of the *Kyowakai* included:

-Spring and fall hall clean-up, maintenance of the ground and Hall;

-Annual spring picnic, a tradition begun from the years *Issei* years;

-The *Shinenkai* or New Year's party;

-Large community activities, like a 50th anniversary of community members. "The *Kyowakai* organized the big events, like a 50th," a *Nisei* woman explained, "but the smaller ones, like a 25th, other community clubs did those. We saved the big ones for the *Kyowakai*."

-And special events, especially those that had to cope with an emergency like a death or crisis or illness.

People often wonder what it means to "take care of a funeral." The details are enormous, planning extensive, and numerous arrangements to be made. For example, 1958 had to be a busy and difficult year for the *Kyowakai*: three funerals, three members lost, three special meetings called to work out funeral arrangements.

In the *Kyowakai* minutes from November, 1958 were the listing of the names of participants in one funeral. These names with some explanation provide insight into the role of one's community and the complexities of "taking care of your dead."

Funeral service, Nov.28, 1958 for Mrs. R. Yoshida.

Chairman: Richard Masuda. The chairman helped orchestrate the funeral, welcoming family and friends, helped with the Buddhist rituals, and lead the community in paying their last respects.

Incense offering: the following list of participants offered incense, a Buddhist ritual much like giving a type of condolence to the grieving family. These individuals represented the other various community organizations and their members.

Del Rey Sunday School: JoAllen Iwatsubo.

Del Rey *Kyowakai*: Juuichi Kato.

Del Rey Japanese community, 1969. Following the war, Japanese Americans returned to Del Rey and once again the community was rebuilt. By the 50th anniversary of the Hall, a new generation, the Sansei had been added to the community.

Del Rey *Howakai* (Buddhist study group): J. Hata.
Del Rey ABA (Adult Buddhist Association): Carole Matsuo.
Fresno *Betsuin* (Buddhist Church): T. Yamashita.
JACL (Japanese American Citizens League): Tom Nagata.
Friends: Toku Hirata.
Choji: a final message of condolence given by the community to the family, said by Masuichi Nagata.

Ushers were also required since funerals were widely attended with often hundreds paying their last respects. Ushers were needed to help with seating. Ushers included: Howard Hayashi, Johnson Shinamoto, Mike Inaba and Gary Ito.

The *choba* was a committee that handled all the donations given at a funeral. Just about everyone or every family contributed to the grieving family to help cover funeral expenses and ease the pain of death. Money was sealed in a simple white envelope and handed to the *choba* committee when you entered for the funeral. The *choba* committee made a list of names and amounts for the family so that thank you's could be quickly written. *Choba* included: Nori Nishigawa, George Yoshimoto, Yoshi Takeda, Paul Fujita and Mitsuo Yamato.

With any disaster in the community, the *Kyowakai* called special meetings to discuss plans for action. For example on April 6, 1965 a special meeting was called about the fire at Bert Mori's grocery store that had just taken place, destroying his business. After much discussion a motion was made to give $50 to the Mori family to help them through that difficult time. In addition, it was decided that the entire cabinet go to "Bert's house for the *kaji-mimai* [fire investigation] and clean up as soon as possible. The following nite was chosen."

Del Rey Buddhist Sunday School

In 1952 the Buddhist Sunday School in Del Rey was restored. An active group of mothers and some fathers met and sought to establish a regular Buddhist education program for their children, with summers off, of course, due to harvests.

The Sunday School quickly grew with the post war baby boom and swelled to nearly 100 students at one time with often over 150 in attendance on Sunday mornings. Of course children grow up and depart, by 1986 the Sunday School was discussing disbanding, they only had 2 or 3 students with a handful of dedicated teachers.

In addition to running the Sunday School, other activities were undertaken by the organization. For example in 1953 some of them included (taken from meeting minutes):

May 17, 1953. ... the final matter discussed was in regard to the "old clothes drive" for relief work in Japan. Items to be collected are: 1. men's and women's clothing, 2. children's clothing, 3. shoes, and 4. blankets and linens.

Dec. 6, 1953. The group decided to form a "sunshine" committee for the main purpose of remembering one member and their families whenever they should become ill or otherwise. After due consideration the body unanimously agreed to send out "get well cards" to any sick member here after. First on the "sick-list" to be remembered was...

Dec. 20, 1953. Our first rehearsal for the coming *nenmatsu taikai* (year end festival) has been set for tomorrow night. We have a program, mostly musical as follows:

1. Sunday School *gatha* (songs) by the nursery and primary and intermediate group - a. *Hotoke Sama*, b. *Tsuki ga deta.*

2. "Winter Wonderland" sung by the older girls and boys accompanied by Yoshi Okamoto.

3. Christmas songs by the primary children - "Santa Claus is Coming to Town" and "Jingle Bells".

4. Sunday School *gathas* by the older group (Jr. and Sr.) - a. *Nobiyo Nobiyo*, b. "When we see the Golden Sun".

5. "White Christmas" orchestra and song.

6. Christmas Recitation by the primary children. Verses read by Kay Ishii.

Distribution of the Christmas gifts will be made after the program. Refreshments of cake and pie along with hot chocolate and tea will be passed out to everyone.

I never did quite understand why we had Sunday School. I'd study my Buddhist texts and read that there really didn't need to be a church, Buddha nature was in all of us and not necessarily in the temple or altar or religious paraphernalia.

So at a young, exploring and questioning age, I'd skip Sunday School, telling my mom I was sick and stay at home with dad, watching him burn some old vine stumps on a chilly fall morning or play outside in the dirt, waiting for my brother and sister to return home with mom after Sunday School.

All the while I was also waiting for something, punishment from Buddha for skipping church. I never got any and I'd say to myself, "See, I was right, Buddha don't need me to go to church, he's in me, right in me when I play in the dirt or watch the smoke and flames rise from the stump pile." Later a Buddhist minister told me that it was a "Buddhist" thing to do, very philosophical for a youngster.

And he was right. I was shocked the Sunday I was in Japan and strolled to one of the biggest Buddhist temples in Japan. It was Sunday and I didn't see any kids going to Sunday School. I didn't see little Buddhist readers and *gatha* books. All I saw were ministers in their robes, lighting incense and chanting. Then it occurred to me, this Sunday School system was an American invention, a model of the Christian catechism and educational system, a rote learning of ideas and parables and dates and names. They didn't have Sunday School in Japan, but then again in Japan it was hard not to be Buddhist, especially when you died. No matter who you were, you had a Buddhist funeral.

But in America it was hard to be a Buddhist: questions about life were often met with deep, philosophical answers instead of clear and concise convictions in neat packages that fit well with American society. I did learn a lot though in Sunday School, and perhaps without that understanding, I would have never begun to appreciate the joys of a child playing in the dirt or the wonder of a dancing flame.

ABA Adult Buddhist Association

I once attended one of the ABA meetings and didn't understand much that was being discussed. They were like a big family having lived in the same place for decades and listened to each other speak for years and years. Now they understood each other so well that they seemed to skip words, everyone seemed to know before hand each other's position on issues so they summarized arguments with simple, "ummh" or "ahhh." That's all they needed to say and everyone knew what that person meant. It certainly saved time and meetings were concise without a wasted word.

The ABA wasn't really the name of the organization, the Del Rey Buddhist Society was correct but I'm sure hardly anyone went by that name, it sounded too formal and distant for these country folk. In fact they used to call themselves the YABA, Young Adult Buddhist Association but I'm also sure that someone a few years back brought up the point that they were no longer that young and should drop that part of their name. I don't know if they took a vote on it, the minutes don't have it recorded but I imagine there was a long silence after that point was raised, mixed with a few "ummh" by the menfolk and it was unanimously passed following this involved discussion.

Their constitution of 1956 reads, "the purpose of the ABA shall be to encourage and advance the principles of Buddhism and to promote unity and friendship among members." I think they believe in both parts of that statement but tended to concentrate on the ladder aspects a bit more, of course doing it with Buddha nature all the while.

If the Sunday School was concerned about Buddhist education, the ABA was concerned about the social life of the Buddhist Japanese of Del Rey. Social meant pot lucks and picnics and gatherings and also concern

Young Buddhist League basketball champs, 1948-49. Sports flourished through the years and community organizations provided the structure. Basketball survived the war and emerged the dominate sport for not only the *Nisei* but also the *Sansei*. A championship year would be remembered by a team and solidified a sense of community, the champs from Del Rey in 1949. (Courtesy Jim Harada)

for their members. Written in the constitution were bylaws covering funerals and hospitalization:

"Funerals: floral or monetary offering of $10 to members and immediate family, residing with said family and parents will be given.

"Hospitalization: a remembrance in maximum amount of $5 will be given to all members with the misfortune of major surgery, major accident or serious illness."

The money was to "be a little something to help the family in their time of need." Today we find it difficult to understand that, especially the dollar amounts but back then, not only was a dollar worth a lot more but these were for the most part poor farm families. The money did mean a lot.

They were a homogeneous group, all about the same age, all Japanese and Buddhist and mostly all farmers. They became just a big family and as you scan through the minutes of their meetings you can sense the aging of this family by tracking their social calendars.

In the 1950's with the baby boom there were lots of baby showers. This trend tapered off in the 1960's and replaced by 25th wedding anniversaries. And when these ran out they were substituted with the 60th birthday parties. Del Rey gained a reputation for a fun, partying group. Not all communities worked together like this but not all communities, as a *Nisei* woman explained to me, "had all the same people, all poor in the same way... we didn't have any big shots and that made us all alike, and maybe like each other more."

There were other activities the ABA became involved with some even political like the 1972 Prayer Amendment in Congress. The ABA had organized a letter writing campaign against the prayer amendment. The amendment failed and the minutes note the effort by the club.

Typical activities included (from the 1973 minutes): Jan.- membership drive; Feb.-snow hike; March-clamming, tentative to be discussed later; April-community picnic; May-parents day pot luck; June-graduation and Sunday school picnic; July and Aug.- *Obon Odori*; Sept.-(blank but we presume the raisin harvest filled the days and weekends); Oct.-*Betsuin* (Fresno area Buddhist Churches) food bazaar; Nov.-nominate officers; Dec.-*nenmatsu taikai* (end of the year festival) and installation of new officers.

Today the key officer is the secretary. With an aging membership, folks forget meetings, dates and activities. Reminders have to be sent out frequently and still people miss meetings. And at meetings, the secretary's minutes play a vital role. When it comes time for discussion about an annual event, like a picnic and the menu, they always simply refer back to last year's minutes and plan the same food and drink.

Perhaps that's why it took years to cut down on the number of cases of "soda water" needed with less and less *Sansei* children attending, and the beer because less and less of the menfolk drank with concerns over health and diet. Used to be they needed a couple cases of beer but now everyone quickly dozes off with their first one and the old metal trough remains full with a case of beer floating around in the melted ice by the end of the day.

Youth Organizations

Youth organizations were vital in the world of young *Nisei* and *Sansei*. Before World War II and immediately following it, the YMA, Young Men's Association and the YBA, Young Buddhist Association sponsored social events such as dances or "blow outs" as they called them. Hundreds of *Nisei* couples met at these gatherings, one of the few time strict parents allowed their children to attend since "all of the kids would be Japanese and that was OK."

In the late 1950's a new organization in Del Rey was formed, the U & I Club, an organization dedicated, as a *Sansei* woman explained, "to the sole purpose *Sansei* would hang around together and meet other, good, nice Japanese kids." Hence the name "U & I", a sort of symbolic metaphor for inducing a sense of community. The U & I Club lasted for a few years, and for the high school *Sansei* it did meet their needs, almost all of them accepting the wishes of their parents as proper and correct.

In 1960, a Jr. YBA (Young Buddhist Association) club was formed, partly an outgrowth from the U & I days, and the youth of Del Rey became affiliated with the West Coast network of other Jr. YBA. The club functioned the same, a social club for *Sansei* to meet other *Sansei*, especially at "sock hops" or "sing alongs" with other Jr. YBA's such as Fowler, Reedley or Parlier.

There were also conferences to attend, a regional one in Fresno every fall and a statewide one once a year. These conferences tried to instill new understandings of Buddhism. For example in 1966 Del Rey had to think of two possible themes for the November conference. One was "Buddhism, the Gateway to Wisdom" and the other was "*Sangha* [brotherhood], a Step Towards World Peace." They were supposed to think of a third one or be fined by the conference committee in Fresno, but the minutes read the Del Rey Jr YBA President would try and think of something last minute.

The themes, keynote address, and workshops at these Buddhist conferences were informative. The *Sansei* participants were polite and courteous, dressed in new outfits and shirts and ties, sat through the day long affair and got their name tags stamped or punched verifying their attendance, and thus allowing them access to the dance that evening (which, of course, was the main reason a lot of them were there).

Once at a conference in the late 1960's, a radical group of Japanese American anti-war college students from San Francisco descended upon the

Junior Young Buddhist Association Conference, 1966. A generation later and the conferences continued. Perhaps changes had not been that great, teenagers still gathered to meet each other and strike amazingly similar poses with a generation before.

500 innocent *Sansei* of the valley and exposed everyone to the war and politics and long hair and jeans.

This created an uproar from the *Nisei* parents and advisors of the Jr. YBA, they were shocked by the invasion of these long haired "hippies" (even though they were all Japanese and Buddhist). A week following the conference an emergency meeting was called and the *Nisei* parents voiced their anger by attacking the long hair and jeans.

The jeans clashed with the innocent black slacks of the boys and the sleek skirts of the girls; the jeans with patches worn by the outsiders contradicted the hand-me-down white shirts and black ties of the boys and the new shoes and first-time-worn make up of young girls. Jeans just didn't fit at the Jr. YBA conference and after a lot of shouting and threats of boycotting the next conference, a dress code was passed to never allow jeans at any conference ever again. The issue was settled.

The *Sansei* handled the whole affair rather well, especially at the conference. The dance was successful as boys met girls as they had in the

YBA. CONFERENCE NOV. 12, 1966

valley for years and to those "progressive thinking" *Sansei*, the exposure to politics and social issues would be valued. For most *Sansei* though, the jeans were clean and very, very few of the innocent *Sansei* mixed with these long haired, older outsiders anyway.

The Del Rey Jr YBA sponsored their own activities, dances, and swim parties. Fund raisers were popular, not only was money raised for parties but also for causes. In 1963 a discussion was held to sponsor foster children overseas and years later the club donated to the Biafra hunger relief fund. One of the first fund raising ideas was the selling of Christmas cards. A Buddhist youth organization selling Christmas cards? They sold well.

Sports were always popular, they had long been part of the Japanese American tradition with prewar baseball teams and basketball tournaments. Although the Jr. YBA was a Buddhist organization, there was an open policy about allowing Christian Japanese to play too. A type of "free agent" clause about "Buddha nature" being in everyone and the fact that one didn't have to know a lot of Buddhist teaching to be a Buddhist, this allowed most everyone to play despite some accusation about stacking teams

Over the years, little had changed since the U & I days.

CHAPTER 7

THE NEW COMMUNITY
AND A LETTER TO THE *ISSEI*

The New Community

Mrs. F. Matsubara, a *Kibei:* "The biggest change in community? Well... before *Issei* do things Japanese way and *Nisei* before the war not old enough. But after war, it more business, everything done the American way.

The American way. What did that mean for the Japanese American community? One over-riding, universal denominator was change, the family changed, the community changed.

Mr. N. Hiramoto, a *Nisei:* "We all used to be one big family, the Del Rey community. Could talk free, never have to hold back, that's how it was.

"But it's all different now, even my own family, different. Used to be we're all same but now, with *hakujins* [caucasians] and the grandkids, like we don't know each other and have to watch what we say. At gatherings, only thing we do together is help ourselves to the food."

Change was part of the natural, growing process of a family and community. Change affected every aspect of life from the way you raised your crops to the way a Buddhist wedding was done.

A *Nisei* woman in her 50's talked about change. She paused, thought for a moment, her eyes blinked as she concentrated, her lips grew taut and a soft "hmmmm" escaped from her throat. "The biggest difference, post war I mean," she said, "I guess you can say the *Nisei* just got older."

In the community you can hear two voices. One was an older, *Nisei* voice: "We *Nisei*... we're close knit, we do things together and feel like family. The Del Rey people felt like 'our people,' what ever we decide to do we can do it together. Like when we do something, want the other Del

Reyans there, I always want them there, I feel more comfortable, just like seeing the others, more secure.

"Even our children, they got that secure feeling from being from a small town. It's always nice to see other people you know, especially us country folks. It feels like we're all one, even keel, no higher up or lowers. You feel like you belong, like you're one. I know other people from other communities all say, 'Gee, you Del Reyans sure get along good together.' And I say, 'We are all just like family, no one has more than the other.'

"We can all work together. We cooperate on about everything, I hardly ever hear anyone saying no. Like election time and our club officers, I've heard one person say, 'I can't do that job, I'll trade with you...' So people trade jobs to work things out well."

Mrs. V. Ishikawa, a *Nisei:* "Today... our community? We've gotten smaller because all the young people are gone. It was in it's prime, peak when *Sansei* were in school. I think it's sad but not our choice, all the young people went away and there's no more children. More old people now... As long as we *Nisei* are alive though, our bunch will be intact, then after that I don't know."

But another youthful voice speaks of uncertainty, with change ever present. Mr. S. Matsui, a *Sansei:* "I know the community is well and healthy. Whenever I come home I see the get togethers and the 60th birthdays... But when these 60 year olds pass away, it's going to be hard to replace the cornerstones of our community. I think of these people... and the *Sansei* don't have the ability to maintain Japanese. Like language, *Sansei* don't know and once you lose the language you lose a lot of the culture."

Mr. G. Nishikawa, a *Sansei:* "The Japanese always got along together but they also got along well with other races. We needed to get along to get further along ourselves. We realized that and took advantage of that as much as we could.

"In the future... we say community but I'm not sure I would call it community, in the sense we had before. I think there's more of an integration with others, there isn't quite the same segregation there was before... Language was a barrier and they kept more to themselves. Younger folk are much more integrated 'cuz they were educated side by side with others. More diversions and we may not have the time to spend for community."

THE REUNION

They spoke of a reunion, a reunion of the Del Rey Japanese American community, a gathering of the past and present residents and a renewal of friendships. Their paramount concern: they had to meet before the old ones died. The "old ones" used to mean the *Issei* but now the *Nisei* had entered those ranks and a sense of mortality found a way into their thinking.

At first it was to be a gathering of the old community, with only the *Issei* and *Nisei*. "Why would the *Sansei* want to come to a reunion?" they asked. Yet perhaps more than anyone else, the *Sansei* needed that sense of history, a sense of home and community. After some discussion the *Sansei* were allowed to come and the reunion was transformed into something different: it became a reunion of family, children returning home for a journey into the past.

But family carried different meanings. "Child care?" they asked, "who needs child care?" Had they forgotten that this was a family reunion with small children included? Or was it simply that the *Nisei* had different notions of parenting? (During a following meeting, the real question arose, "What do you mean child care?").

"Send the invitations to just the *Nisei* parents. We save money that way," they added. Of course those parents would talk with their children, of course they would tell them of the reunion, but had we forgotten the distances between family and the miles between siblings and their parents? And would something be lost in the translation? Would they speak of the reunion with the same enthusiasm we shared, that feeling of community and shared memories? In the end the parents were entrusted to convey the message, in their own way, with their own words, and rightfully so.

On an April weekend, a banquet was planned and the following day a return to the Hall. "The Hall?" they asked, "Why go there? Who would want to go back there? It's old and practically falling apart! Besides we can see it anytime."

It took a soft, quiet voice that made the swing vote, an old *Kibei* man who had kept quiet during most of the meetings, sitting in the corner, away from the discussion at the table. He finally stirred and said, "Ah, I think we should go to Hall, the people come from a long way, they think they get to see the Hall." He paused, lost in a brief thought, perhaps recalling the glory of the Hall, the times when it was the heart of the community, the center of a people's memories and experiences. "The Hall, might'y important you know."

We would get to return to the Hall.

The responses began rolling in. Letters accompanied registration, excitement stirred as members as far away as the East Coast and Hawaii confirmed their plans to attend. Yet others reacted indifferently, they felt alien, wondering if "this was going to be reunion of just the old-time community, before the war." Some questioned, "Why should I go, to see the same people, nothing special to me. We'll just boycott." Boycott? We hadn't realized we stirred such emotions.

That night the banquet tables were beautiful and a community gathered once again: handshakes, hugs, smiles, laughter, coupled with awkward moments of silence as faces weren't recognized and names forgotten. For some, just as important as "who was there" were "those who weren't there," unexplained absences, differing attitudes about community, and fears of lost friendships.

The *Issei* bowed to each other and seemed to slip into another world with conversation and memories only they knew of. Proud grandparents carried bewildered grandchildren as families exchanged greetings and needed introductions, for much had changed.

For the evening's program and entertainment, we introduced the entire community. Everyone in attendance was introduced with a brief update on individual histories, a recognition of a familiar face, a renewal of community. Applause with comments accompanied each name, the room buzzed with energy. Since individuals were introduced by families, usually small groups stood with each introduction. But one name brought sighs and jokes of disbelief for it seemed as if half the room stood with this one particular family, a gathering of one clan with four generations represented.

A few had stood proudly and waved while others shouted greetings and told a brief story. Many, though, simply quietly rose and bowed to the community. A shy gesture, a soft smile, you sensed a type of pride in them, perhaps from the unexpected recognition or could it have been a sense of belonging, for this was the community they had once called home?

The conversations continued, a cherished, souvenir banquet program had listed all in attendance with the personal updates and comments. These programs were carefully tucked into purses and saved for future reference and renewed reminiscing, memories carefully packed within each page.

The families slowly departed and grew excited, the next day they would return to the Hall.

She was glorious in the morning sun. They had cleaned her, painted the interior, prepared her for the return of her family. The Hall stood in the warmth of that April morning, earlier that morning a group of individuals had scurried about, preparing for the arrival of the others with a fulfilling breakfast and smile.

She had come to life that day, filled with conversation and children running and babies crying. It had been years, many, many years since such a large gathering had filled her interiors. The sounds of children playing seemed to give her energy, a natural, simple reincarnation of life.

People sat and ate and talked more. Those that had left the area were astonished at how well the Hall looked, it seemed as if the years had been good to her. And those that had stayed were just as astonished, perhaps they had been mistaken, the Hall wasn't as old and dilapidated as they had grown to believe. *Sansei* walked their children around the yard, trying to remember the games they used to play along the sidewalk, and describing the meaning of this place where they came so many Sundays in a row.

A local television reporter came, the story carried interest for them, meanings for a wider audience. Interviews were done, the camera recorded the history being celebrated. The reunion had come to mean more than just a gathering of a individuals, it now carried a story for many to share in.

A single story captured the meaning of it all. A *Nisei* man had explored the Hall grounds, searching the exterior walls along with his memories. He finally located what he sought, it wasn't large nor conspicuous but it had survived the years and generations. He proudly pointed it out to us, a discovery that carried more than just memories, it was a sense of the past embodied in a few simple nicks in the wall.

In the wood siding you could see a cluster of nicks, slices once cut into the wall and painted over many, many times. "That," he explained, "was where we played during Japanese school. At recess we used to pitch pennies right there, at those nicks, trying to see who could get theirs to land closest to the wall."

The nicks survived, a monument to a time past and a symbol of the spirit of community. They would now live forever in his memories and perhaps ours too.

The sounds of crickets at night, the morning fog hugging the vine rows, a marriage with nature and her impulsive weather. This is a country way of life fewer and fewer know or understand. This is a rural voice that has diminished in volume to a faint whisper.

Country folks had always understood these different rhythms, a tempo dictated by seasons and not time clocks or paid vacations. And as a group they were outsiders to the city. The city was something you visited, sometimes with envy and other times with intimidation. "We were *inaka* [country]," folks explain and say that with a pride. "We enjoyed living out... we didn't let it bother us and took life for what it was. We enjoyed life."

But today they are a smaller minority and their shrinking numbers have given birth to a set of different relationships. For those that have left, memories and bittersweet emotions for the farm life remain. Others who still have family in the *inaka* may come home to the place that connects them with their past, sometimes with a sense of wonder and joy and other times with a depression as they see decay and deterioration.

Yet for those that remained, the overriding emotion is difference, a difference that separates and becomes an overwhelming barrier, and yet a difference that provides a source of intense pride and identity for community and her people.

A LETTER TO THE *ISSEI*

To the *Issei*:

Time and death have thinned your ranks, you no longer occupy whole rows of tables at picnics or potlucks. And less and less Japanese is heard or needed at church services.

But that is why I have to ask you about life, questions of the past history and the changing spirit of family and community. I have to ask these questions and discover answers before your waiting has ended and your stories are lost forever.

How will I remember the scenes of your youth? Will I be able to describe your building of Del Rey Hall, the work of skilled hands and strong backs that molded a wooden structure that has withstood 60 years, like a monument to your belief in community? And your founding of a Buddhist Church here in America, the strength and perseverance you required for such a vision and challenge despite the barriers before you?

The founding of the Del Rey Hall, 1919. "Will I be able to describe your building of the Hall, the work of skilled hands and strong backs that molded a wooden structure that has withstood 60 years, like a monument to your belief in community?" (Courtesy George Fujihara)

And of your bringing of the Christian beliefs to a Japanese community, the conviction of your values and strength of vision to understand the need for a Japanese Christian community along side the Buddhist?

Can I recall the flavor of your picnics in the foothills and the *shibai* (plays) and *samurai* movies, times when your community paused from its work and gathered to drink and play and be entertained? Wasn't that a vital part of your life, a balance between work and the social and "spiritual" worlds with the sweet taste of homebrewed *sake*?

Could I report on the drama of other times, the bitter debate between the Buddhists and Japanese Christians, a division that forever split the Del Rey Japanese community? The excitement as other Buddhist Churches in the surrounding area were also built and established, the Japanese community prospering and growing? And the pain of witnessing the hall during World War II when it was temporarily seized by the government to house wartime farm laborers, the same government that had incarcerated and exiled you because of your race?

And will I remember the stories of your children, the *Nisei*, and the memories triggered today at reunions and gatherings? Will I be able to

describe the growth of the Sunday School when the Del Rey Hall buzzed with activity and was full of running, squirming children? When the *nenmatsu taikai* (year end festival) lasted for hours and filled a December evening as a community gathering to celebrate the completion of another year?

Or the community pot lucks when the hall was jammed with families, a full five rows of tables crowded up against the walls, all the men seated along one side and the women on the other side with children in between? And the food tables that were almost sagging from the collection of food to be shared, the *nihon* (Japanese) wives with their *sushi* and *teriyaki* and the more American *Nisei* with their experimental dishes like pasta or meat'n potato casseroles or even later Mexican food?

Could I retell the tales of the Del Rey YBA days and their first conference that attracted hundreds to Del Rey Elementary School before the war? And how about the latest rage at that time: ping pong and the tournaments sponsored by various communities, and Del Rey's table that still remains in the back of the hall, a monument to a past generation and era?

Will I be able to relate the feelings that many in the Del Rey community hold dear? Like a sense of pride when they won the contest at the Fresno *Obon* for their costumes, an attitude that Del Rey might be small in numbers but, as they called it, "still mighty?" Or like a sense of security that reveals itself during tragedy with the comforting knowledge that the community will come to help you and your family during that time of grief and pain, an emotional insurance that no amount of money can buy?

And will I remember the experiences of my generation, the *Sansei?* Will I forget what happened in the last ten years when change seemed to accelerate and a distant future suddenly arrived and a different sort of reality closed in upon us?

Who were the leaders of Del Rey that had passed before us? What happened to those who dedicated an entire life and hours of service to our community, only to pass away in a slow, draining process? Were they, like true *sensei*, still trying to teach us something in their final hours?

Why do I think of the 25th wedding anniversary parties of the Del Rey *Nisei*, how they began as the women's night out, and later changed to include the men when a waitress once questioned the ladies during one of their festive dinner celebrations, "if it's an anniversary party, where's the men?" And how those *Nisei* women decided, "why not include the boys?" Or the 60th birthday parties that aren't for males only and my realization that my parent's generation actually enjoy parties just like everyone else? Yet I can't help but wonder who will be at my 25th wedding celebration and what will Del Rey be like at my 60th birthday party?

I sometimes wonder too when will the Japanese of Del Rey once again gather for a reunion? We met in 1985 for a grand collection of familiar faces that stirred warm memories in all of us, a community renewed its spirit, a sense of history born in all of us, a collection of not just the *Issei* and *Nisei* but a gathering of family including *Sansei* and even *Yonsei:* can we continue to meet as a community in the future?

And where have all the *Sansei* scattered to? Have their professions lured them away, and now the slow, quiet pace of the *inaka* (countryside) become out of step with their life style? And what of their children, will the *Yonsei* come to know the meaning of "Del Rey" or for that matter even care?

And how can we continue to function as a community? With shrinking numbers, we face a different reality. Funerals bring us together more than celebrations, declining numbers make it difficult to be represented at Fresno area functions. And even the hall, the grand old hall, new and difficult questions are raised, can we continue to support such an aging friend?

So these are my questions and I do not expect answers. A silence lingers when I think of you *Issei* and these questions, and in that pause lies a wealth of understanding and insight, all in a moment of wonder and mystery.

This is the history I wonder about, a history of the everyday and of the ordinary, a history of the rich yet subtle colors of nature and farming, a history of traditional families and communities in an ever changing world.

This is the legacy I wonder about, a spirit that remains alive even if only in our minds and souls and captured in a few scribbled words in a letter.

This is the Del Rey community, a rare family farm community with a life style fewer and fewer know or understand. Even those born here have grown distant and foreign - the dust and sweat and natural forces alien to the offices and technology of city life.

But what will become of it all? You, the *Issei*, will soon die and we shall follow. Yet perhaps even in your death you teach us all that change is part of our life and of Japanese culture? You, the *Issei*, have left us a history, a spirit that lives within our memories so long as we continue to ask and wonder. And in you, the *Issei*, we find the simple nature of a country people that continues to guide us in our daily lives. You shine in our future.

SECTION II

CULTURE

Culture. It's like watching an *obon* (Japanese summer dance festival) and the young *Yonsei* boy about 5 or 6, all dressed up like a little *samurai* with a *hapi* (Japanese jacket) and *geta* (wooden sandals). Except, the headband across his forehead, the traditional *hachimaki* with *kanji* (Japanese characters) written on the white band, it's upside down and the *Sansei* mother doesn't know it because she doesn't speak or read Japanese. But they whirl and turn and clap to the sounds of Japanese folk music and it all makes sense.

Culture is like a mysterious creature, at times it is elusive, ever on the move and changing, and other times it seems to just sit there, wallowing in tradition and custom. But culture binds us, gives us meaning and provides us with foundation; culture has been described as "webs of significance" that surrounds, entangles and supports our daily life, a matter of learning "what it is we have to know" to belong within a family and community.

Often we think of culture as just those festivals and art from a nation or region, that's why in the course of interviews many said: "Culture? Naw, I don't know a whole lot about that stuff." Yet a few minutes later they'd be explaining about various Japanese foods and how they were made at New Year's celebrations, or the proper sequence of the seating of relatives at a funeral, or the years of education received at Japanese language school.

Some of this culture will be displayed in the following pages, stories that capture those gestures and visions, all flecks of culture that differentiates who does and who doesn't belong. Culture is constantly in flux, a part of it securely entrenched yet another part changing, evolving over time with the influx of new ideas. The cultural language spoken by the family farm community is presented here, meanings and structures of significance sifted out of a people's thinking.

CHAPTER 8

THE MAGIC IN A NAME
AND GROWING UP JAPANESE

The Magic in a Name

"After all, you're *Nihonjin* (Japanese). That's why we gave the kids Japanese names, I want to make sure they know they're *Nihonjin*." Mr. N. Haramoto, a *Nisei*.

We all live with our names, they travel with us constantly like a shadow. But a Japanese name in America brands you as different, foreign, alien: a reminder of who you are and where you came from. You tolerate mispronunciations, raised eyebrows and comments like, "Why don't you get a normal name?" Within our Japanese names we carry a part of our heritage, our histories.

A lot of *Nisei* have added an American name for use by non-Japanese, a sort of adopted public name. At home you were Ichiro or Fumiko, at school you became James or Florence. The *Nisei* tried to dodge a lot of the teasing and pain by giving American names to their children, a few still clung to Japanese names but usually it was innocently hidden as a middle name. And yet today *Sansei* have often given a Japanese name to their children, a middle name they feel preserves that sense of history.

Names, married to our faces; names, we need them daily; names, they contribute in their own way to who we are, to our identity. There's magic in our names, a power hidden in the names we wear.

Mr. M. Masuda, a *Kibei:* "When we lost the Sanger ranch, give it back to the former owner in 1915...or 16? When we lost it I went to my friend, well... not friend but distant relative, they brought me to this country.

"These people... a couple, they a far relative you know. My father ask them to take me to United States. So I know them very well. So I went to their home and they said, 'Why don't you work'... He a gardener you know... 'Why don't you stay here and do gardening a little bit.' So I did that for months.

"They're a religious, a Christian family. So they got me to be a Christian for a while. They have *hakujin* (Caucasian) friend, a Christian. She call me Matthew. Matthew, after that I use Matthew as my name too."

Mrs. T. Asakawa, a *Nisei:* "My real name is Ryuko. But I got Thelma because when I was going to school, when I first started school the teacher couldn't pronounce my name, Ryuko. So she gave me her mother's name."

Mrs. K. Nakamoto, a *Nisei:* "We lived on a ranch and the old lady there named me. That's why I always said to my dad, 'How come you always gave me a name like that, you can't even pronounce it.?'

"He said, 'No, the *hakujin* lady... she gave it. After all, we all lived and worked there."

Mrs. D. Yanagi, a *Nisei:* "Dad could speak some English, he had schooling in Hawaii. Well, not real fluent I would say, but he could make people understand and he could understand. When I was born he got to give me an English name. I guess he didn't know much English names so he just took the word dollar and dropped one of the "l's" and named me Dolar.

"When I went to school the teacher said, 'There's no such name Dolar, it must be Dora.' That's how I became Dora. See, so close to 'Dollar' she thought it was a mistake. Of course, Dad made up the name and on my birth certificate and marriage certificate I used it, Dolar. I thought, well, maybe one day I'll just change it to Dora but I figured why change it? Dad gave me that name."

Mrs. V. Ishikawa, a *Nisei:* "I was against naming my children with a Japanese name. I think because I never liked my Japanese name, maybe that's why. People always teased me because it rhymed with a bad word in Japanese. And now our granddaughter... they named her with my Japanese name. When they wrote and asked what were some good Japanese names I said any name but mine. And they turn right around and use it!

"I think I never thought about a Japanese name for my children because, I don't know if you understand this but when we *Nisei* were being raised, we were so busy being Americanized. We kind of, not that we resented it but we didn't like it when we had to say our Japanese name. So

I got so I lied when people asked what my initial stands for and instead I used to make up an American name.

"But as much as I rebelled and any name for my granddaughter but that, I was really honored."

Mrs. J. Oyama, a *Sansei:* "No, we won't use a Japanese name. We figured our last name was Japanese enough, why make it any more complicated?"

While studying in Japan, I toured the nation with a group of California students. At a Kyoto temple, we stopped to sign a registry of visitors, a dozen of college students from California writing their names in Japanese.

The *hakujins* wrote with katakana, a simplified Japanese alphabet often used with foreign words. We *Sansei* wrote our family names in *kanji* characters.

I remember firmly gripping the pen, slowly etching my name on the white parchment, deliberately stroking my family's name just as I had learned from my father and *obaasan* (grandmother). After the final stroke I leaned back and smiled, I had been told that my family characters weren't very common and for that reason I felt a little special.

Behind me stood Fukuda-*san*, our Japanese tour guide. The sweat beaded across his upper lip, his fat, round face swelled in the heat, he tried to conceal his discomfort and not be bothered by the heat. "You young *Sansei* must learn Japanese culture," he had often repeated to us, singling out the Japanese Americans as if we carried a special burden. "And you must learn of Japanese thinking, of respect," he added.

Fukuda-*san* leaned over the registry, the small table bore his entire weight and seemed to groan under his mass, a few drops of sweat splattered on the pages. "*Heiii..* who is this?" he said, "is this Japanese?" He laughed and his rolls of fat shook under his tight shirt, rippling with each sneer. "This last name, did one of you students make it up?"

"It's mine," I answered and glared at the tour leader.

"Oh you," Fukuda-*san* said, still taking deep breathes between chuckles. "I'll teach you the right way to write it tonight. You can't go and keep inventing *kanji* here in Japan." Fukuda-*san* glanced once more at my writing and laughed, "Well, at least everyone will know my American Japanese tour group came here." Snickering at his own joke he motioned everyone into the temple grounds.

I had learned my name from *Baachan* (grandma). I remember our writing lesson. She sat at the dining table, the chair seemed to engulf her

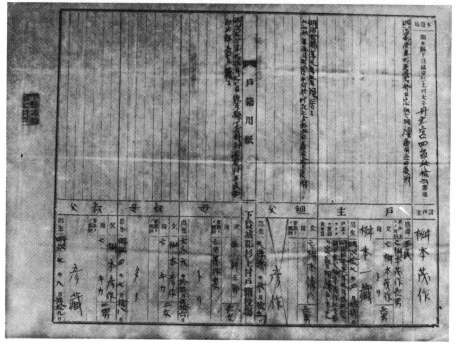

The family *koseki*, a registry, 1918. A *koseki*, the family registry, 1900's. The *koseki* provided a documentation of who you were, the household you belonged to, the family you were part of.

small frame, her black cotton pants and faded flannel shirt hung on her wiry body.

I sat next to her, blank sheets of typing paper and two pencils before us. *Baachan* looked at me and half smiled, I wondered if she remembered the morning's conversation when mom had explained about my wish to learn how to write the family name. Mom had admitted that she didn't know how to write our name and later I was to teach her. Now at the table, I sat ready for my lesson. *Baachan's* sunken eyes surrounded by a web of wrinkles stared back at me.

I handed her a pencil and waited, wishing I knew some Japanese. Finally I said in English, "OK *Baachan*, show me, OK?"

She gripped the pencil as the veins in her hand swelled and her knuckles grew white. As she wrote, her pencil dug into the paper and almost tore it in a few spots. She stopped and pushed back in her chair studying her work. She had scribbled five letters of the Japanese alphabet, letters, not characters. None of her strokes were smooth nor even, her

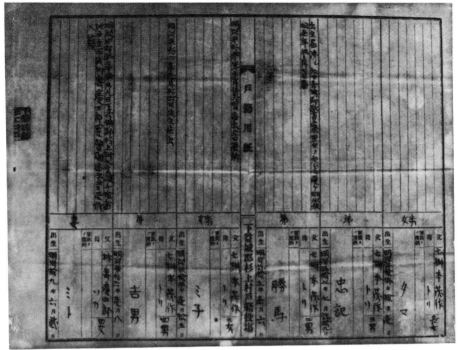

My grandmother's name is on the last page, in the lower right hand corner. Her marriage to Hikazo Masumoto was written on the first page, lower left corner. He was a second son. At the time of the *koseki*, they were considered to be "under" the household of my grandfather's eldest brother, the number one son. Everyone belonged to a single household and each household had its master. My grandmother clung to these sheets of paper, carefully tucking them in a back corner of her dresser. They were all she had of family, they were her identity.

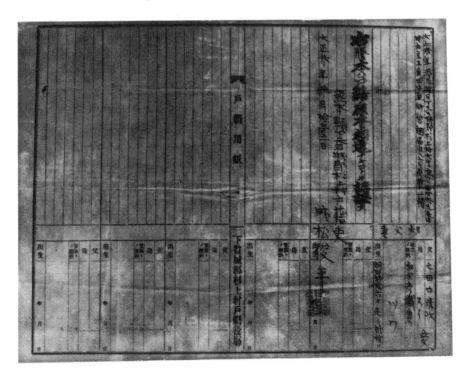

lines wavered and stopped short of connecting. *Baachan* put down the pencil and stared out of the window, gazing at the vineyards.

A few months later I learned the family name from Dad. He explained that only *Jiichan* (grandpa) knew how to write it. Dad though was unsure of all the strokes but thought the characters looked close enough to be right.

GROWN' UP JAPANESE

"I don't know if I was raised Japanese. I didn't know what was Japanese and what wasn't." Mrs. D. Maruyama, a *Nisei*.

When you ask about culture and being raised Japanese, a lot of country folk don't understand your questions. For them the idea of culture remains buried in customs and tradition or narrowly confined to the arts. Yet being raised Japanese (or Armenian or German or Mexican or most any other ethnic group) envelopes you, it's all encompassing to the point you don't think of it as being any different than the rest of the world. It's as if you didn't know better and accepted it as being just part of the way everyone is raised, just like all the kids.

A *Sansei* explained that like most Japanese Americans he grew up with *shoyu* (soy sauce). He put it on everything from eggs in the morning, to a lettuce salad with *shoyu* dressing, to beef and fish submerged in the black liquid. *Shoyu* belonged on the dining table right next to the salt and pepper.

It came as a shock to him when he first discovered that not everyone else used *shoyu*, it was conspicuously absent from other tables. And a further shock was that not only was it missing but they didn't even know what it was (this was in the 50's and 60's, before alternative foods like *tofu*, soy bean curd, and *sushi* were popularized). He remembered eating in a restaurant and debating whether to ask for some worcestershire sauce for his beef, a meager replacement for *shoyu* and could possibly ruin a fine slab of beef, yet he felt he had to do something.

Now you can buy *shoyu* at your neighborhood grocery, but they still don't call it *shoyu* and it's an American version, it tastes sweeter he claims. So he still buys his *shoyu* in the square gallon tin cans by the case at Central Fish Store.

The old days. It was always a generation or two before you came of age, a time when folks were raised differently, with an inference of a better way. Those were the good old days.

Mrs. V. Ishikawa, a *Nisei:* "We were taught a lot of mannerisms. Say, for instance, when somebody brought something my mother would say, 'Now don't open it till they go home.' Now that seems to me to be Japanese-y.

"And then that we were not supposed to talk unless spoke to and if I said anything my dad said, 'You're always talking out of turn or talking back.' And what's considered being open and conversing now was considered talking back. I remember that, my dad was famous for that."

Mrs. F. Matsubara, a *Nisei:* "Well, Japanese style? Our food was always Japanese style at home and my folks always spoke Japanese. And they always told us, 'don't be rowdy, be quiet and respect elders and that's all. That's all Japanese tradition."

To be brought up the old way. If you're Japanese you'll call it being raised Japanese, if you're German it will be German and for Armenians it's the Armenian way. The old days, it was an era of respect for elders, of hard work with no complaints, of no questioning authority.

What people called it didn't matter though, the fact is people were raised that way and they believed it was part of their culture or heritage and others couldn't have undergone nor endured a similar upbringing.

Mr. G. Sato, a *Nisei:* "We were probably no different than the other kids of other cultures. But we thought we were... only Japanese families were this and that way. We were country kids you know, most of the time with our own kind. Didn't know a whole lot about other folks. But that's the way it was in those days."

Mr. G. Oyama, a *Nisei:* "I swear, my folks planted weeds to make sure I always had more work to keep me busy. You know how Japanese folk are about work, you're only happy and healthy if you're working,"

Jack Hata, a *Nisei*, and his wife Tomi, sat across from me. I asked, "Were you brought up Japanese?"

"What do you mean Japanese?" he said.

"Ah, you know," Tomi Hata interrupted, "you were."

"Why?" he said.

"Because your mother did everything, cater to men folk and he still carries that over."

"Oh?" he said, "you think I'm the chief?"

"Like in Japan. The menfolk important, everything catering to them. Whatever they want. That was carried over to him," Tomi said, pointing to her husband.

Jack laughed and began to say, "So, I just sit down and..."

"And he just sits down and eats and leaves everything on the table. I mean that's the way they were brought up," Tomi explained.

"But you do it, don't you?" said Jack.

"Well, that's the way I was brought up too. It was my work to take care of you. I was taught to keep busy and work, even if it is to pick up after you. But I'm sure glad I taught our daughters to be different," said Tomi.

Jack turned to me, shrugged his shoulders and said, "I guess I can't win."

Nihongo (Japanese language). It was part of growing up Japanese for an entire generation.

Most of the *Issei* knew very limited English, the rural farm isolation shielded them from the English speaking world. Almost all of the *Nisei* knew some Japanese and attended Japanese school, some for six days a week, after regular school. The *Nisei* saw an important part of their world through *nihongo*, part of a cultural legacy they grew up within.

"While growing up, I wasn't sure of what was Japanese," said Mrs. F. Yoshioka, a *Nisei*. Compared to what I consider what was really Japanese-y, I don't think we were really Japanese-y. The only thing was that my mother didn't speak English. We all had to know Japanese."

To many *Nisei*, language wasn't cultural, it was simply required. Spoken at home or in private conversations, the Japanese language was part of being Japanese, uneventful, almost unimportant.

But to *Sansei* who didn't speak Japanese, it carried special meanings and connotations. Mr. S. Mitsui, a *Sansei:* "Whenever my folks used Japanese, it meant either they were mad at me so I'd sit even more quiet and let them lecture me or it meant they were talking about something they didn't want us kids to hear. It was really comical."

Few *Sansei* became fluent in *nihongo* and within a single generation, much of the language was lost. Growing up Japanese meant knowing a few words in *nihongo*, but an understanding of Japanese culture was not centered around language. Thousands of *Sansei* grandchildren never had a conversation with their *Issei* grandparents. Never.

Sometimes only when you leave a place can you look back and see exactly what you had. Many *Sansei* left the valley for education and work and discovered the world where being born and raised out in the country, on a farm, it was unique: like being Japanese it marked you different.

Mr. F. Yamashita, a *Sansei:* "It took me a while for me to realize that being born and raised out in the country was unique. 'A farm?' people would say, their voices raising and immediately romantic images flashed through their minds, barnyard chickens and churning butter and fresh milk. Hell, we never had any of that stuff, only a few dogs and cats."

Few *Sansei* had chickens or fresh milk or butter, but they did have a rural culture, a different type of perspective you grew up with. Being a "country" *Sansei* meant you probably spent some time under a grapevine either playing as a little kid or hiding in the shade to escape the hundred degree summer heat as a youngster or resting and cooling down before you had to go back out into the fields as a working teenager.

Interview with Mr. S. Mitsui, a *Sansei* now living in Northern California.

Question: were you brought up Japanese?

Mr. Mitsui: "Sure, definitely."

Question: In what ways?

Mr. Mitsui: "I think my parents really stressed religion. The Del Rey Buddhist Church was a very important part of my growing experience. I'll tie that together with the fact my parents also spoke quite a bit of Japanese in the home. That had set a tone inside the house. I think there was quite a bit of culture, and we didn't even know it... like even ideas of how you get married. Just about everything in our upbringing was very Japanese influenced. It made a very positive, a big difference in me."

Question: In what ways was it positive?

Mr. S. Mitsui: "I think, at least for myself, I know that my parents stressed a lot of independence. And that independence, I think works to my advantage now. I think early on, there wasn't a great deal of dependence on my parents, which is good. They stressed that you are a person and that you have all the tools to succeed."

Question: What do you mean my independence? And how is that related with being Japanese?

Mr. S. Mitsui: "Because my parents worked in the fields a lot. OK, you sit there as a kid and had to make up games to play on your own... we didn't have much TV or a lot of other things, just ourselves. And that happened to all of us country kids. Sure, we were Japanese because of church and *nihongo* [Japanese] language and all that... but we were also farm kids by ourselves.

"Sure, you may have played a lot with your brothers and sisters but it wasn't like your parents were always taking you to the park on Sunday afternoon or everyday watching you play. You did a lot of things on your own, without interaction of your parents. That's what I mean my independence and it's still is part of me today."

CHAPTER 9

EVENTS AND CELEBRATIONS

The first time you attend a Japanese celebration or festival in Del Rey you may feel as if you've stepped back in time.

At the annual New Year's pot luck dinner, as soon as you walk through the front doors you're greeted by rows of tables, covered with white butcher paper, and the majority of men sitting along one side, dominating their row of tables and on the other side of the room are the women positioning themselves along their wall. In between the two is a sparsely settled land, seating for those late comers who were bumped from their respective sides and room for the young children and *Sansei* couples. As you settle in your seat you can't help but think of the hundreds of dinners before, where all the men still sat on one side, arms crossed over their chests and all the women on the other, patiently sitting, heads slightly bowed and hands clasped in their laps.

There's a sense of tradition in these celebrations, a culture that penetrates the soul and almost humbles you; there's something going on that's a lot larger than your own beliefs; there's a spirit that embodies the occasion of a family and community celebration. Culture comes alive and lives in our celebrations.

The Community Picnic

Picnics have been part of the community ever since the early *Issei* days. These picnics were held in the spring, in the foothills or park and away from the farms and work. They were a day of leisure, of games and of laughter.

Mr. G. Fujita, a *Nisei:* "We'd go all the way over near Shaver Lake. The family would take the old model T and oh, we had a big time. All day

The Del Rey *Kyowakai* annual picnic, 1920's. Held in the foothills with a lumber flume in the background, the Del Rey Japanese community gathered for a day free of work and worries. Skits, plays, drinking and races were held, a celebration of life and family and community. (Courtesy Emma Hatayama)

Sunday. We wanted to get away from all the people because the first generation wanted to get drunk. By the end of the day they wanted to sober up and come home. That was the sole reason they went way up there where there was nobody, that was the main reason.

"The men sang and clapped like this... [clap, clap]. Usually just the men, they were rowdy ones. The women watched and took care of the kids. We had games, the older ones ran half mile races... and there was prizes, anything you can buy for a certain amount of money... pencils, erasers, tablets, books, a ball.

"Oh we looked forwards to it. Anytime we had a picnic we'd also get new shoes you see, we looked forward to that."

Mrs. V. Ishikawa, a *Nisei:* "We always went to the foothills for the picnics. We went to the same ranch, it belonged to a farmer, one Japanese family used to live and work on his place. Because of this connection, he'd let us use his place. I don't think we paid but it was like a cow pasture and you had to watch for the 'do-do's.'

"We went about 10:00 or so in the morning, just about the same way today. But it was bad, we had to clear the fields, the men would take shovels and stuff to clear the place because we kind'a had to find a level place for the kids to run.

"They always took soda water but our own lunches, everybody had their own lunches, you know *bento*. See, today we all have pot luck... In our generation, the mama's finally got smart, we got tired of doing all the cooking for everything at the meal. It's more fun with pot luck and we're such a small community.

"The games... we always just ran. I don't remember anybody playing anything else, no softball, it's up in the foothills remember, not very good for softball. The parents all ran too, the old ladies did spoon races where they run and carry something in a spoon and try not to drop it. The prizes were very menial, pencils, tablets... and we were glad to get the pencils, we didn't get much in those days, it was really something. You know I don't remember the prizes much because I had a girl friend and she was always fast and I was slow and finished second all the time. I could never win and so she always got the first prize and I never found out what it was like to choose.

"It was all Japanese food. But families didn't compete, you know, who brought what and who had the best *sushi*... we really didn't have a lot. Every mother did the best she could and packed her lunch. It was usually *sushi* and chicken and a lot of *nishime* [vegetables]... like New Year's food.

"Even after the war we still went up to the foothills."

Mrs. D. Murashima, a *Nisei:* "Everybody took their own food. Today we're more organized, the men barbecue the chicken... but back then it was really rough on the women, you know everybody make their own *gochisoo* [food]. So that's rough when you have to make all your own... See, this way today it really simplifies it and you can enjoy it."

Mr. R. Matsubara, a *Kibei:* "The big picnic, we used to go to ranch in foothills on Sunday. People bring *bento* [lunch] and we have running games and *sumo* wrestling. The *sumo*, young men. In those days mostly young men you know, even the *Issei* now, they were young in those days.

"All kinds of prizes, not toys but pencils and tablets, things like that. The adults had races and they used to have that pulling ropes... a tug of war... the girls on one side and the boys on the other... and we used to have numbers to add up who ever adds up the fastest would come to the line and be the first one. No, I don't remember Japanese games like *hana* [card game] there."

Over the years the picnic has remained a tradition, it has switched locations to a park instead of the foothills but a lot was still the same. One event in the picnic was the raffle. Prizes were collected from merchants and businesses that Japanese Americans patronized. A few weeks prior to the picnic, community members went to these businesses to solicit donations.

The 1957 Picnic Donation List:
Standard Oil Co. Sanger $5.00 cash
Royal Jewelers   1 wrist watch band
Okamoto Jewelers   1 candle stand
Arie Barber   3 bottle hair oil
Yokomi Fish Market   1 rice cake, *aji*, cookie
Komoto Department Store   1 Japanese Tea set
Aki Co.   1 sprinkler, 1 garden hose
West Fresno Floral   1 house plant
Sanger Nursery   2 camellia plants

Selma Nursery 1 azalea
Bert's Del Rancho Rey   18lb. rice   25lb. dog food
2 25 lb. sugar   2 giant Tide soap
Parlier Lumber   1 electric heater, 12.95
General Petroleum, Parlier   assorted cleaner material and leather cleaner
Budd and Quin's Station   3 tractor toys
Tokubo Fish   4 candy
Del Rey Hardware Co.   2-5ft. hoses 2 pak plant food
3 pliers   1 sprinkler   1 corn server
Hilco, Sanger Branch   garden hose
Sanger farm supply   garden hose 4.45
Ray and Grant's Service   1 car polish
Gibbs Tractor (Case)   1 shovel
Joe Morita, Selma   1 gal Wesson oil
Federated Store   1 towel set
Del Rey Packing Co   1 box raisin in carton
Garry Packing Co   1 fancy pack ass't fruit
Nicks Service Sta. $2.50 service card
Tidewater Assoc. Oil, Selma   1 case oil weed oil
Enoch Packing Co   1 box raisin in 15oz. carton
Yosemite Nursery   5 plants
Honda Garage   car goods

The 1974 Picnic Donation List:
Seiberts Oil Co.   paper towel
Selma Nursery   flower plant
Phillips Petro   grease gun
Farmers Supply   1 case soap, 1 gal. *shoyu*
Sunnyside Packing Co. $25.00 check
Selma Ag Supply   Water hose
Baggie   12 sacks fertilizer
Moriyama Trucking   1 gift
Rain for Rent   Sprinkler heads
Bill Smith Motors   car polish
Hallowell Chev.   snow chain
Bank of Tokyo   2 boxes of gifts
O'Neal Irrig. Supply Co.   2 rakes, 2 hoses
Controlled Irrig. Corp   Sprinkler
West Fresno Florists   plant

Harada's Landscaping   plant
Honda's Garage   fire extinguisher
Parlier Lumber   skill saw
Payless (Mr. Wilson)   tennis racket
Sanger Nursery   tackle box, hose, 2 thermos, 2 shears
Benny's Toyota   mini mats
Farm Machinery   12 toy tractors
Elmer Schmidtgall Jr./Heinlet Helzer $5.00 check

The 1980 Picnic Donations List
Alvin Anderson   1 case motor oil
Farmers Market   1 case *shoyu* (4-1gal),
1 case paper towel (30 roll), 12-5# sugar
Selma Ag.   1 two gal. hand sprayer
Farmer machinery   16 caps
Moriyama Trucking   1 tea cup set, 1 serving container
Central Fish   2 vegetable press, 2 salad makers
Sanger Nursery   2 pocket knives, 2 garden magazine
Heinle Service Station   5 qts. oil and 1 oil filter
Inaka Sushi   10 exchange cards for *sushi*
Sunnyside Packing $25.00
Sanger Ford Mercury   1 lub. job and oil, filter change
Calif. First Bank   6 coffee mugs
Honda Auto Supply   1 electric lantern
West Fresno Floral   1 dry flower arrangement
Jim Harada   1 Japanese plum, 3 juniper
1 box wood plant
Farmer Buying Service   1 pair boots, 2-1 gal. cooler
Fresno Ford Tractor   1 case motor oil

If you look at history in different ways, these lists can tell you a lot about how a community has changed. Certainly you can speculate on why the list has shrunk, either less and less folks were around to solicit the donations or more and more business folded and weren't around to donate. It was probably a little of both, the community lost members, more retirements and less business with the local merchants.

But equally important, a lot of the little "mom and pop" stores folded, traveling to Fresno became routine instead of an adventure. So places that Japanese Americans used to patronize, like the Del Rey Hardware Co, have gone. In fact when the Del Rey Hardware Co. closed and they had a final sale, all kinds of antique dealers flocked to the sale. They found bargains in those small, authentic items that either fit or repaired their antiques, parts that were no longer made because that company had long ago folded but these were the items that had cluttered the shelves of Del Rey Hardware for all these years. So when the Hardware store closed its doors, the picnic donation list lost a lot of gifts and a little bit of the community too.

The menus for the community picnics were simple and required only a few lines in the meeting minutes: "Chicken was barbecued and supplied by the community as a whole, the rest pot luck style."

Over the years the community members came to understand their individual roles: who were the good cooks, who liked to experiment, and those that would bring the best Japanese foods. Some *Nisei* women would talk as if they were terrible Japanese cooks and never dare to bring Japanese style foods. They'd try taco salads and leave the Japanese foods to the pros: the *Nihon* (Japan) wives, those younger women who had recently married and come from Japan. Over the years everyone had begun to identify foods with people so just by looking at the tables covered with plates and heaping bowls of food, you could more or less tell who had come to this year's outing.

Picnic Menu from March 3, 1962 minutes:
"Eighty chickens were to be purchased and 15 cases and the left over soda water (total 30 cases), 2 cases of beer, 2 gallon *shoyu* [soy sauce], 5 lb. sugar, garlic salt, a 5th of sherry wine and charcoal for barbecuing. Each family were to bring *musubi* [vegetable dish], *sushi* or *inarizushi*, enough serving for their own family. Group 1 and 2 dessert and Group 3 salad. $60.00 were for kiddies prizes and races. Picnic assessment was decided as same as previous years, $3.00 single, $5.00 couple and $10.00 family."

Picnic Menu from Jan. 30, 1979 minutes:
"The annual picnic date tentative, first choice in March 25 and next choice March 18. Menu: 45 chicken, 2 1/2 case soda water, 1/2 case diet soda water, 2 case beer, 70 lb charcoal, 2 gal *shoyu*, 5 lb. sugar, garlic salt, 1 dry sherry wine, 1 roll heavy foil, 1 roll paper towel, 5 fresh garlic. Prizes $90.00 was allotted. Group 1 and 2 dessert and group 3 salad. Assessment for picnic - $10.00 family, $5.00 couple, $3.00 single.

Tradition lives in these menus. Questions about the "Group 1, 2, and 3" opens the door to a history lesson. The community was long ago divided up geographically into groups of 10-15 families. These divisions helped structure and organize the community, the geographic divisions were important at that time, neighbors could easily work with each other due to their close physical proximity. For example hitching a ride from your neighbor was essential, especially when your group was *toban* (in charge of an activity or occasion). *Toban* meant you had to arrive early to set up and be in charge of all the details, like starting the charcoal at a barbecue or setting up tables and chairs and turning on the heater in the hall for a New Year's pot luck dinner.

Glancing through the picnic minutes, groups 1 and 2 seemed to always make dessert and group 3 the salad. Perhaps this too became a tradition, much like the menu. Chicken was still the main course, chopped up the night before and soaked in a *teriyaki* marinade overnight. The special recipe still called for a bottle of sherry wine and garlic.

But the numbers have changed, less and less people attended the picnic. It was hard to imagine 30 cases of "soda water" for the kids and consuming 80 chickens in addition to all the other foods. The 45 chickens and 2 cases of soda (one case diet soda) in 1979 symbolized the changes, most of the children had grown and left the community, the picnic mostly for aging *Nisei* who loved to take home the extra chicken for left overs since "it's hard just to cook for two," as one *Nisei* wife explained.

And another sign of the times was that it used to be only pouring rain that would force a move of the picnic from the park site to inside the hall. But today with an overcast sky and slight threat of rain, phone calls were quickly made and the picnic would be moved indoors, much to the relief of older bodies. There's a few more children at the picnic in the recent years. Some of the *Sansei* visit home and bring their children with them. It can point to a revitalization of the picnic, still a family and community gathering but perhaps with a new meaning, a chance for a new generation to come back to see where parents and grandparents were raised and worked. Perhaps even one day the community shall see the return of the 30-40 cases of "soda water" era.

Oshogatsu, The New Year's Celebration

In Japan *oshogatsu* is a three day holiday of temple visiting, eating, drinking and visiting friends and family. The tradition continues in Japanese American communities like Del Rey, it remains both a family and community event. On New Year's Day, families prepare Japanese food, invite family friends and neighbors over, and a celebration comes to life. A few days later, the *Kyowakai* has an annual pot luck dinner with more food and drink. This is one time of the year you don't plan on dieting. *Oshogatsu* means family and community celebration to welcome the New Year, a time to reflect and continue a tradition.

They sat and recalled the celebrations and festive memories. Both in their 70's, memories were slow to surface but the topic of *oshogatsu* seemed to bring them to life.

"*Shogatsu?* Ah, that's a real big thing you know," he said.

"*Shogatsu* was about the only holiday we had," she added. "We were all too poor, couldn't afford any other holiday."

"Especially Hiroshima people, they really celebrate," he continued. "Ah... they make lots of *gochisoo* [Japanese food] you know."

"Yes, Hiroshima people... we all celebrate but they did a lot. There were so many of them around here, they're all from the same places too. I guess they wanted to out-do their friends maybe," she said.

They both paused, wandering in their thoughts, then she added, "Lots of family and friends came visiting. Mostly the men came, the wives don't come, they all stay at home and the men could go around and drink. They didn't eat very much, they just drank a lot."

"Oh yea, we celebrate two, three days. See, in Japan everybody do almost one week. Yea...," he said.

"Sometimes they had *shibai* [Japanese play] at the hall," she added. "We had *mochitsuki* [making of rice cakes] too... friends get together, all pound the rice, make about 100 pound sack for one family. And if there's four, five families you can imagine. It was an all day job. I remember we put them in *kanae*, those big crocks. Put them all in and then put water. Yea, it'd get mold so they take out the mold, scrape it off and add more water a few weeks later. It'd last quite long, at end they get sour. They used to eat a lot of it for mornings. My father used to eat and it wasn't just one or two, he'd eat a half dozen or more."

The couple then grew quiet, possibly drifting off into memories of the *oshogatsu*, celebrations that shined in contrast to a lifetime of hard work in the fields.

Mr. G. Fujita, a *Nisei:* "*Shogatsu*, it was a biiiigggg deal, open house deal. I remember...we were Christians with Christian friends and we celebrated Christmas but *shogatsu* was a big deal.

"*Mochitsuki* at *shogatsu* time was one of the biggest deals they had. Done mostly by family, the bachelors too, they helped out. One of the most festive times for us all.

"Never miss, everybody take a week off. Even when we were teenagers, that was one of the traditions we carried on. I mean we... from New Year's eve until about a week later, if we slept 2-3 hours we were doing good."

Today families and the community still celebrate *oshogatsu*. It's one time of the year the *Sansei* children often try to return home, for family and as many explained: "for the food." The three day festive spirit has been condensed into a single day and some of the meaning of the holiday may have been forgotten, but the traditional array of food, *sushi, chashu, yokan, kamaboko* along with other foods that symbolize the beginning of a new year, such as red lobster for good luck or black *azuki* (beans) for good health or *somen* (noodles) for long life, all these foods bring home families and memories, a fusion of tradition, culture and good times.

Some still travel and visit neighbors and friends, dropping in for a drink and a toast for good luck in the coming year and a quick plateful of *gochisoo*. Of course though, these visits are now sandwiched between bowl games and half times, a new rhythm interjected into the celebration.

And a week later, the community still gathers for their New Year's pot luck dinner. A toast begins the meal, a gulp of champagne and a heaping of New Year's food. As noted before, it's not a time for dieting.

The *Obon*, Summer Festival

Colors flash as the dancers spin, turn and dip in their bright *kimonos* (Japanese dress costume). In their hands the *kachi-kachi* (wooden clackers) crack together with the drum beat and rhythm of folk songs. The music echoes from the Buddhist Church grounds, a strange blend of Japanese song and dance and the backdrop of a summer evening in Fresno's west wide.

With each summer comes the *Obon Odori*, the annual Japanese festival with folk dancing in the streets. For many Japanese Americans, the *obon* holiday is a time to honor family ancestors, a reunion with the spirits of the past. Through lively and colorful dance, Japanese perpetuate in memory and display gratitude to their ancestors.

Obon originates from a blend of folk culture, legend and Buddhist beliefs. It celebrates the idea that ancestors return and briefly visit the living, even if only in memory and symbol. Colorful lanterns light the way for spirits to return home and the dance symbolizes the joy of this spiritual reunion.

Drums beating, hands clapping, feet skipping, all these join in a fusion of motion and spirit. An illusion is created: the entire community dancing, including the blur of a great grandfather or grandmother dancing as he or she may have done. *Obon* provided a spontaneous outlet: a time of celebration and rejoicing.

Obon dance movement reflects a sense of freedom, the motions are relaxed and simple, the rhythm quick and upbeat. Normally the dance is performed in a huge circle with a *yagura* (stage area) in the center where teachers maintain a steady example for others to follow. Spectators are encouraged to join the dance, their sometimes rough movements add a festive element.

Many dances involve accessories complimenting the hand and body motions. The *kachi-kachi*, named for the sound it makes, are two narrow strips of wood that are held in the hand and cracked together. These produce a clean, crisp sound, especially when hundreds of dancers snap them in unison.

Brightly colored towels with red, blue and gold designs are waved through the air, twisting and flapping as if energized by a sudden summer breeze.

Fans with colorful and elaborate designs add to the spectacle. When skilled dancers wave these fans, they seem to glide through the air in accompaniment with the floating music.

The *Issei* brought the *obon* with them. These pioneers struggled in the fields of California, often working for cheap wages. The *obon* was a Japanese tradition they looked forward to, a slice of their homeland recreated in the San Joaquin Valley. The *Nisei* soon became part of the festival.

"The *Obon* was one of the few times the boys could visit and be with us girls," said one *Nisei* woman of the time before World War II. Our *Issei* parents were very strict, but during the practices before and during the *obon*, we were allowed to visit. It was a big thing for us back then."

The larger Japanese American communities held an annual *obon*. Pockets of Japanese in the Fresno, Fowler, Parlier and Reedley communities maintain the summer tradition. Other valley communities, Bowles, Dinuba and Visalia once held their own *obon* too. The Fresno *obon* is the largest and draws participants from outlying communities.

During the 1950's, the Fresno *obon* grew in scale and size. *Nisei* had begun their own families and hundreds of *Sansei* participated in the event. A common sight were groups of young children dressed in proper attire, mimicking the older dancers but always a few steps behind and a number of counts off, nonetheless a lively addition to the festival.

During the peak years of *obon* a two block section of Kern Street in front of the Fresno Buddhist Church was sectioned off. Spectators packed the sidewalks and noise filled the air as friends and families gathered and visited. The dancers traveled in a huge oval circle slowly passing through Japan town and by the hundreds of smiling faces.

The *obon* was the grand summer festival, especially for many who were struggling to reestablish themselves following the war when they had been shipped off to relocation camps. The freedom in dance, the rhythmic music and the flashing colors contrasted with the emotional scars left by the war years.

A competition was held between the various communities such as Fresno, Fowler, Del Rey, Bowles and Selma. Awards were given for the best group costume, each community designed and wore special *obon* costumes with the hope of winning a trophy, recognition and community honor.

"I remember, they had a contest for each community to make the best *obon* costume," said Mrs. D. Takeda, a *Nisei*. "Well, we in Del Rey,

Obon festival, 1930's. "A competition was held.. each community designed and wore special *obon* costumes with the hope of winning recognition and honor." (Courtesy Clair Nagamatsu)

we're such a small group, we jumped on the wagon right off and beat everyone. We contacted Mrs. Kimoto in Fresno who helped us make our outfits, we had all black with hats... No one else was on the ball and us in Del Rey, we all had the same outfit, all ready. We beat those others to the punch and won first place at the first contest. We're small in number and beat all those others. And you should have seen them the next year, everyone, Bowles, Fresno, Fowler, boy did they have costumes. Well there's no way we can compete against that. You know, they never let us win again... but we got first that one time and we'll remember that one."

The contest was eventually discontinued after the competition grew too fierce and overshadowed the festive spirit.

A common sight at the *obon* were *Issei* sitting together, exchanging stories about their families, pointing to children and grandchildren as they danced past. Some sat Japanese style and watched the dancers, their haunches touching their heels, elbows bent and resting on their knees. They would sit like this for hours, clapping hands to rhythms, perhaps silently returning to Japan with each song.

Rings of spectators surrounded the *obon* dancers. Many were husbands and fathers of the dancers, greeting friends and neighbors and discussing their harvest and farms, utilizing the time to renew friendships. A dual parade of faces encircled each other, the dancers on the inner ring while on the outer rings, friends chatted and moved on toward the next conversation.

For children the most important food sold at the *obon* were the snow cones. A tradition evolved at the Fresno *obon*, snow cones were sold by the *Byakudokai*, a Japanese community club. Children would grow excited, not because of the dancing but from the thought of an annual treat. Picture dozens of children, dressed in clean, stiff Japanese *kimonos* or *hapi* (Japanese jackets), with bright, clown colored red and green mouths and lips from strawberry and lime snow cones.

Over the years the size of the *obon* has decreased. A natural attrition occurred, fewer and fewer *Issei* remain alive to attend and many of the *Sansei* have lost interest in the dance. Few men now participate in the *obon*. However, the Japanese American community remains in transition, the next generation of children, the *Yonsei* are beginning to participate.

The *obon* of the 1980's points to a new tradition: the celebration of Japanese American history and experience. For many Japanese Americans the *obon* music stirs memories not of Japan but of the *obons* of years past. The *obon* tradition includes the rhythms of Japanese music echoing through the West Side of Fresno and the small communities of Fowler, Reedley and Parlier. The *obon* remains a living yet ever evolving tradition.

CHAPTER 10

GOCHISOO AND BROWN RICE *SUSHI*

Gochisoo, Good Foods

Name five things about Japanese culture here in America and odds are someplace on that list will be Japanese foods. But it's not always the food that's important in terms of understanding culture, sometimes it's what happens around the food that's crucial.

Mrs. I. Kagawa, a *Nisei:* "When I got married my mother in law always lived with us.

"I never once did make *botamochi* [sweet rice cakes]. I'd put the *azuki* [sweet beans] on, you know, the beans on and grandma took over. I never asked her but every time I put on the azuki... each time with *botamochi* I put on the *azuki* and that's all I did. Grandma finished it up.

"Until she was gone, I never made it myself.

"The same with *osushi*, grandma always there. I helped her but grandma always had the lead. But of course you always have respect for the elders and you just let them do as they wish."

Like an additional flavor, meanings are carried with food. Foods you grew up with , foods attached to holidays, foods that don't simply reflect a culture, they are the culture.

Mrs. D. Misawa, a *Nisei:* "I guess in my own way I stressed culture to my kids. I don't know if they'll remember it but Girl's Day and Boy's Day I made *botamochi*. Every year... so that they'll know what it was... I would do this. Not that the boys were particularly fond of the food but the girls loved it. But I always made it, tried to impress to the children that March third, three and three is Girl's Day and May fifth, five and five is Boy's Day. That's what I did for them."

Mrs. K. Yanagi, a *Nisei:* "*Oshogatsu* [New Year's Day Celebration], that left a big impression on my children. To this day they all want something for New Years, the New Years Food and all that.

"And you know *yokan* [sweet gelatin], it takes a lot of hands to keep stirring it. I carried that tradition on until just a few years ago with everybody gone now.

"And when my oldest went away for school and not too much contact, they stressed the New Years themselves and they made *sushi* and all that. Well, I just thought that was terrific. That's something that must have stayed with them."

For many, cooking has remained a cultural tradition, a surviving ritual passed from one generation to another. Family recipes, specialized techniques, secret ingredients and seasonings, all part of a tradition and passing these cooking methods to the next generation has become part of the rites of passage for many, especially some *Nisei* women.

Imagine this training: an *Issei* mother takes her daughter aside one day and begins to teach her all about life, mainly how to cook the proper and right way, especially with "their" foods. "Their" meant those special Japanese dishes you just can't buy and will have that homemade flavor. Over the years the daughter becomes proficient at meal preparation so that one day, when she entertains her future in-laws with a glorious dinner that she has planned for weeks, her future mother-in-law nods her head in approval and the daughter and marriage-to-be is approved.

But it didn't always happen that way. Mr. D. Abe, a *Sansei:* "I remember my *Baachan* [Grandma], she was a terrible cook. I don't think she taught any of her daughters to cook and I don't think anyone ever taught her how to cook. Oh, she could handle a shovel like a pro and work from sun-up to sundown out in the fields but in the kitchen, she just let mom do all the cooking. You remember, she came from the countryside in Japan and they didn't have a whole lot back then, her life was more farming than homemaker. I guess it all worked out though, grandpa needed a strong back with him in the fields more than a great meal waiting for him at home."

Mrs. D. Murashima, a *Nisei:* "No, I didn't learn how to cook Japanese foods much from my mom. She was ill a lot in her last years so I learned more from trial and error I guess. Some baking I learned from high school. My brother, he encouraged me to bake I think because he's the one that probably wanted to eat. But I feel that I owe it to him. He was very encouraging. Later, after I got married, my mother-in-law was the one who helped me on some things. She was good to me.

"But you know, a cook is what your family makes you. If your family praises you, you're going to do your best to make it again. If they turn up their nose on something you'll say, 'forget that, I'm not going to make that again!' That's really how I learned."

Mrs. I. Matsubara, a *Nisei:* "I learned to cook first from my mom and then the Del Rey *Fujinkai.* There was a woman from Bowles, she used to come and teach like *sushi* and *manju*, things like that. I was still young, before the war and I got married. Lots of people attended from the community. They continued these classes, bringing in experts to help us *inaka* women out."

Brown Rice *Sushi*

Following my graduation from college, I lugged home a newly found "organic" mentality. Home meant an 80 acre family farm outside of Del Rey, and "organic" roughly translated into doing things the most natural way, like switching from processed fertilizer to animal manure. A fundamental part of this mentality included changes in my diet and nutrition and one specific change involved brown rice. Being Japanese American my family had eaten white rice daily, but now I had converted to the anti-white rice cult and my goal was to enlighten my family to the wonders of brown rice.

On the second day home I shocked everyone and volunteered to make the dinner rice, opting for the brown rice alternative. The family gathered for the meal, my parents, grandmother, and a sister seated around the dining table filled with plates full of *teriyaki* beef, *tofu*, stir fried vegetables and steaming hot brown rice. One hour later with a pot full of the rice sitting cold in the center of the table, I got the message my brown rice campaign was in trouble.

My grandmother finally asked, "Ah, did someone burn the rice?" My sister burst out laughing.

My dad added, "You know, *Jiichan* [Grandpa] ate regular rice his whole life and died at 88. If white isn't supposed to be good for you then maybe I should eat more of what isn't good for me." A hungry look complimented his statement.

Returning from the kitchen, my mom carried a reheated pot of white rice leftover from lunch and we then began the meal. A realization struck me: you did not substitute brown for white rice at dinner, a special meaning we attached to the white rice, a meaning that seemed to go beyond nutritional differences.

Within the context of a Japanese American family and community, a vital relationship existed between white rice and the surrounding environment. What occurred around the rice, the way and manner it was cooked, served and eaten all added to its special "flavor." A specific taste for white rice had been developed, so eating brown rice instead of white for dinner was not the same thing and such a change disrupted the pattern within the entire meal.

Part of the message contained in white rice was the traditional way it was served by Japanese American families. At our meals rice was a type of centerpiece, it was not only served with each meal (my dad ate it for breakfast with his eggs), it sat in the center of the table, my mom serving us our portions in *chawan*, a specific bowl we used only for rice. There also was a specific order of serving, my dad was first followed by the male children, then my sister and grandmother and mother last. These rituals had evolved from Japan and it was "the way it was done in Japan," according to grandmother. In addition, during my childhood the entire process by which rice was brought into the home strengthened a linkage with Japanese culture. The white rice we bought was called "Japanese rice," it was thicker and more sticky than regular supermarket rice (which we called "Chinese rice"). Our rice came in 50 or 100 pound sacks, though grown in California, the rice always had a Japanese name with bold *kanji* (Japanese characters) printed on the outside. Dad always purchased the rice at the farmers' co-operative he belonged to, a local co-operative formed by Japanese American farmers after World War II out of a need to pool resources and buy their own supplies, a backlash against the racism following the war.

Rice became a strong daily symbol of Japanese tradition, one of the few that survived the years. This made me wonder about my brown rice disaster. The significance of my brown rice was not what it was but rather what it wasn't. If meaning was derived through differences, the way I had served the rice was quite simply not Japanese, it lacked an affinity to "being Japanese." Another realization occurred: since the taste of food went beyond any one sensory pattern, perhaps if my brown rice was incorporated within another pattern, a distinctly Japanese pattern, it would

Hot dog *makizushi*. "Two cultures have clashed, the dual worlds of American and Japanese traditions."

have been palatable. Then the method I packaged the brown rice played a vital role for community and cultural perspectives were framed within the foods around us.

I thought of my brown rice and wondered what frame it could belong within. When compared with white rice, the imagery of brown rice seemed to reflect impurity. In addition I understood brown rice was once a peasant's food in Japan, unhulled it was considered less refined than white. White rice acquired a flavor of status, when *Issei* came to California, such an orientation could have easily been carried over with them. However at college, brown rice had devoted followers who argued the merits of brown verses white rice. I believed them, yet there was an irony in my thinking: the very stripping of the nutritious hulls from rice added a Japanese-American flavor to me. Eating white rice felt like home, indeed whenever I came home I did eat white rice: to be Japanese American you eat white rice.

The packages of meanings surrounding food can and do change, new patterns can emerge, new codes that bridge changing cultural beliefs.

I had seen an example of this in a cartoon from a Hawaiian magazine. The cartoon depicts a scene where two cultures have clashed, the dual worlds of American and Japanese traditions. In the first frames, a child enters a kitchen and asks his mother, "What's for lunch?" The mother is preparing *makizushi* (a type of *sushi* with rice rolled in black seaweed).

She answers her son's question: "We are having *makizushi*." The son immediately pouts, "Yuck, I want hot dogs!" and pouts more. Later, in the last two frames, the mother calls the son to lunch. He jumps from the television and runs to the table. There, the mother wears a wise smile and to the son's surprise, she has his "hot dog" on his plate: a wiener wrapped in black seaweed instead of a bun.

The cartoon pointed out a solution that bridged the differences between cultural dietary patterns. The acknowledgment of differences had led to a birth of new cultural forms, one that is not American nor Japanese but a fusion of the two. In the cartoon, the packaging of food mediated the difference between cultures, altering taste and acceptance. This packaging involved the wrapping of cultures around each other, foreign elements in specific combinations that maintain familiar cultural references: like a hot dog *makizushi*. Cultural meanings are then encoded into food, people package their foods in unique ways necessarily incorporating cultural dimensions and interpretations. Food becomes a social metaphor, assigning meaning to behavior. In this sense, a hot dog wrapped in seaweed becomes a type of cultural mediation.

Perhaps then my brown rice also needed packaging, a frame that mediated the natural food and Japanese American communities. I imagined a type of "brown rice sushi," a metaphor of the two cultures much like the "hot dog makizushi." By encasing the brown rice within a *nori* (seaweed) wrapping, a literal and symbolic wrapping of brown rice within Japanese tradition would be achieved, a birth of a distinctly Japanese American type of *sushi*. The *nori* differentiates the plain brown rice and provides a point of identification, a cultural frame. Brown rice would then no longer be a substitute for white rice on a dinner plate, but rather a creative, alternate form of making and serving a food.

Yet my brown rice *sushi* required a certain social context in which it could be introduced, an environment or situation open to change. The opportunity occurred at the annual Del Rey Japanese community New Year's potluck, a traditional gathering of the twenty or thirty Japanese American families from Del Rey, usually held on the weekend following New Year's Day.

We met in the Del Rey Japanese Hall, an old wood floored and walled structure built early in the century by Japanese American families as a meeting place for the community and a home for the Buddhist Church. The pot luck was for both Christians and Buddhists. Inside the hall, long rows of tables ran the length of the interior with butcher paper spread on top as a table cloth; the adult men sat in one row of tables against the east wall, the women sat along the table hugging the west wall and on the in between tables, children and younger adults sat. Ten years before, four or five rows of tables were needed to seat everyone, the community had been large, perhaps with 100 people at the pot luck and dozens of children running and chasing each other before the meal. But over the years less and less came, many *Issei* had died and the *Sansei* had left for college and work.

The food was the centerpiece of the evening, it was spread across two head tables with the various food dishes jammed next to each other, salads first, then rice dishes, followed by main entrees with desserts last and drinks on a side table. The like- foods were grouped next to each other, chicken dishes in a small circle, pumpkin pies rubbing crusts. Patterns had evolved at these annual gatherings, the good cooks always made the Japanese food, others brought the American foods like meat balls or fried chicken and recently enchiladas and taco salads had become popular. The "*Nihon* wives" (women born in Japan who had married *Nisei*), tended to dominate the Japanese food circuit, often in near competition. Some of the *Nisei* women joked that they no longer had to bring Japanese food (which they felt required much more time and detail) since the "*Nihon* wives were so good at it." I read a sigh of relief between such lines, American food could be served in all sorts of manners but Japanese food demanded a strict and proper appearance and taste.

I believed my brown rice *sushi* could be introduced within such a setting. I was one of the few *Sansei* who attended the gathering, one of the few sons who had returned to the family farm, and that evening I would be attending with a *hakujin* (Caucasian) friend who had been seen at other community events with me. Within this context I felt I could break frame and introduce my *sushi*, a new package for the community.

From the outset, community traditions began to dictate the evening's course of events. As soon as my companion and I walked through the double door entry, people looked up, smiled and waved; they enjoyed seeing "young folk" at their gatherings so I was often told. My friend carried the *sushi*, she had helped in the cooking and being a nutrition educator had interest in the brown rice *sushi* experiment. A woman took the plate from her, commenting on how nice it was for her to bring something, and directed us to be seated. They asked what food we had brought and we answered with brown rice *sushi*. The woman smiled and peeked under the foil cover at our plate and quickly a dozen women surrounded her, curious and not wanting to be left out.

After a short welcome from the Del Rey *Kyowakai* president, we began to eat. The *Issei* were asked first to get their food, followed by the men and children with the women last. I was categorized between the adult men and children but waited in order to observe the popularity of the brown rice *sushi*. As it happened to turn out, four or five plates of *sushi* were on the table, all of them except mine were *inarizushi* (white Japanese rice stuffed into small jackets made from soybean curd); this *sushi* looked like miniature rolls except they had rice within the tan soybean envelopes. The *sushi* I had brought was called *makizushi* (rice rolled in black seaweed with strips of vegetables in the center), each *sushi* was a flat, circular piece with brightly colored food in the center with black seaweed rolled on the outside. But instead of contrasting white rice I had used brown.

As the lines of hungry *Issei* and men stood around the head tables, they searched the plates, picking and selecting their food. The brown rice *sushi* stood out from the other rice dishes, simply at a glance because it was the only *makizushi*. Many of the people stopped as they picked up a piece with their chopsticks, and held it up in the light seemingly studying the color. By the time everyone had a first helping, as usual, all the *sushi* including mine was gone.

After dinner I began asking what people thought of the brown rice *sushi*. Some were surprised and had wondered why it looked different, others commented on its slightly different flavor. Later a friend of my mother decided to conduct a series of interviews of her own. She approached the keenest judges: the "*Nihon* wives." Their response was polite and clear: the *sushi* tasted different. Some said the rice was too hard and should have been cooked longer. Others were concerned about the dirty look of the rice, it wasn't white and clean. But they agreed it was pleasing and enjoyable and they were happy to see "young folks" make Japanese food. In addition most said it was the first time they had eaten brown rice. A few others wished there were more of the *sushi* to try.

The brown rice *sushi* package became a potential vehicle for dietary changes, a forum to negotiate change in traditional eating habits. The introduction of and exposure to new ideas and values was accomplished only within an authentic context, a sense of culture was maintained along side of dynamic change. Food became a means of passing old while creating new tradition, ideas allowed to penetrate the community while existing cultural practices were never fully abandoned. The clash of my "organic" culture with the Japanese American community was mediated through food.

As communities develop, change is not a passive process but actively given and received in innovative ways. New meanings and metaphors are introduced and created, adding to the process of cultural production. Understanding the packaging of these meanings, the fusing of the new and old, the innovative within the traditional, may provide us insight as the ways communities are growing and changing. Upon examination we find rural communities, such as the Japanese American farm community, are exploding with life and energy.

CHAPTER 11

CULTURAL RELATIONS

"Harvest time, dad hired outsiders. I can hear my father saying, '...here comes the Mexicans, hide your shovels and tools.' It stayed in my mind. Even to this day, any of the workers come and there's a shovel out there, it's gone the next day." Mr. G. Fujita, a *Nisei.*

"Now take the Armenians for example, they're a little bit different, almost selfish. Japanese and Armenians, we're too different." A *Nisei.*

"No, there wasn't a lot of prejudice in my life. Del Rey people were very nice and friendly. Japanese know others and we're all like one family." Mr. I. Matsui, an *Issei.*

"In a way I have an inferiority complex, you know *hakujins* [caucasians] always thought they're better... we felt a little inferior somehow or they made us feel that way. So with me that could never change. I know I'm their equal but sometimes you kind'a think...well....(she laughs softly)." Mrs. D. Morishima, a *Nisei.*

On the whole the people of Del Rey got along pretty well. There's been a history of cooperation, a number of agricultural cooperatives exist, farmers working with and for each other. A lot of people don't realize that Sun Maid raisins was not a private corporation but instead a cooperative owned by 2,000 small and large raisin growers, historically overcoming differences and working together.

But, as the lyrics of a song in Fiddler on the Roof "...of course there was the time when..." Racial discrimination, cultural impasses, community problems, Del Rey was no better nor worse than anywhere else. So long as there were differences, people have incorporated that into their thinking, almost as a given, a part of human nature.

Mr. N. Hiramoto, a *Nisei:* "The biggest difference between *hakujin* and *Nihonjin* [Japanese] is their culture. We have old traditions, like if

Del Rey Hall founding, 1919. The Japanese and non-Japanese of Del Rey "got along pretty well" as leaders of both communities attended the opening of the community hall with a symbolic union of the flags as a just background. (Courtesy George Fujihara)

others do something for you, we have to return that favor. *Hakujin*, well... hell, they have none of that stuff. It's the culture, that's important

"Then when I went to Japan and saw our culture and civilization, oh man, it's far beyond the so-called caucasian race.

"The trend now is more our way. The caucasian races are beginning to learn our traditions more, and they're improving themselves. I'm glad to see that. The background of our civilization is so far beyond their race so they're willing to learn."

Mr. M. Ishikawa, a *Nisei:* "We Japanese are different. Like in conversations... a lot of hakujins seem to talk loud, as if they yell a lot. And others, they just keep chattering away, maybe they don't like silence, they don't like to hear nothing."

The differences that folks talked about, they often arose due to the isolation, sometimes imposed and other times self imposed. There's a pattern of relationships based on non-contact and segregation.

Mr. G. Fujita, a *Nisei:* "The only time we were around other races was in school you know. Otherwise, like I said, we kept to ourselves. We didn't go visit our neighbors. We just knew them, that's all. My folks, all of our parents kept to themselves and didn't talk much with others. And even in school, like high school, I was still among my own group."

Mrs. V. Nakamoto, a *Nisei:* "I grew up knowing only Japanese. Weekends we went to Japanese school and saw Japanese. And the rest of days we went to public school and saw other friends but even then we looked for other Japanese."

Mr. J Hata, a *Nisei:* "The Japanese community was a tight knit family deal. I remember Sunday School and stuff like that, we all get together. Oh gosh, I remember the picnics, going to picnics. It was really nice, just a regular gathering, just like family outing what it was, it's a real close knit community. At that time you were isolated, you were really isolated you know. Just the Japanese family, oh sure you made some American friends but it was strictly Japanese, mostly Japanese."

Mr. T. Kumashige, a *Nisei:* "Yes, the Japanese community works well here. The only reason it works so well in this part of the country is that during our period we had so much racial prejudice against us. This is where we always stood together. We had to whether we liked it or not. We always had our picnics and own affairs and that's why the community remains so important."

It's hard to say which was first, because of the differences a people and their communities grew separated and isolated, or because of their isolation the differences were amplified and legitimized.

Mrs. V. Ishikawa, a *Nisei:* "I think it's nice to mix with the American people and everything. But I have several very dear American friends but I have them in different little boxes, I don't know why.

"I draw a line somehow, as close as we are, I have a very, very good friend but I don't know what it is, because she's *hakujin...* I don't know why. Maybe it's because my social life swirls around the Japanese community too much that she doesn't fit in with my cause."

Mr. G. Fujita, a *Nisei:* "The trouble around here, the early Japanese people, they were just working and working and working. They didn't get to know their neighbors or anybody. The neighbors were suspicious of them.. and that's why they were evacuated. So the whole thing after the war was to let the people know who we are."

A *Nisei* described: "Del Rey, we're all just small, we're just farmers, all of us."

Just farmers. More than anything it binds folks in this part of the country, a shared history that slices through generations. The differences remains but the shared history offers hope, a sense of a past where individuals worked together in the same profession, the same calling.

That doesn't mean everything was and is fine, folks here aren't blind to their differences. But in little ways the farming culture and today their shrinking community and squeezed economy, those remaining on the land band together and a rural farm culture emerges along side of one's ethnic roots, just as vital and significant.

Mr. R. Matsubara, a *Kibei:* "The Armenians,they're sort of like Japanese I think. That's what I feel. We knew some and they real nice. They came to farm here same time *Issei* but they learn little more English than Japanese did, maybe that why they in business more. But they not treat us badly. Some people maybe bad but most were good."

Mrs. D. Murashima, a *Nisei:* "The young folks will do the best they can and keep the community going. Especially because we're farmers and used to helping one another. We have to try and bring in others into the community, maybe not all Japanese but who cares? Anybody that's interested in preserving some of our community, we should invite."

There's an *Issei* woman, in her eighties, she makes you think twice about lessons of the past. Despite a life of struggle and prejudices and discrimination, she radiates a warmth of understanding that makes you feel guilty to even talk about cultural differences.

She spoke of returning to Del Rey following the war and four years of exile, four years of life behind barbed wire. She and her family returned and sought a place to live until they could move back into their home. Their farm and home had been leased out, a desperate agreement hastily signed in the final days before evacuation. Another caucasian farmer and his family lived in their house and wouldn't move out until the lease was up, almost a full year later.

But the *Issei* and her family were simply thankful to still have ownership of the land, so they tried to find a place to sleep anywhere and were refused rooms in town. The townsfolk didn't want any Japanese in their place. Finally, the *Issei* tried a neighboring farmer's place and he was indignant about the treatment given to Japanese so he housed them.

The *Issei* woman only remembers how kind and understanding these neighbors were, not the action of others. The *Issei* woman was so grateful that they hadn't lost the farm and she expressed deep joy that even the car they had lent to a packing house right before the war was going to be returned. "Imagine that!" she expressed.

In The Fourth Grade

In the fourth grade at Del Rey Elementary, I sat next to Jessie Alvarado. We'd cheat on tests together, he'd open a book so I could read the answers then he copied my answer.

But that was before they told me he was Mexican and I was Japanese. Our cultures were different they said, like he ate tortillas and I ate rice and our grandmothers each spoke a different language.

That was before they told me his family were farm workers and mine were farmers. We were supposed to be on opposite sides, something about human rights, even though we both sweated and itched the same during the summer when we picked peaches.

That was before they told me he was poor and I was rich. It made me feel guilty yet confused. I guess his brother's Chevy Impala wasn't as good as my brother's '58 Ford with the V-8 engine. But was I supposed to feel sorry for Jessie?

That was after the fourth grade when Jessie and I cheated together. And I wonder what they have told him since then.

CHAPTER 12

BEING JAPANESE: *GAMAN* AND *ON*
(PERSERVERANCE AND OBLIGATION)

There's a story about an *Issei*, a lonely bachelor who immigrated without family. They said he was a hard worker, quiet but intense, speaking with fast hands and a never-ending endurance. Every evening though, after a bath and meal, he would always sit outside, apart from everyone and stare at a brilliant red sun as it set in the west.

Someone once asked, "What are you looking at?"

They said he just sat silently for a few minutes, the red and purple hues of the sunset surrounded his silhouette , a lone figure kneeling before a flaming orange canvas.

Finally he said that the sun, the sun setting in our western sky was just rising in Japan. The same sun he watched daily would be shared with his family in Japan as they awakened. He explained it was comforting to know that and it gave him both a peace of mind and strength to keep working in the fields day after day.

Stories like this were often repeated to *Sansei* children, especially when they complained about the heat and dirt and sweat while working in the fields.

Through the generations, an image of what it is to "be Japanese" has evolved, a fusion of the old and new, of Japanese and American ideas, a blend that often resulted in both a comforting yet unsettling connection with the past. No different than other communities, Japanese American traditions in Del Rey have evolved, changed, and been maintained, all combining into what a people believe is "being Japanese."

Mrs. V. Ishikawa, a *Nisei:* "Our parents, the *Issei*, were more Japanese than the Japanese that are there in Japan now. I know some Japanese from Japan and they're more modern than my ways because their way of thinking. Our folks were raised in the old fashioned way in Japan, the olden days. So it's really old stuff... that upbringing is what they put on us.

"For instance, to show you how opposite it was. OK, for instance when pie is served I'm never supposed to say, 'Please have some, it's delicious.' Instead I'm supposed to say, 'This is not very good but please have some.' Now why would I serve someone pie that's not very good? See, out of politeness, it's so opposite.

"When my dad used to reprimand me about different things, I used to say,'Golly, here you send us to American school and we learn one way and we come home and you try and teach us the Japanese way, what do you think we can do anyway? You're getting us all mixed up."

"For the *Nisei*, it was rough because our parents were so different. The *Issei* were from the old, old Japan. We really had it rough. I bet it was harder on the older *Nisei*.

"Then, at the same time dad wanted to teach us to be more Japanese... I don't know if I should say this, it's just tales I heard... but Dad wanted to teach us Japanese ways and used to tell us stories... we heard this one *Issei*, he wanted his family to be American so bad they threw all their chopsticks away. Dad used to tell us that story I guess just to remind us."

Mrs. L. Nakamoto, a *Nisei:* "Japanese traditions? I just took it for granted the kids *(Sansei)* understood. Isn't that funny, I never thought of explaining. You know what it is partly, in our days, we weren't that open with our children. Whereas now, I see them constantly explaining things to their own children, the *Yonsei* and we didn't do that.

"In fact I have even been called on from my children, 'You were never open with us,' they'd say. 'A lot of things you talked with dad and we weren't informed, you're never open, that's what's wrong with you. You never express yourself, you never say things.'

"But then I felt it was not for them to know some things. I sort of drew a line. Whereas I noticed my daughter doesn't draw those kind of lines. I can see the difference how she's raising her children. I can see why she objects to the way we did.

"And she's right. I am reserved to a certain extent because I've been raised differently. I was told not to, not to express myself. When I used to talk or say something it was talking back. That's how all *Nisei* were raised.

"We *Nisei* had a hard time. I know *Issei* physically had a hard time because everything was done by man power and they had a language barrier and they weren't familiar with food and everything. At that we were OK, but as far as our schooling and our thoughts and the way we were raised, what Japanese kid did you ever see that got up and gave an oral report? The third generation is more outspoken, but for us, we really had a hard time."

Gaman

The Japanese word for it is *gaman*, roughly translating into perseverance. The *Issei* and *Nisei* knew it well, a motivation to keep struggling despite hardships, an attitude to strive towards, a state of mind that enables you to rise above this worldly suffering.

Gaman manifests itself in everything, from the heroic battles of the 442nd military troops in World War II to the everyday struggles in the fields with 100 degree summer days or seven days a week winter pruning.

Gaman. Nikkei don't talk a lot about it, and for those who know and understand it they probably don't have much to say, the images and feelings of endured struggles defy words and explanations. For those who aren't familiar, *gaman* remains foreign, an alien spirit.

Mr. R. Matsui, an *Issei:* "Well, when I ready to come to this country, my mother says to me, told me all about *gaman*. My real mother. You go to America... your uncle is pretty hard head you know, you better *'gaman-suru,'* she say to me.

"Here in America, I work pretty hard and help Uncle and wife but she, my step mother... she and my uncle raise me so I should be thankful for them and respect them always. I guess I *gaman* like my real mother says."

Mr. G. Sato, a *Nisei:* "*Gaman?* Oh yes, we had that very much so. Well, just like when we had that fire, burned down my dad's boarding house and all we had. You know, my folks didn't say much except *shigataganai* [it can't be helped] stuff... and *gaman*... you have to be patient 'cuz you know what happened has happened. Nothing you can do to remedy it, you just have to go on. Oh we had it rough I tell you, it's amazing and then during the depression years it was bad."

Mrs. V. Ishikawa, a *Nisei:* "My dad stressed *gaman* but I didn't think it was important at the time. I thought he was full of hot air. Like during camp, I told him, 'You're wrong, it can't be... nothing can be any worse than this,' is what I said. So in other words I wasn't even thinking of *gaman* I guess."

Gaman, part of a legacy of being Japanese American passed on through the generations, part of the myths and traditions a child growing up has to learn and accept either as old fashioned and outdated or as the law, the unwritten code of behavior. With the *Sansei* though, one further generation removed from Japan, one generation more Americanized, there's a question whether *Sansei* have ever known *gaman*.

A *Nisei* college professor spoke of the *Sansei*. He said that when he first began teaching, it seemed all the Japanese American students studied hard and worked hard for good grades. He recalled students walking into his office in tears, terrified about their "B" and their shame and wondered if there were some way they could do extra work to raise their grade.

Today the professor is amazed at the *Sansei* that are flunking his classes and don't seem to care. He's advised them to drop the class before the deadline and avoid an "F" but they don't worry about such details. Despite knowing better, he just couldn't help but expect these Japanese Americans to study harder and work harder; a cultural shock he explained that he has yet to recover from.

Mrs. F. Matsubara, a *Nisei*: "At home we do a lot of *gaman*. Even if we wanted to say something we didn't say it if we didn't think it was right. But now a days the young people, they'll say whatever's on their minds. So I think the *Nisei* are quite different than the *Sansei* and *Yonsei*."

Mr. G. Fujita, a *Nisei*: "*Gaman*... it's important. All those mannerisms, culture, whatever you call it. Japanese has a lot of good things they do, those are important, very important because it's something brought from the past and refined to the point where it becomes sort of a model to follow. Like working hard you know, someone complains and you say *'gaman shiro!'*

"I tried to set a model for my kids. No we never sat down exactly and talked about it but we tried to have that model."

Mrs. D. Murashima, a *Nisei*: "*Gaman* was part of all us *Nisei* growing up. And I kind of wonder if that's what we didn't instill in our children. I really don't know and I wonder because of the fact that we had to *gaman* and we had to... we had to do more than our parents. But as a whole we obeyed our parents very closely.

"And then I guess the *Nisei*, maybe we were just a little more lenient? It makes you wonder. I was strict in certain ways but *gaman*, I don't know if I instilled that in the children. I really wonder."

Mr. S. Mitsui, a *Sansei*: "I don't know if it was... what do you call it? *Gaman*? Or if there was a pride in who we are that we are not going to fail. I don't know if you would call it, perseverance? Or maybe it's pride? I don't know.

Maiko dancers, 1920's. Young *Nisei* girls were trained in traditional *maiko* dance and performed at the Del Rey Hall. Such traditions were an obligation, an expectation to learn. And through their training, even if only for a short amount of time, these *Nisei* were to learn "what it was to be Japanese." (Courtesy Virginia Ichihana)

"And my child? Hopefully she'll have a little bit more happy go lucky attitude than we had. I think we were a little bit more desperate in some ways. I don't think she's going to have the same problems, the same... drive. I don't think that drive will be there. I think that's probably good too, I think that the maturation period is getting larger and larger. Now I'm feeling pretty at peace with myself and it's taken 30 years. Like my parents experienced that at 22 or 24. My children may not experience that until 36 or maybe even later. As long as she eventually gets to that point sometime in her life, that's important."

Gaman may not be something passed on like an heirloom or hope chest. It may be something peculiar to a culture, something that has to be learned. Then perhaps the *Sansei* aren't at fault for their lack of drive or motivation as some *Nisei* describe. *Sansei* never had to live through a depression, a world war, hard times; they grew up in an age of baby boom plenty and they were given just that, plenty. Their challenges were different.

An older *Nisei* farmer once described the new, flashy "Z" car his son just bought and the huge new home the son had built and was moving into, all signs of success and no doubt the son was successful and had plenty. But there was one thing the son never was and probably never will be, the *Nisei* commented. You couldn't tell whether the father was proud of his son or felt uneasy about the material wealth. As he slowly shook his head from left to right the old farmer said, "Nope, my son was never hungry."

ON

ON became an unwritten law for many Japanese Americans, it meant a type of eternal obligation and respect.

For most *Nisei*, *ON* was a code of behavior, an attitude that bound them and dictated actions, like after winning a church raffle they donate most, if not all of it back to the church. Obligation and respect, they became a duty you learned and for *Sansei* it became a sensibility larger than reality, an ideal and standard you were forced to live up to.

Mrs. D. Murashima, a *Nisei:* "In Japanese school we were taught about obligation and respect. We learned it as *ON*. *ON* is a little bit more than just a debt of gratitude. You cannot explain *ON* in English. There's no real actual word. But our first duty was to parents, teachers and country. That's where our *ON* rested on.

"See, when the war broke out and the men were asked to go into the service, that's part of it. We were taught that we owe our respect, our *ON* to our teachers, parents and country.

"We learned this at Japanese school. The teacher always said that. Teacher impressed that on us. It stayed with us for the rest of our lives, it just comes to you that way. Like us, when we were kids... you young folks call us *Nisei* by our first names but you think I'd dare call an *Issei* lady by her first name? Oooohhh, that was disrespectful. I know when my kids first called the reverend by his first name but when they did, I hit the lid. I said, 'What?' No, that was disrespectful, to us that's wrong."

Mrs. V. Ishikawa, a *Nisei:* "My mother was very ill and wanted to go back to Japan and visit. A grandmother had raised her and my mother wanted go to her grave before her end came too. You know Japanese believe in going to the cemetery and they walk around it three times or they have some kind of superstition. And she was hell-bound to do that, she wanted to do it.

"And she told my dad when she sort of got better that she had to go to Japan and she was going to go. So just my father and mother wouldn't go, they wanted to take all the children and my brother got furious. He said he was not going to Japan and he was staying right here.

"My brother was a headstrong person and he was not going to go and I remember he told dad, 'I'll stay with the neighbors, the Tanaka's. I'll be fine without you.'

"My dad said, 'They have five children of their own, they can't take care of you too.'

"Then my brother said, 'Well, just leave me a sack of rice then, I'll manage.'

"That was the first time I saw my dad mad and I saw him chase my brother with a pitch fork because he was disobeying. He was to obey dad at all times."

Mr. S. Mitsui, a *Sansei:* "Obligation. I think it's even more emphasized now, not for the *Sansei* but with my folks' age, the *Nisei.* I see it a lot more now because it's like whenever there's anything bountiful in our family, it's passed around the neighborhood, within our family, whatever our immediate group that my parents are associated with. I sort of see that more now than ever, maybe because they have more now to pass around.

"My world is different. Not done to the same extent nor to the same degree nor the same large crowds. But there is that idea that... for instance, that I take fruit back home with me and I don't just take it home and hoard it. I take some to work, take some to my friends and whatever. That may be an off-shoot of my folks and obligation, maybe it is."

Ms. A. Nishimiya, a *Sansei:* "There's always this family need for me, I had it for varying degrees all through my life. It just depended pretty much on the situation just how strong that need was.

"There's still this very strong tie to the family so there's always this need to go back to the family. I think that's influenced the way that I thought for my future, that the family is a very essential thing for me, so I guess that devotion has always been there just to varying degrees depending on the situation.

"Also there's still a very large sense of obligation to community. There's a big feeling that they were very comforting for me, very supportive for me so that's the type of community I want my children to grow up in. The community is important as far as socialization because you get a lot of learning that you don't get anywhere else. So that's a big factor for me later on in life.

"Again, there's a feeling of obligation that the community is still there and I have to repay them in what ever way I'm able to do it..."

CHAPTER 13

EDUCATION: EXPECTATIONS
AND JAPANESE SCHOOL

Expectations

"We didn't have a choice, we had to get an education." *Nisei* woman in her 60's.

For many Japanese Americans, education became a type of bi- cultural expectation. Bi-cultural because most *Nisei* at one time or another attended two schools simultaneously: an American school to learn English and all about America and a Japanese school to learn Japanese and all about being Japanese.

"You were expected to learn everything at school," said Mrs. K. Sasahara, a *Nisei.* "Everything!"

School meant not only public school and a weekend Japanese school but also special classes in the Japanese arts or traditions where teachers were brought in from the city. Del Rey even had a series of Japanese cooking classes where one learned the secrets of cooking and the proper way to prepare Japanese foods. One series of classes began in the thirties and another in the fifties.

But it was Japanese school, the grand network of cultural education spread across the West Coast, in large cities and rural pockets like Del Rey, that instilled within an entire generation what it was to be Japanese.

Mrs. D. Murashima, a *Nisei:* "Japanese school wasn't emphasized by our folks, we were just expected to go. We were obedient children I guess, we did what our parents told us we must do. And so I don't think we knew any differently, we knew we were just to go to Japanese school and then to American school.

Mrs. I. Kagawa, a *Nisei:* "Education was more-so for the boys. Because you know one thing I remember, when I was going to high school

I wanted to take Spanish. My mom said a girl doesn't need the Mexican language. See, that's the kind of attitude they had so I didn't take Spanish and to this day I'm sorry.

"But when it came to Japanese school, all the kids were expected to go, boys and girls. At least there we were equals."

Mr. G. Sato, a *Nisei:* "We took it upon ourselves to get educated. Like you hear about these generation gaps how you couldn't talk with your parents and all that. You know we had all that, worst than most of the people because of English and Japanese... but still you took it upon yourself to get educated.

"My mother and dad kind'a pushed that Japanese education fairly well. It wasn't a thing of 'you better go' or anything like that. We were taught to like school."

The legacy of education was intensified due to relocation and the denial of a generation to live out their hopes and ambitions. The *Sansei* inherited the burden and en masse entered not Japanese school but the college ranks.

Mrs. D. Yanagi, a *Nisei:* "I don't know why I didn't send my children to Japanese school. My son once asked me that and I said, 'Well, you're going to the university and if you want to learn Japanese, you can get it there.'

"But after the war and we came back and... I know Sanger had Japanese school but I never did send my kids and that was probably a mistake. It didn't hurt us any, we came through life and we struggled but it doesn't hurt to struggle. So my children would just have to struggle with Japanese at the university instead."

Mr. G. Yanagi, a *Sansei* (Mrs. D. Yanagi's son): "Education was emphasized probably more family wise and that emphasis was very important. Nothing was really expressed hard but that your brothers and sisters did well so it was expected that you would do well too.

"It's probably in one way a Japanese influence on us, a real family thing. Why? Probably so that the kids would have it easier than the parents because of the folks' experiences, their struggles and need to survive.

"And their need to make their children fit into society. Children had to be that much better and smarter to survive and I think that's why they sent us to college. To learn all those things they never learned."

Ironically, the exodus to college meant a restructuring of rural communities, new professions lured *Sansei* away from home and family, the limited job market in rural areas forced the educated to leave. An entire generation was exposed to a new world with new potentials and new relationships, all away from home and community.

"I guess it's funny if you think about it," said Mr. K. Kimura, a *Nisei*, "here I send the kids off to college and they do well and now I'm working even harder on the farm, all alone and just hanging on."

Mr. S. Mitsui, a *Sansei:* "My education was a positive influence but it wasn't to the point of making everyone a good eagle scout. It was an alternative, like something hanging over your head saying either you're going to get an education or end up on the farm all your life. So with those alternatives you say, 'Well, I think an education is not so bad.' You say that especially at the end of a hard work day in the fields.

"The goal of our parents was to educate us so we would not become dependent upon the farm, to become independent of the farm so we could strike out on our own and be independent. It was pretty firmly planted into us, that we were to go to college and get educated. Something our folks didn't have, the opportunity they missed."

Ms. G. Nagao, a *Sansei:* "My parents expected me to go on to school although they didn't have the slightest idea what work I should do. They knew it was old fashioned to just have education for the boys and they wanted me to study something worthwhile, like the sciences. But at the same time I really don't think they felt I'd be a professional. They just knew education was important but... I was a girl too..."

Japanese School

Japanese school: it evokes memories from most *Nisei*, it was an expectation of the *Issei*, and yet in a single generation it has nearly fallen into oblivion. We are not talking about a sociological acculturation process or theoretical analysis of cultural maintenance. We are talking about what most *Nisei* kids had to do every Saturday for at least a few years of their lives, or in some instances, six days a week for what probably seemed like an eternity.

Japanese school: an education in addition to "American" school; an education chiefly in Japanese language; a place to meet your best friends and play. If the rest of America had a new world open to them during a

1920

Del Rey Japanese Language School. The learning of language and culture was a vital part of education. The Nisei en masse attended such language schools without question and over the years the faces matured and the school grew with the community: more students, more classes and more honor.

1924

1928

Following the war, most language schools closed and never reopened. The majority of Sansei never attended such schools, a generation lost language and along with it a Japanese education. (Courtesy Virginia Ichihana)

1935

Saturday at the movies, the *Issei* and *Nisei* had their world at Japanese school.

Mrs. D. Murashima, a *Nisei:* "I must have gone 10 years to Japanese school. Mom didn't let us start until we were two years into grammar school. I guess she didn't want us to struggle, our brains to struggle. She kept us out for two years before we started... I think... all I know is that my Japanese school classmates were a few years behind my American school ones.

"I remember we respected our teacher very, very much. She had the authority and what she said goes. We were obedient to her and as a child I thought very highly of my Japanese school teacher. She was strict and in a way still, I admired her 'cuz I thought to myself, 'Someday I'm going to be a Japanese school teacher,' which never materialized.

"The two teachers were very different. We had two when the first started, then we had three later on. The principal took the older kids, the other had the younger ones. They divided us up by grades. When you started you were in first grade, everyone was six or seven when you started, generally you didn't start when you were much older.

"We just thought it was just normal for us to go to Japanese school as well as American school. I guess our parents wanted to educate us in the Japanese language."

Mr. N. Hiramoto, a *Nisei:* "Japanese school was on Saturday and Sunday. For a while we had it at 4:00 after school, we used to walk over to the Hall and we had one hour of Japanese lesson and then we'd go home. Everyday. That lasted until the teacher left to go back to Japan, in the early 1920's.

"There were quite a few in class. We had vocabulary, like first grade words, and then we learned the alphabet, '*Ka,Ki,Ku,Ke,Ko...*' And then we learned *katakana* and *hiragana* and *kanji* [various Japanese writing styles].

"Even the *Kibei*, the bachelor men came out and sometimes helped and participated."

Mrs. T. Hata, a *Nisei:* "The discipline was there at Japanese school. We needed that discipline, we were just kids. I think that was just as important to learn as the language, maybe that's part of why our folks sent us too, to learn Japanese discipline."

Mrs. D. Yanagi, a *Nisei:* "Japanese school left a big impression on all of us. I'm sure it had something to do with us as well as our own parents. The teachers taught us the way of the Japanese. Like so... you know when Japanese and China were having a war, we would sing these songs like *katekureo...* I think that's what it was called... you know, war songs. That had some impression on us.

"So we got quite an education to a certain extent, and yet we're different. Our thoughts and way of thinking is different from the Japanese in Japan. We have such a mixed education, a mixed way of thinking.

"Like Christmas for instance. In Japan they never have Christmas. But here we go to American school and we sing all those Christmas songs and it gets embedded in you but we really didn't know exactly what it meant."

Mrs. I. Kagawa, a *Nisei:* "Oh yes, discipline was there. They disciplined us pretty well. The one incident that I'll never forget, towards the end of the school year we always practiced for *gaku ekai,* that's graduation, the eighth grade graduation and we would all put on something. Some people would learn speeches and a lot of people had to learn something and say it. They had some plays or something like that and the teacher would have to figure it all out... we would put on skits and we would have to polish everything up and memorize things.

"There was this one boy that was standing up on the stage and practicing his speech. Well, in his storytelling he's supposed to say, *'Hyaku dete ike!'* [Hurry, get out!] but he said it softly... *'Hyaku dete ike'* ...quietly.

"And so the *sensei* [teacher] said, 'that's not the way to do it, you can't do it like that...' So she then yelled, *'HYAKU DETE IKE!'*

"And you know what happened? One kid was in the basement all this while, I don't know what he was doing down there, playing when he wasn't supposed to I guess. Well, he just ran out of there and flew into the hall.. because the *sensei* had yelled and he thought he was getting in trouble and you know how the *sensei* seemed to know things all the time. Oh, everyone laughed when he really ran out of there.

"The *sensei,* they affected us a lot. Once there were two boys that were mischievous. They always used to get the dickens and they both had the same first name. One got the blame a lot for something he didn't do and the other did.

"One time this one kid got called and he didn't do anything. Well, you know after that he became a very, very quiet sort of person. He wouldn't hardly say boo anymore. To this day he's very quiet, not married or anything. Japanese school left a big impression on us."

The story began with the line, "I used to walk five miles to get to Japanese school, both on Saturday and Sunday, in the rain, no matter what the weather," said a *Nisei* farmer. I braced for more tales of sacrifice and persistence, of the struggle to get educated and inherited baggage my generation was obligated to carry. But then he shifted directions.

"But just as soon as I could I quit Japanese school. Wasn't learning much. I quit to go to work in the fields."

I leaned forwards, intrigued by the honesty and asked how he'd managed to quit.

"Well, the folks of course expected us to go to school but when I got so I could make a little money for the family, well, we needed whatever little we could make so they let me work instead of school. But they kept the younger ones going though, but I was lucky."

Mrs. D. Murashima, a *Nisei:* "We started at 9:00 in the morning on Saturday and I believe till 3:00 in the afternoon session. We took our lunch and that's the big joke. We can't remember all what we learned so we say, 'Oh, we went to eat our lunch."

Mrs. F. Matsubara, a *Nisei:* "As a young person I don't think I ever thought about Japanese school, it was just that Saturday and Sunday you go and weekdays American school. I went 'cuz my folks sent me, it was more playing though and seeing your friends. I'm not sure I learned very much."

Mrs. V. Ishikawa, a *Nisei:* "I don't remember the exact amount but we paid tuition to go to Japanese school. Something like, for instance, the more children you sent, the cheaper it was per child. But still, almost all the children I know went.

"It was so much writing, like *'Ka,Ki,Ku,Ke,Ko...'* and all that jazz. And then it was a matter of writing and teacher would write on the blackboard and we would have to copy it and then we have to get up and read. Oh, it was so hard to read. I never did like it, it's that terrible... I just wish I could.

"I could hardly wait for recess. I loved recess because there were kids from all outlying districts, they were all Japanese, it was fun. We all got to meet together. I bet there were a good 50 students just in Del Rey.

"At recess, we'd play games and as we got older we were famous for going down in the basement. The basement wasn't used as a classroom at that time. We used to go down there and one girl, she would start and say, 'let's have a program.' She would make anyone with a talent... sing or dance... she'd make us do things and entertain. I remember she'd line up the benches and we'd used to play like we were going to have a program."

Regrets

I once asked my mom why she never sent me to Japanese school.

"We didn't think you wanted to go, to give up your Saturday mornings. You seemed to love those cartoons... we couldn't tear you away," she answered.

A generation of suffering and sacrifice manifested itself in allowing me and the majority of other *Sansei* to stay at home and watch cartoons. I gained a fantastic knowledge of those old shows and expertise in trivia games and lost a generation of learning to be Japanese.

Mrs. I. Kagawa, a *Nisei:* "The *Nisei*, we over-did Americanization. Everything goes with the times. We change. Like I said, if I thought Japanese language was going to be so useful, I would have sent the children on to Japanese school too but... I didn't know.

"Like we went to Japanese school since we were little but a lot has left me. All those years we went and especially the *kanji* [Japanese written characters], I can't remember hardly any... I'm kind'a ashamed. Because we're not constantly using it I guess we didn't retain it. And like I said, we tried to Americanize ourselves, trying to be accepted.

"I think now though if we had the foresight we would have sent them. I know some of my children now ask how come you didn't send me to Japanese school. And I say, 'Now listen, if you want to learn, you're still young enough to learn so get in there and learn."

Mrs. F. Matsui, a *Nisei:* "We should have taught our children more Japanese. We were more Americanized. They started Japanese school but all their friends quit so they quit and that's too bad. One son, he really regrets it now but we couldn't make him stay because his friends quit too. Oh, he really regretted it now."

Mrs. L. Nakamoto, a *Nisei:* "Everyone began sending their kids to Japanese school in Sanger. I asked our daughter to go and she said, 'No, I don't want to go to school seven days a week.' I don't know if it was wrong that I asked her, I should have just sent her but I guess it also was laziness on my part because that meant I would have to make an effort to send her. I don't think I worked at it that hard. And it's kind'a sad 'cuz as I grew up I was sorry I couldn't remember how to read and write more. I was sorry I didn't remember and yet I didn't try to push it on to her because I thought, well, how much did I learn? I really didn't retain it.

"Now I wish I had but that's a thing of looking back. It's too late now. And later, all this change came on afterwards, you know... how it wasn't important to know Japanese because it was from the wartime... and a little bit later I would realize how important it was. Japanese things weren't emphasized that much back then, it wasn't brought forth with the caucasian people where as it became the thing now.

Mr. S. Mitsui, a *Sansei:* "Japanese school was more forced education than public school. Because it was Saturday afternoon and that wasn't much fun. I thought it was a waste of time because we were way too young, let's see, I was about seven I think. It wasn't valuable as it could have been. Maybe if the attitude of the kids or the teachers was different... It probably would have been more valuable later on in life, maybe even now."

CHAPTER 14

RELIGION AND DEATH

Once a Buddhist minister told a group: "You farmers are fortunate. Your life on the farm, working with nature and the earth, your life is Buddha nature."

I thought about this for a long time, trying to understand what he meant. Was it the isolated, independent life of farming coupled with the closeness with nature and the elements? Or was it the uncontrolled, unpredictable life we live?

The more I thought about it, the more "Buddhist" the reverend's statement became, abstract, philosophical and at the same time with a type of simplicity, just like farming. I couldn't help but think of working out in the fields, especially in winter when you're pruning vines with the valley fog all around and overhead and you can't see more that a couple hundred feet in any direction. A sense of silence envelopes you and you relate it to Buddhism: a silent, individual spiritual understanding of the world. No words, no doctrines, no scriptures. Just the fog around you and the sound of your pruning shear slicing through the canes and the mist of your breath floating before you like incense: farming and Buddhism as a way of life.

Japanese American Buddhists in the valley rarely talk about religion. They have been taught that their *Jodo Shinshu* sect of Buddhism permeates all actions, all life, it's ubiquitous. Perhaps that's why folks don't talk about it, "it's always with you" they contend. And when it comes time to send their children to church, without question they were Buddhist too, no baptism or confirmation classes, it was a birth right.

Mr. N. Hashimoto, a *Nisei:* "Religion is up to the individual. When you think about religion, it's very important. Because... it isn't the future of your life you're worried about, it's here, right now, just as we are talking. That's the difference between Christianity and Buddhism. Buddhism, we have to be thankful of what we have here. Anything nature gives us was a living thing once upon a time. And we ought to be thankful, they sacrifice their lives to support our lives. And this is the thing that's important and once you realize you begin to appreciate what Buddhism is."

Mrs. V. Ishikawa, a *Nisei:* "I felt Buddhism was important. It was brought down upon us and with my children I never gave them the option really to choose. I had a Christian friend ask me, they couldn't understand how we got the kids to go to Sunday School so regularly. I said, 'It's not a matter of choice, it is no problem.'

"Well, what this lady was doing was driving her children to a nearby church and just leaving them and expecting they stay. But in my case it was sort of out of need I began going with them and stayed and got involved. See, I think it's true with most of us *Nisei* mothers... going to Sunday School was just as much good for us as it was for the children, we learned right along with them. It just became a way of life I think and actually... we're not that religious but it became our social life and we worked around it, everything involved the whole family too. Now, the children are gone but we still look forwards to going to services, it just became our life."

Mr. L. Murashima, a *Sansei:* "Buddhism has taught me to think more logically as opposed to being a Christian where there's a single deity that everybody almost depends on. In that respect there's more dependence on the self with Buddhism... but I think the big thing about being a Buddhist was it being a social process. It was another link for the family, for the community, to get together and learn the rules of the culture."

When I was a college student in Japan, one Sunday I ventured out to discover how the Japanese Sunday Schools taught Buddhism. I felt comfortable with the language to ask a few questions and observe the workings of the church. At a neighborhood temple I paced for hours. The normal flow of visitors wandered inside, lit some incense or sat and listened to the monks chanting inside, but there were no signs of classes, no evidence of children learning their lessons.

Had I missed the class time? Perhaps this was a holiday and vacation time? Or was it like in Fresno where every so often they held a mass service at the Fresno temple and children from the rural areas like Del Rey traveled to Fresno for a large, combined service?

Sunday, a week later, I rose early and caught a train to a larger temple in the heart of Tokyo. Approaching the gate I saw families strolling in and out and felt today I'd get to see the Sunday Schools in action. Inside the

"You farmers... your life on the farm, working with nature and the earth, your life is Buddha nature." A Buddhist minister.

familiar smell of incense filled my nostrils, and the sounds of a dozen or so monks chanting provided a rhythm to my walk. But the scene was the same, folks strolling about, monks chanting, but there was no organized service, no worship hour posted and no Sunday School.

Sunday School was an American invention. In Japan you don't study about Buddhism, you simply live it.

This may sound strange, but it's hard to live like a Buddhist in America. There's a lot of spiritual competition, other religions that are packaged well, presented simply for the average kid to understand. The problem is that Buddhism seems to be a quiet religion, almost non-verbal in doctrine. Such a quality makes it difficult for a child to grasp, especially with the surrounding Christian world in America and the structured catechism of the other churches.

Mrs. D. Murashima, a *Nisei:* "Buddhism was brought down on us... or rather we grew up with Buddhism. Though we didn't exactly understand the religion really... I know a lot of people say they can understand Christianity better than Buddhism but with Buddhism we're living it everyday and everything we do is Buddhist but that kind of thing you can't understand when you're growing up.

"But then of course when the children come along and they began to be old enough to go to Sunday School, I figured well, we got to get in there and give them some religious teachings, knowledge of the religion. That's why I took to helping teach the children, because we wanted our children to learn but I think we teachers really gained more from it than the children. Because in order to tell them anything we had to know what we're talking about so then we would have to cram ourselves and study up on what we were going to say so we wouldn't be so dumb. In that way we benefited a whole lot and as the years went by I thought, 'Gee, I wish I had known a little bit more when I was teaching those kids,' I always felt that way.

"We had the advantage and I just hoped the children learned something from what little knowledge we had because we were learning right along with them actually."

"My goal in life," a Buddhist reverend said, "is to no longer be a minister." He paused, anticipating the confusion on the listener's face, and then he continued telling about his vision.

He explained that a Buddha nature lies in the "self" in all of us and each individual must come to realize this type of enlightenment. His role as a minister was just as a teacher, and there was nothing sacred about that profession.

"Wouldn't it be a wonderful world without all us ministers?" he asked and smiled.

When you're a Buddhist here in the valley and especially in the small, rural pockets of Japanese Americans, you automatically joined a community. Not simply a spiritual community but rather one based on ethnicity, a Japanese American Buddhist community. The two were fused together, each instilled an identity, a sense of community outside the mainstream of Christian, white America.

A lot of *Nisei* educated their children in Japanese traditions via the church. The church became the standard bearer of the community, a blend of the religious spirituality with Japanese traditions and customs. And for most *Sansei*, there was no need to differentiate between the two. The celebration of Boy's or Girl's Day was a Buddhist holiday just as the *Obon* was a Japanese custom. Religious meanings were blurred into a cultural understanding and identity.

Yet the Japanese American ethnic church was not an isolated, separate community like the Amish. The Buddhist communities in America have been for the most part accommodating to outside influences to the point they have invented wedding ceremonies, special mother's day celebrations and end-of-the-year parties that closely resemble Christmas pageants.

"Weddings are our invention," a Buddhist minister explained. "What Buddhists would like to do in a wedding ceremony was entirely up to the individual. Most have copied the Christian/American one with vows and music and dress.. and let me be honest here, we Buddhists don't copy them very well.

"I remember one wedding a long time ago where the bride wore a fine, flowing silk wedding dress with ruffles and layers of lace... But she forgot that her reception would be at a Japanese style restaurant where they all sat on the floor. Oh, she had a difficult time that evening, trying to keep neat and unwrinkled while sitting on her knees, bowing to guests with a dress billowing for miles all around her."

Being both Japanese and Buddhist in America meant to be different and with that difference came a special sense of one's heritage and community.

If a Japanese Buddhist in America was a minority, then a Japanese Christian was a minority within a minority. As Japanese Americans were converted to Christianity, groups formed and congregations assembled. Some met in each other's houses, some grew large enough to organize and build churches. Often though, the church was constructed in a larger population center, like Fresno, with rural bands of followers scattered through the countryside. These Japanese gravitated together as a Japanese Christian community, ethnicity a dominant factor in organizing; few Japanese Americans joined other, established churches, and instead they chose to form their own Japanese one.

Mrs. M. Masuyama, an *Issei:* "In the 1920's, a Christian reverend from Fresno came to call on us and encouraged us to attend church in Fresno. We were unable to go since we had little children and I had to work. However, the Reverend called on us frequently. Later, another minister from Japan came to this area and we were all baptized. Some active Christians started a Sunday School in Del Rey and the Reverend and others came from Fresno and conducted services on Sunday afternoon."

Mrs. F. Fujita, a *Nisei:* "Oh it was hard because our boys were Christian. We went to Fresno for Sunday School, so far to drive and all of their friends were Buddhist here in Del Rey. But it was required, we had a good church group in Fresno and we understood. There weren't many Christians in the Japanese community you know but we all understood."

Mr. M. Fukuda, a *Sansei:* "I always wondered why we were different, all the other *Sansei* kids went to church in Del Rey and we went to Fresno. My father once told me about the Christian services out there in Del Rey, a minister devoted enough to come way out here. That helped me understand a little, about the meaning of devotion and belief."

Mrs. T. Kimura, a *Nisei:* "Our family became Christians later, I won't go into the story here but my husband had a rough time and the Christians helped us a lot. Yes, they helped a lot. And each community we lived in had a strong group of Christians, they were the first ones to come visit and make us feel at home. I don't think the children understood what that meant but it was important to us.

"The rest of my family were Buddhist but religion didn't make much of a difference. I don't remember any time when it did. Two of our oldest children were married in a Christian ceremony and the other two married Buddhists and were married in a Buddhist way... see it really didn't matter much.

"Once I remember some of the *Issei* women in church talked to the minister... about a memorial service for their late husbands. The minister wasn't trained in anything like that, you know, memorial services like the 7th day service and 3rd year and 5th year... it was a Buddhist belief but very important to these *Issei* widows. The minister was good and understood and made up something like a service. Oh were the *Issei* women joyful, they cried and cried and said how grateful they were to the minister for that service."

"Buddhists and Christians have been fighting each other for centuries. It's nothing new to Japanese folk and Del Rey was no different." Mr. N. Sakamoto, an *Issei.*

Not every Japanese American community suffered from a division between Christians and Buddhists or the debates and arguments concerning religious differences. Not everyone in the community will admit to such a bitter time and recall the tragic stories of broken friendships and even families. Few *Sansei* though know of this past and carry with them this sense of history. But in Del Rey, religion separated families and friendships and was a force in community development and cultural understanding.

Mr. R. Matsubara, a *Kibei:* "Well, Christian big shots... They... *Nani kara kenka natta na...* [What did they fight about...]? Oh, Japanese school... for a while Christian and Buddhists share the Hall for Sunday School. Uh... I don't know too much details... they head strong people, I'm not sure about what started the fight... Oh but there lots arguing in the Hall."

Mr. G. Fujita, a *Nisei:* "I don't know if I should say all this, I don't want to bring back bad feelings. In Del Rey, we were all Buddhists. Then in the 1920's and 30's, a Christian Reverend from Fresno came out and converted a lot of Japanese, he came out on weekends. At that time the Buddhist Church was going on. So when Christianity came in there, there was a fight. Oh, it was a violent fight. One man was a Christian spokesman and they really went at it. They shouted and everything.

"That's why there's still some funny feelings in Del Rey and probably a lot of other communities. I can't understand it, religion is your own belief, it doesn't need to divide a community.

"Both sides wanted the Hall on Sunday for their church. So they said one Sunday, the Christians and next one the Buddhists. But the main conflict stayed. Later the Buddhists wanted to take the *butsudan* [Buddhist altar] into the Hall and they fought more. It all centered about the use of the Hall 'cuz everyone built it, everyone should use it

"The *Issei*, they stayed up all night arguing. There weren't too many Christians, Christians always a minority... so they needed to talk a little louder, trying to make a good defense. Some families were even split, one brother a Christian, the other a Buddhist."

Mr. N. Hiramoto, a *Nisei:* "A big squabble came about... oh some big trouble makers. All, the Christians and Buddhist and all that. Well, they... I don't know, what the hell... little Napoleon wants to be big Napoleon you see... that's the whole darn trouble.

"Oh, one guy had no kids but wanted to make big issue out of it, over the Japanese school. See, on one Sunday they had school and then on the next week the other side, Christians and Buddhists. Now how can you have Japanese school, Saturday it's OK for both sides but Sunday, one group on one Sunday and the other on the next? I thought what a bunch of *bakatare* [crazy fools].

"The community got split, Christians wanted to be big guys and Buddhists too big for their own good, that's what happened."

Mrs. D. Yanagi, a *Nisei:* "I heard about the argument and how terrible it was. Some of those *Issei*, they seemed pretty quiet but once they got at it, oh, they were strong headed. Afterwards the community was never the same, we all lost a lot."

Forty years later the issue had been settled, as if a bitter feud has been finally settled with most of the original combatants dead and gone. But this final settlement did jolt old memories and brought to the surface some deeply rooted values and concerns. A sense of the past stirred within a community, not just memories but the meaning behind the arguments, spiritual meanings that live at the core of the soul.

For decades the Hall had remained community property and was taxed accordingly at a much higher rate than a church property. Until recently this was of little concern, lower taxes and an active, large community gave no reason for a symbolic name affiliation with an established church to be made.

But with a reassessment and higher taxes that drained a small budget, talk of some sort of tie with a church arose and after some quick discussion, a designation as a Buddhist Temple was assigned. On paper the Hall was to be titled a Buddhist Church although some wanted to call it simply a Japanese Mission. As a mission some felt the Christians would be accepted and acknowledged. Others felt that since the large majority of the remaining community were Buddhist, the appropriate temple designation would suffice.

Besides, many felt that it was only a name change. Yet you could almost feel the dead souls of the *Issei* stirring from their deep sleep.

Death

"You Japanese are preoccupied with death," a non-Japanese friend once said.

She was right. When you consider all of the detailed arrangements involved with a Japanese funeral, the huge family gatherings and dinner following the burial, and the seemingly countless memorial services that were held (on the seventh day, the 49th day and the 100th day after the death we were supposed to conduct a service... and on the first, third, and seventh years, and then I loose count). Japanese are preoccupied with death.

But Japanese folk don't quite see it that way. Actually many feel that, if anything, Japanese have a positive attitude about death. All of the memorial services, though tragic and sad, nonetheless are accompanied by a grand family reunion and community spirit.

Picture this: a huge funeral with hundreds of family, relatives, and friends with sad faces and tears, followed by a burial combined with yet another brief service. At the conclusion of these events, a family spokesman stands and thanks everyone for their kindness and support during this sad occasion, and then invites everyone to dinner. For some reason, everyone then goes to a nearby Chinese restaurant and for a few hours a grand meal is served and conversation fills the room. (It always seemed to be a Chinese restaurant. Someone once explained because a long time ago when the *Issei* first came, only the Chinese had established restaurants so that's when the tradition originated). Despite the gloom and depression of the grieving process, it felt good to talk and converse, a type of celebration of life. Inevitably someone would mention that the one who just died "would have wanted it this way," and all would feel a little humbled and yet grateful.

"You Japanese take care of your dead," mentioned a friend who accompanied me to a funeral and subsequent dinner gathering. I felt that to be one of the highest compliments one could receive. "And you know how to take care of the living too," she added.

Mrs. D. Murashima, a *Nisei:* "When the *Issei* first settled here, I imagine it was mostly men, now of course somebody died. There was no family, no body, see, because they're from Japan. So that's when the *Kyowakai* [community club] helps. When someone dies in the community, everybody goes and so in those old *Issei* days... I don't know if they put a dollar in or what the amount was... but everybody pitched in to the *koden* [donation], helped with the funeral.

"Maybe in those days it went towards the funeral, I don't know because they were generally bachelors, weren't they? But people did this because they had no family and were so far away from home.

"To help one another out, and it helps you financially because of the *koden*. Now if you were a close friend or special friend you would give them flowers but outside of that it's all *koden*, I think it's really terrific, you're really helping that family out.

Issei funeral, 1930's. A community mourns the loss of a member. Perhaps because it was the Depression and hard times were made even harder with a death, family and community, Buddhists and Christians, everyone supported each other and shared in the grieving. The Depression, a great equalizing force. (Courtesy Virginia Ichihana)

"Then everybody begins to help out, so then it kind'a snowballs in one respect. Because, now for instance, if I knew your parents and for instance your parents' folks passed away, we *koden* because we knew your parents. So it kind of snowballs you see. It's really nice because it really helps."

Mr. N. Hiramoto, a *Nisei:* "So many things very important, like a funeral. If they live in our community, we all go whether they're wealthy or not, we try to help them out you see. Co- operation is the most important part. Like at a funeral, what we put in the envelopes, the *koden*, we put cash in it to help defray the funeral expenses. At the end of the service we can pay for everything and that's it. No big bills you have left over. You know, even the undertakers knew Japanese folk were good at paying."

Mrs. D. Yanagi, a *Nisei:* "A close relative's funeral of mine was held at the Hall. The whole community came out, *hakujins* [caucasians] and kids and all. And remember all these people kept coming to the house before the funeral, coming over to help, to cook, to pay respects to the family. Remember the *Issei* didn't have relatives to help out so friends came, every day and night too.

"But at the funeral, I remember some of the *Issei* speakers would carry on and on. I think that's the worst thing, they should make it short and brief. That's not a happy time, if it were a happy time that's different. People get bored when they'd speak, it wasn't just a few words about their friend who just died...

"And not all the *Issei* were good speakers. Some of them were long winded and oh boy, they would go on and on it seems, you know how some people like to talk and not get anywhere.

"Oh yes, we had memorial services. And we were very strong on our food. You know *oshojin* [eating no meat], they were very strong on that. I think when a close relative died we observed it for 49 days. We ate lots of *tofu*, you couldn't eat meat you know."

Mrs. L. Nakamoto, a *Nisei:* "When a family member died, Buddhists were real strong on *oshojin*, that means no meat, fasting. All the ladies from the community would come over and do the cooking, you know, clean up and cook vegetable stuff. *Oshojin ryori* stuff, food that has no meat. They used a lot of *tofu* and *miso* [soy bean curd], and they flavored stuff like that. They just avoided using any meat and they'd cook for the funeral food like that. We had no relatives so friends and neighbors came to help and eat.

"After that we were told to have no meat. So for 49 days...I got so tired of eating string beans with no mayonnaise.. and with your rice nothing... I don't know why I didn't think of getting my peanut butter sandwiches out. I'd survive a lot better but see those days you didn't do things to suit yourself. Later on we had tomatoes and I began to hate tomatoes and we had mayonnaise on pineapple... can you imagine eating that?

"I pouted. I was just a kid and was spoiled. I thought the world ended, I thought the world was the pits. We did it, for 49 days."

Mrs. V. Ishida, a *Nisei:* "When my mother died, the whole community really bucked in to help us. We didn't know what to do. I remember one good family friend, a businessman with a lot of savvy. He came over and took us to help choose the casket. We had no family and it was so nice to get help.

"I remember we went down to look at caskets and this family friend said, 'I know you're grieving and want to do the best you can. But don't feel that way, they're going to show you the best one first so just choose a fairly nice one and let it go at that because they're just going to bury it anyway. And you just want it nice, just be reasonable.' I think that was so nice, a wise man helping us.

"There were so much flowers at the funeral. Well, Japanese still do that but from every organization we belonged to, they sent flowers. Well... Del Rey is small and we went to grade school and even all the teachers came out... and both the Japanese and *hakujin* [caucasians] came out. And the flower wreaths from the school, they sent flowers too."

Mr. M. Ichioka, a *Nisei:* "I can't remember when it started, but at a funeral they passed out a can of coffee, or was it tea? Everybody that comes gets a can of coffee or tea. A small pound can or a can or box of tea leaves. It was either, I don't remember which one. It's like a thank you, we've been to different funerals since then and some people pass out coffee or tea, which ever you wanted. I guess every head of the family got one.

A sort of repayment I guess. After the war, one funeral, they gave a book of stamps as a thank you."

Mr. N. Hashimoto, a *Nisei*: "Memorial services are to remind you. It's easy to begin to forget, once someone's gone, you're missing something but hard to know what it is. But with a memorial service, like the 7th day, 49th day, one year, three year... it brings you back: they're still here. They're not actually here but your feeling will be here. I think that's tops."

Mrs. V Iwata, a *Nisei*: "I feel a memorial service is to gather family. It's really for the remaining ones. We would have these memorial services and say, if it's going to be the 17th year and my brother was in the army and always moving around. Well, if it were the 15th year we still would have the 17th year service early because my brother would be here and may have to leave. So one day I thought, 'Gee, it's really for us. The relative that passed away, doesn't know anyone. It's to remember, but it brings us together.

"It was said once by a speaker, I heard one minister stress that it's really for the living. The ones that are left, it does gather us and it's nice. It almost has a social, family tie value plus the religious, plus the remembering."

At the funeral of a close friend, a young *Sansei* girl age 22, a group of us stood outside the Buddhist Church, waiting for the casket to be brought out, the same place we had stood numerous times after a wedding ceremony, waiting for the bride and groom to emerge. It felt odd not to have a clammy handful of rice in our palms.

But most of us were in shock. Our friend had died of a disease, not a total shock since we all knew of her illness but still a shock, it was our first death of a peer. Somehow we had missed the lessons to be learned at the number of funerals of relatives we had all previously attended and the dozens of memorial services for uncles and aunts, most of whom we barely knew or never said more than a few words to since their English was so limited and our Japanese was null.

Next to us two, *Issei Obaasans* (Grandmothers) greeted one another. As one walked out of the church and saw her friend, she bowed. After walking closer, the other one recognized the face and returned the bow and they exchanged greetings. They spoke rather loud since their hearing seemed to have faded with their age.

"How are you? It's so good to see you."

"I am fine and how are you? It's good to see you."

"When did we see each other? Was it at Nakamura-*san* or Yamamoto-*san?*"

"Oh, it wasn't too long ago, wasn't Ogawa-*san's* before Yamamoto-*san?*"

It took me a while to realize they were talking about friends who had passed away, this was their funeral list, their timeline of sorts. Then they slipped into a conversation of their mutual friends who had all gone, they both were happy to see each other, happy to still have a friend to greet and exchange conversations at these funerals.

Then one said, "Next time we save time and just list our friends that are still alive. It will go faster."

They both laughed at this, a laughter that troubled all of us *Sansei* who stood nearby. We all gathered in an uneasy silence, tears in our eyes and blank looks cast on our faces. We were all unsettled by the two *Issei Obaasans*, they seemed too loud, their laughter totally inappropriate, perhaps they weren't serious enough about this death of our friend.

Of course the irony was that these two old women had felt death many times and probably were at ease with it. It was we *Sansei* who were too quiet, we weren't serious enough about death and instead stood apart from everyone else, a huddled group of souls in fear and shock and unthinking.

Japanese traditions surrounding death are not limited to the Buddhist religion. There was a minister from a Japanese Christian Church who was faced with an unusual request from his congregation. Unusual in the sense that his ministerial training had not prepared him for such a challenge, but not unusual from the Japanese community: they wanted a Christian memorial service for their family members who had passed away.

The minister was challenged to create such an entity and the result was a Christian program that blended with Japanese traditions. A mediation had occurred, two cultures coming together and a rise of a new vision of tradition: one that is alive and continually evolving.

CHAPTER 15

CULTURAL DELIVERY AND FOLK MEDICINE

Cultural Delivery

No one prepared us for this. I should have been forewarned when one of my wife's relatives became concerned about our pregnancy and asked, "Gee, are you sure those kind of babies turn out OK?"

Those kind of babies meant a product of an interracial, intercultural marriage: a Japanese American Buddhist with a Wisconsin German Lutheran. I said intercultural because our differences went beyond just racial, they necessarily involved a merger of two cultures, two worlds not always in harmony. And those differences were never more evident than during labor and delivery.

Time: 5:00am. Labor contractions were five minutes apart. Marcy (my wife) and I left home and arrived at the hospital. The nurse suggested that we walk around and told us we still had a long way to go, the cervix was only at two centimeters. He reminded us it had to dilate to ten centimeters in order for the baby's head to fit through and it normally dilated only about one centimeter per hour.

"And remember," he added "labor and delivery will be demanding. Be nice to mama no matter what."

I naively nodded my head in agreement.

To pass the time we talked about names. We had agreed that one name would be a Japanese one, I hoped my child would maintain a connection with his/her heritage and identity, a consciousness.

"But my family can't even pronounce most of those names, we have to be selective," Marcy reminded me as we continued to walk through the hospital. "They still pronounce your name wrong half of the time and can't seem to figure out why someone would use the name 'Moss'."

I reminded her that were we to have a girl, one name would be Rose, after her grandmother, her mother and Marcy's own middle name. But whenever I heard Rose with a Japanese name like Yoko or Mariko, I kept thinking of 'Tokyo Rose'.

Someone should have warned us that traditions could be painful and this child would be a blend of two cultures sometimes in a not-so-smooth blend, even with his/her name.

The next wave of contractions forced us to divert our thoughts and attention.

8:00 am. The contractions had become steady, three to five minutes apart. Dilation had progressed to four centimeters and so did the labor: Marcy's temperament had grown short.

"What do you think it'll be, a boy or girl?" I asked to distract from the pain.

"There you go again with that boy-girl question," she complained.

Bad question on my behalf.

At first I had wanted a boy, part of an image I held of Japanese tradition and the little *samurai* son, coupled with a country image of the son taking over the family farm, the passing on of a legacy. But then, with two disastrous years in the farm economy and the increasingly vital role of Marcy's work as a health educator, I grew to understand what a lot of *Nisei* farmers had once felt: no one would want their children to struggle like this, children should go to college and get out of the fields on to a better life. A girl would do us just fine.

"But what about a woman in today's professional world?" Marcy snapped. "A lot of women are treated unfairly, and if she's part Asian, what about that quiet, passive image she'd have to contend with? You may not see all those things but I can." She paused and took some deep breaths, a method used to cope with the pain of a contraction.

Then she continued, "Look at the Japanese community pot lucks, with all the men on one side, arms crossed, talking, nodding their head and all the women on the other side, aprons ready in place, busy with the foods and cleaning up."

She was right, at those pot lucks two worlds existed on each side of the room, we always tried to sit together at the middle table, between the two forces. Even worse though, a lot of folks didn't expect Marcy to help out like the other women because, "after all, she was *hakujin* [Caucasian]." And at the serving tables someone would kindly suggest to Marcy that especially for her use, they did have some buttered white bread at the end of the line, past the *sushi* plates.

I shrugged my shoulders and suddenly wasn't sure which I hoped for, a boy or a girl. The differing worlds we lived in contained different realities, contradictions that continued to confront a lot of our basic beliefs.

Luckily, a contraction kept us from getting any angrier and we started our breathing exercises again. The subject was dropped, left unresolved with dangling questions. Though we didn't like to think it, with some things we just didn't have all the answers.

11:00am to 2:00pm. The contractions became monotonous and we both grew weary. Dilation had advanced to six centimeters, but was holding constant. Marcy tolerated the periodic pain but the lack of progress troubled us, we weren't used to things out of our control.

We began talking about the pain, whether to fight it and try to think about something else, or accept it and focus upon it. I told her it'd be very "Japanese" to focus on the pain, to accept it as part of the process much like suffering in Buddhism. She said this long labor must be part of the bargain, sort of like karma, an easy nine month pregnancy and today we were paying the dues.

I began to think about coping with pain, an Eastern approach to suffering as part of life vis-a-vis the Western world of science and medicine. Here in the hospital we were suspended in a world that seemed to deny pain, as if with drugs and medicine we had overcome nature.

Before coming to the hospital, Marcy had drunk a lot of a special tea one of my aunts had given us. "To speed up the contractions," my aunt explained as she gave us the brown paper bag with some dark seeds inside. "It may not stop the pain but will help it along."

At first we were hesitant, we had no idea what was in the bag and we didn't understand what was meant by "helping the pain along". Then we tried it and at least it helped to occupy time and enabled us to relax a little more at home. Later we wished we had the tea with us, a little bit of family here at the hospital and a little dosage of spiritual medicine.

Folk cures were foreign to Marcy, such spiritual healings were alien to her upbringing. Yet throughout my childhood I had received all kinds of "medicine" from family and friends, superstition and faith blended together as an elixir and placebo. Marcy and I had different orientations, and for the longest time they had never met.

Once, though, we visited with her relatives in the Midwest and discovered back home they regularly used some sort of folk cures, trading remedies was part of being a neighbor and friend. A new world of tradition, culture and a sense of community opened to us. Our narrow vision of modern, Western culture was confined to a Californian view with communities only a generation or two old. Perhaps our intercultural union wasn't as distinct as we thought, a growing sense of history was accompanying this birth and child.

7:00 pm. The contractions had surged to one right after the other, this was the transition stage beginning at eight centimeters. Everything increased in intensity, the pain, the emotional swings. The nurses feared we might still have a long wait.

If we thought the pain was difficult before, this stage was beyond belief. We were constantly in breathing patterns trying to deal with the pain, our emotions were drained. Conversations became jagged and rambling, blunt statements were made out of context, often with piercing truths.

"You gotta relax, you can't stop the pain, all you can do is relax."

"You can't feel the pain, don't tell me to relax."

"Tell me where it hurts. How the hell do I know where it hurts?"

"Don't touch me, just be there. God, oh God it hurts."

God. The contraction ended and we rested for a few minutes, knowing the next would soon arrive. I momentarily slipped into my thoughts, "God? What can he do? I don't even believe in the almighty God so what can he do? Is he punishing my wife because I don't believe?"

"I'm sorry," I blurted out loud.

Marcy rested and my thoughts wandered back to an early conversation we once had about religion and this unborn child. Would we baptize the baby? Do we believe he/she must have a place in God's Kingdom through infant christening?

I knew her family would be waiting for us to decide, an eternal question left unresolved. With this one issue there was no indecision, no tolerance of anything lesser. Either we did baptize or we didn't, no grays, no in betweens.

Suddenly a surge of insecurity rose within. Though I knew our families had religious differences and we tried to bridge the schism such as incorporating both Buddhist and Christian ministers in our wedding ceremony, a barrier still remained: I was not Christian and Marcy was not Buddhist.

Perhaps Marcy's family had accepted that in me but with their own grandchild? Their belief would be absolute: salvation for this child must include baptism. And in their church one didn't wait very long, you baptized infants so their soul could be saved. The infants didn't choose, the family accepted such responsibility.

I stared at Marcy's face contorted with pain. With every contraction and the terror that swept over her face, a sharp tightening surged within me. I felt challenged, responsible and punished.

For two hours the ordeal continued but after his examination the doctor informed us Marcy had not progressed at all, we were still at eight centimeters.Marcy was ready to concede, to give up and so was I.

"Listen, you gotta believe," I heard myself whisper to her. "You gotta believe." She nodded and a renewed look of determination grew on her face; I remained still, surprised by my own comment. Gradually we broke into a rhythm, like a chant, breathing and believing with each contraction.

I thought about the baptism issue and realized there was no answer, just a belief in what we chose to do would be our best decision. Our life as a couple and soon family would always be filled with differences, many unresolved and unanswered: that was the spirit of our future, of our beliefs.

The baby was born at 11:50 pm, after over 20 hours of labor and a difficult delivery. There came a point where with blind acceptance we fought through each severe contraction and the wailing pain while pushing. Afterwards we couldn't help but think of our mothers and grandmothers and the different type of labor they too experienced, one at home with little of the medical world around her and the other alone in an operating room. Now we too were inducted into a family lineage.

Nikiko Rose Masumoto was born 8 lb. 10 oz., a large baby with a huge head. We concluded that all of our words and conversations must have filled her head and no wonder she had trouble squeezing through.

With her birth a new tradition had begun for both of our families, an interracial child in an interracial family. Culture was not to be denied but delivered. The two cultures Marcy and I were raised within may not always be in harmony, yet despite the unsettled affairs, differences could be mediated. With the arrival of Nikiko Rose, a sense of history was instilled, a family was created.

Folk Medicine

I don't know of any community with more urban medical professionals in one generation and yet back home on the farm, there remains a bazaar collection of folk cures and spiritual healing.

In the Japanese American community the two stand side by side, armies of *Sansei* doctors and nurses coming home to their *Nisei* parents and grandparents with their mystical teas and herbs or unlicensed specialists and advisors. Both generations live in two worlds, one public with Western medicine and professional status and one private, at home with apothecaries on kitchen window sills or healers whose offices are living rooms. There is something mysterious about it all and perhaps that's how the spiritual medicine works, mysteriously.

Imagine the university researcher, a scientist working on a project, searching for a cure for cancer who comes home to drive his mother out of town, to northern California to a "witch doctor with herbs" as he called it. It's not that his mom was sick, she just wasn't feeling great and heard from one of her friends about this woman healer. So she asked her son, the medical researcher, to drive her north and get some of the medicine. Obediently he carried out her wishes and they journeyed together. Later, he could only recall the healer's home as "being smelly" and his mother got her medicine.

Then on Monday, back at work, he told everyone that we went on an adventure with his mom and before he could elaborate, they all agreed what a nice thing that was, to give up a weekend for your mother. All he could do was grin in response to their compliments.

Picture the family that believes in *okae* for stomach aches, a type of rice gruel, not the most pleasant in taste. Or *jorei*, a healing touch where visitors quietly sit with the ill, touching an arm or leg or back, meditating and in their spiritual union and solitude the healing occurs. Or imagine using *okyuu*, a cleansing by burning incense which doesn't sound too bad until you realize they burn little spots on the body to heal, sort of like an acupuncture with fire.

Then there's stories of the *Issei* and their medicine. Like burying *nasubi* (eggplant) to cure warts, as the *nasubi* rots, the wart gradually disappears. Or bitter teas made from bitter herbs. One family used to buy such herbs from a peddler. This "doctor" would travel around the countryside just like the old snake oil peddler and sell his elixir, and unsuspecting children would be subjected to bitter teas and oils. "It taught you not to be sick," said a *Nisei*. A case where the cure was worse than the illness.

And we can't forget the *okaisama*, a little statue many *Issei* kept in the kitchen near the stove. *Okaisama* was like a little god that watched over certain things, an extension of *Shinto* belief in California. There were farm

Issei inspection certificate, 1918. She had arrived in Seattle, Washington and entered quarantine, a period of waiting, delays and bewilderment. All immigrants experienced such an introduction and welcome to America and one wondered what Japanese folk medicines and cures were employed to insure passage through quarantine.

okaisama in addition to the house ones and some became specialists, like the stove *okaisama*, the protector of the stove, one of the most important parts of the home. "We used the stove all the time" explained a *Nisei* women who many a time as a girl witnessed her mother standing before the *okaisama*, clapping her hands and then returning to her work. "That stove, we depended on it."

Today I wonder if there's a VCR or television *okaisama*, especially during football season.

Part of the curing spirit in these folk medicines was the fact that it was Japanese in origin. Anything remotely connected with Japan carried a magic within it. And when passed on to the next generation by family and friends at Japanese gatherings, perhaps that magic was increased and amplified.

Kinoko was an odd, white fungus that looked a lot like *mochi* (rice cakes). You soaked this fungus in water and drank the solution like a tea. This medicine traveled throughout the countryside of Del Rey one year via family and community, relatives passing it on to relatives, the medicine introduced to communities at Buddhist activities or *Kyowakai* (community club) meetings. You tried it because it was given as a gift from a relative or close friend, a gift of healing. Part of the cure may have been the spirit behind the tea - a true folk medicine.

We call it today the placebo effect but the name isn't important; what people believed was important, part of a healing tradition in our families and communities.

Finally there is one folk medicine that cuts across differences between the generations and doesn't belong to one ethnic group per se. Amazingly, people overcome minor aches and pains with this, and one's mental health vastly improves as folks forget their troubles and problems. Some even claim the mountain air is the best thing for them and swear by the exercise they get, especially with their right arms. Of course, we are talking about the miracle of Reno or Las Vegas gambling trips and the magical sounds of jackpots and the robust pounding of the heart with a blackjack in your hand. For a lot of Japanese Americans gambling fever isn't a disease. It's a panacea like the *Issei* knew with their games of *hana* and trips to Chinese gambling dens.

SECTION III

THE LAND

Abunai Kusa

There's a type of weed called Johnson Grass that my *obaasan* (grandmother) used to call *abunai kusa. Abunai* means dangerous and *kusa* means grass: dangerous grass.

She called it dangerous not because it was poison to humans but rather it was poison to a farm. Johnson grass is a voracious grower and it spreads rapidly and deeply. Uncontrolled, it will grow and monopolize sunlight, suffocating vines and choking roots. It's almost impossible to kill Johnson Grass and the only means to keep it in check is to chop off the stalks and stems and dig up as much of the roots as you can and even then, when new sprouts emerge, you have to repeat the process.

"You can't ignore them," she'd tell me, "they dangerous. *Abunai.*"

And to a struggling farmer they were dangerous. The land meant everything and Johnson Grass was a poison, a special poison to the land. Today we have new herbicides to kill Johnson Grass but when the *Issei* were farming, they had a different relationship with not only the land but also with their weeds. Some weeds were indeed *abunai.*

The land has been and always will be central in the lives of farm families and their community. Ordinary people become artists with their farms, carving out not only a living but a way of life, that's what makes them different.

The tradition of family farms unfolds in the following pages. This is not a history of dates and chronological events but a story of a people and their work and life, ever changing and evolving amidst the eternal *abunai kusa.*

CHAPTER 16

DREAMS IN A LAND

"Me? Oh no, I never dreamed of a farm or land, nothing like that. In those days we never thought of those things, no, nothing at all. Now-a-days young people are smart and think ahead... but me? [She smiled and covered her mouth with her hand as a giggle escaped]. Me? I never dreamed. I was sure dumb!" Mrs. D. Murashima.

After a day's work with the hundred degree heat still lingering from the burning afternoon sun, I kick off my work boots, the mud caked on the sides crumbles onto the dirt. My feet suddenly breathing as the air suddenly cools them and the sweat escapes. My shirt clings to my chest, damp and wet, and a coolness begins to creep along my back. I sit and rest, knowing a full day's work is behind me.

I catch myself dreaming of better harvests, better weather, better prices. Then I scold myself for such fantasies and try to anticipate the disappointment and plan for the future. Dreams are strange creatures for farmers, they drive us through depression and disaster and hunger, and then they tease our optimism with hope.

But the farmers from this valley don't talk about dreams, we all bitch a lot and at the same time talk about the next year: better harvests, better weather. And our dreams remain, part of a legacy we inherited, part of a vision we hold sacred, part of ourselves we cling to.

The meaning of my dreams creep into my mind and I allow them to visit, contentedness rises within and for a moment, for that one moment while sitting on a bench in the back of my house, shoes off and sweat drying on my back, all is as it should be. Perhaps that is why we continue, we work from moment to moment with the land, the dreams fill us like a song or vision and for a brief moment, all is as it should be.

The *Obaasan* (grandmother) dreamed. She dreamed of the day she could shovel *abunai kusa* from her land, from her farm. The dream never

DEL REY
CALIFORNIA

DEL REY
"Where Raisin is King"

Del Rey Chamber of Commerce promotional pamphlet, circa 1920's. Many communities published these pamphlets hoping to attract new growth and development. "Ha. They were what the dream was supposed to be," said one long-time Del Rey farmer. (Courtesy Ken Swanson)

materialized. The Depression, the war, economic and political obstacles kept a tiny 95 pound old lady from fulfilling her dream. But over the years her dream evolved from a simple goal or hope to something else, something very personal. She spoke of her dreams as an opportunity that had filled her life, a wish that still provided her with pleasant thoughts. One sensed that long ago she had accepted her fate without ignoring her dreams. Both lived within her and created a contentedness.

To the *Issei*, dreams were tempered with reality. Their entire life had been a gamble, a risk: to leave a familiar country and culture and venture into a new world, that in itself was a dream being realized.

Mrs. V. Ishikawa, a *Nisei:* "Dad first came to Hawaii and then here. I had seen of ads of Hawaii and asked him, 'How come you left such a nice place like Hawaii?'

"And he said, 'Well, we just thought we'd do better over here.'

"I then asked dad why he didn't get his own place, and he said he could never swing it, never had the money. That's when he told us all these stories about people who did try but... it's better not to fall on your face then there's no trouble... those people tried and went broke, they were shamed. He didn't like risks... I remember later when the old folks started going on those Reno trips he came home and he didn't even like it... He said, 'Ah, it's not fun, just lose money, not for me.' He just wasn't the gambling type. He just wanted more security and I think he wanted that because he had such a sad childhood, his mother and step mother had died in Japan when he was very young.

"My dreams? Probably to pay off this place, get it paid for. We didn't have big thoughts... I remember one *hakujin* [caucasian] man told us when we first bought this place. He said, 'Listen you kids, I'm happy and I know you're excited, but don't ever expect to get rich farming. You will just make a good living. Just count on that and you will never be disappointed...'

"And that's exactly right, we made a good living, raised our children, got them through school... say that must have been our dreams! We were never that verbal, we never discussed it."

A lot of *Issei* claimed never to have dreamed, that their life was such a struggle they "were too busy or tired to dream." But I'd watch them in their latter years, tending their gardens, working with their plants and soil and nature. They didn't need to tell me of their dreams--their sharp eyes while pruning a *bonsai*, or their quick hand when raking leaves, or their steady prodding pace, hands clutched behind their backs, leaning forwards like old

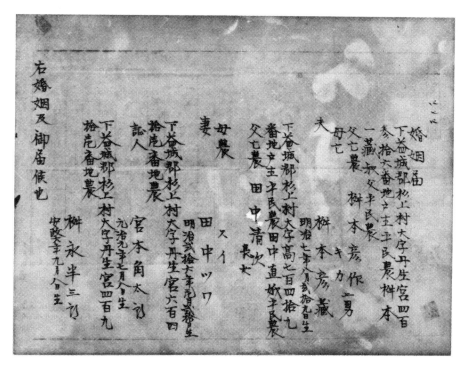

The marriage certificate of Hikazo and Tsuwa Masumoto, 1914. This document not only recorded the joining of husband and wife but also told a story in itself. He had returned to Japan to marry in 1914, the date of the certificate. Shortly afterwards he once again left for California. According to her passport, she joined her husband four years later in 1918 to share in his dreams.

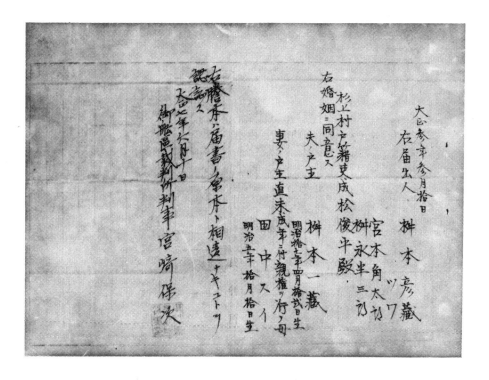

people do as if they're walking against the wind, their special walk as they strolled through the vineyards and orchards--all this told me of their dreams, to live out in the country, maybe on a place of their own and of course, to die there.

There were times when one generation's dreams clashed with those of the next. Mr. G. Sato, a *Nisei:* "I dreamed of being a doctor. Some caucasian friends encouraged me to study and be a doctor and I took those pre-med courses in high school. But then dad got sick, he was an invalid and that just popped everything off. So I had to stay on the farm, I was the only son. No, I never questioned that... I just made up my mind that staying was one thing I had to do.

"I also had dreams of flying so I took it up on the side.., by myself. That was one of my dreams, I wanted to fly. You gotta figure it cost $7.00 an hour to fly way back in '34 and '35 and that was a lot of money when you're making only ten cents an hour... well, I had to save a lot and I got my license. No one knew I was flying, my parents didn't approve."

Mr. R. Matsubara was a *Kibei*, educated in Japan but an American citizen by birth. He spoke deliberately and slowly, pausing with each word or phrase, a slow pace, very controlled. His wife sat next to him, patiently waiting for his answers to my questions, adding her thoughts when she felt necessary, helping to jog his 70 year old memory. We sat in the kitchen of their suburban house, the only house in the neighborhood with an elaborate Japanese garden outside and a backyard full of *bonsai*, orchids and vegetables. The yard was not jammed with these plants, rather all were ordered and set as if they each had their own specific home.

"What kind of dream did you have after returning from camp?" I asked.

"After camp," she said, "our main goal was to buy land but we had to raise the children too you know. So we didn't get it right away. Our children were all born before we went into camp."

"So the land was your main dream?" I asked.

"Well...," answered the *Kibei* man. "Then we like to get kids a good education. That's a main thing you know..."

"In your life, do you think your dreams were reached?" I asked.

"Oh, I think so," she answered and glanced at her husband. "At least we got the ranch."

I paused then asked, "Were you disappointed that none of your sons took over the farm?"

"Kind'a..." he answered and paused. "Maybe... son take over ranch and I didn't have to sell the place..."

"Would you have liked to retire on your farm?"

This question was first met with silence, a silence that was part of their answer. She finally spoke, "He would have liked it but I didn't mind. I like the town, everything so close..."

The silence then returned and he stared out a few feet in front of him, a weak smile clung to his face, his old eyes were glassy but he remained still. She again broke in and said, "I didn't feel so sad but I think he did... It was his baby."

In many ways *Sansei* dream in the same way as did their parents and grandparents. They don't talk a whole lot about their dreams, especially those who stayed on the farm and in the community. They've done a lot of thinking and planning, new varieties of peaches or plums to plant, new grape rootings and spraying techniques, thinking and planning and that's sort of like dreaming.

But Japanese in general don't talk about their dreams a lot. If you begin to dream too much, I was told, you forget about what you already have. So like that *Obaasan*, farmers silently struggle and dream to themselves because there's always more *abunai kusa* out there.

CHAPTER 17

LAND CLAIMS AND FARM HISTORY

Farm Histories: The Land and Her Farmers

Less than a hundred years ago in this valley, Japanese pioneers began claiming farms from a desolate countryside. Only a hundred years ago these lands were desert: sage, wild grasses and a few hardy oaks dotted the landscape; a dry, parched land spread for miles and miles; and a handful of adventurers dared to settle and work this desert.

In Fresno the rainfall averages ten inches per year and the usual daytime temperature in summer is near 100 degrees, a dry, hot desert. Yet, with the right crops and the magic of irrigation, these lands were turned into a green oasis, miles and miles of orchards and vineyards. That transition all began less than a hundred years ago.

An *Issei* told me about claiming the land, breaking the hardpan layers and his struggle to get enough water to his vineyard to keep it alive. That conversation taught me about "claiming."

Farmers here fool themselves when they talk about "claiming" land from nature. Sort of like trying to convince yourself that you belong, that your hands and back can outwit nature and keep a vine growing on land that it doesn't belong on. But farmers sense it's only a claim, not a right... much like a favor. They borrow this land to squeeze out a living, feeding her with fertilizers and water while at the same time probably abusing her with chemicals and disking and over production.

But the second and third generations on the land kind of lose that sense of "claiming." An *Issei* once explained: "You young folks got it too easy." He was right; but in the end, nature had a way of keeping us young folk in our proper place too: a thunderstorm on your table grapes or showers on unprotected grapes that have yet to dry into raisins, these experiences quickly humble you.

In addition to "claiming," the history of a farm involves other elements, man-made objects like businesses or markets or politics. Farmers are constantly trying to outwit each other with new techniques and developments and methods. And some things, like political policy or market demand, seem out of our control, and we accept it just like it's another part of nature. Right or wrong, we accept it because we're eternal gamblers and optimists, and dumb.

"Farmers are the dumbest creatures on earth," a *Nisei* farm leader once said. "There is no other occupation where we leave so much to chance, so much uncontrolled and we accept so much without question."

He was right too. A stubborn streak in farmers kept them from organizing and demanding and controlling their own industry. I think it has to do with a fragile "claim" they cling to, the belief that keeps them farming and keeps them knowing who and what they are... most of the time.

The history of Japanese American farmers began at the turn of the century, when *Issei* immigrants first came with dreams and hope and ambitions to claim farms and homes. Through the decades, claims were won and lost: farms were named, family names attached to places like the "Yamada place" or the "Ogawa farm."

And if the land could talk, it'd tell of changes and development, of vines and trees planted, of stakes and wire trellis set, of concrete irrigation lines buried and drip systems introduced. The stories would revolve around family claims, a family and a piece of land bonded together and passed on, an inherited obligation for *Nisei* and *Sansei* children.

And through these years a sensibility has evolved, a rich feeling about a certain place, that family farm, simple, yet very real for those that stayed, a fragile claim that remains alive today.

He and his wife sat on one side of the table, a tape recorder between us. Right from the beginning his answers were clear and distinct, as if for years he had them ready, just waiting for someone to ask. He was a *Nisei* farmer, his farm one of the oldest in Del Rey "claimed" by his father.

Why did your folks emigrate to the United States?

"It's a sad story. My folks are from Fukushima in the north. They got this silk worm farm and they make thread at home, you know. All that burned down and he lost a lot of thread there, from other people, they were weaving it. So he got in debt and he said, 'I'll come to America and repay the debt.' And so he did."

Why did he come to this area?

"He liked the land. See, when he bought this place in Del Rey he also had another 40 acres elsewhere in Caruthers. He said the dirt there isn't very good. You have to have 80 acres over there to compare with 40 acres of dirt you have in Del Rey. It was the days of horse and buggy. He'd ride over there with the horse and stay and farm over there and then come home and work. They really went at it.

"When he bought this place he said it was $500 an acre. It was right after the war, the first war and so the land was high and raisins were high."

How did he buy the land, weren't Orientals excluded from land ownership?

"You know the time my father bought this ranch, the Japanese couldn't own land. So he made a corporation and they owned stock. And he and Mr. Nishikawa... see Mr. Nishikawa bought his 40 acres over there, a few miles on the other side of Del Rey and my father bought in too. And then when we kids became of age he changed the title to the boys. That's what we did. There was this lawyer from Fresno and he helped a lot. Ah, he was good to all the Japanese."

Did your father talk about his dreams?

"Well, I don't know. Once he came over here to California he liked this country. He paid off all those debts in Japan. He was... I guess... satisfied."

RAISIN PRICE HISTORY

(SOURCE: RAISIN BARGAINING ASSOCIATION
AND RAISIN ADMINISTRATIVE COMMITTEE)

YEAR:	AVERAGE PRICE PER TON:	TOTAL NATURAL THOMPSON RAISIN PRODUCTION (TONS):
1919-20	$210	144,156
1920-21	$260	138,406
1921-22	$160	115,407
1922-23	$70	190,564
1923-24	$50	236,974
1924-25	$63	137,174
1925-26	$80	159,352
1926-27	$65	221,778
1927-28	$60	234,100
1928-29	$40	214,385
1929-30	$61	176,601
1930-31	$59	157,709
1931-32	$60	138,817
1932-33	$39	215,207
1933-34	$57	160,173
1934-35	$64	140,459
1935-36	$56	166,744
1936-37	$69	149,495
1937-38	$63	202,886
1938-39	$42	238,206
1939-40	$49	201,243

YEAR:	AVERAGE PRICE PER TON:	TOTAL NATURAL THOMPSON RAISIN PRODUCTION (TONS):
1940-41	$56	150,000
1941-42	$84	175,800
1942-43	$109	180,000
1943-44	$157	281,000
1944-45	$194	241,400
1945-46	$195	190,000
1946-47	$309	165,350
1947-48	$132	264,080
1948-49	$131	201,560
1949-50	$124	220,138
1950-51	$260	127,916
1951-52	$161	211,125
1952-53	$151	242,127
1953-54	$153	204,282
1954-55	$165	143,991
1955-56	$162	194,076
1956-57	$187	174,827
1957-58	$263	138,888
1958-59	$311	134,549
1959-60	$198	198,745
1960-61	$211	170,264
1961-62	$201	205,554
1962-63	$266	168,286
1963-64	$240	195,368
1964-65	$234	209,903
1965-66	$207	243,303
1966-67	$202	259,072
1967-68	$290	161,320
1968-69	$260	240,949
1969-70	$261	227,429
1970-71	$278	176,066
1971-72	$319	172,347
1972-73	$500	91,258
1973-74	$700	198,753
1974-75	$605	212,390
1975-76	$606	253,271
1976-77	$1,050	117,605
1977-78	$855	218,813
1978-79	$1,610	74,410
1979-80	$1,160	263,108
1980-81	$1,167	254,657
1981-82	$1,230	224,463
1982-83	$1,300	205,700
1983-84	$572	347,942
1984-85	$619	299,466
1985-86	$588	362,657
1986-87	$700 (EST.)	340,000 (EST.)

The veteran farmers studied the numbers and recalled the years, the collapse of prices in the mid-20's, the low Depression prices, the lost riches of the war years, the rains of '58, the frost of '72, and the naive expectations following a thousand dollars a ton raisin prices. These farmers didn't need photographs of those disasters, just the numbers of a short crop or low price renewed bitter memories and emotions of what might have been.

A lot of people think of the immigrants as pioneers, almost as saints, hard working, industrious, seeking new life and opportunity. When I was younger and heard stories about the great immigration to America and the Statue of Liberty with its plaque: "Give us your hungry, your tired, your poor..." I naively wondered what my grandparents thought of too as they sailed past the Statue when they arrived. But they arrived in San Francisco and Seattle, where there was no statue and only quarantine.

Immigrants were business adventurers, and for some, the land, these vast farmlands, were just another angle, another opportunity to strike it rich in America. A lot of farms were bought and sold in the early days of immigration, the land was good but the money was better. We like to think our Japanese grandparents were simple farmers and they were. Only some also were shrewd business people or at least tried their best to be.

Mr. N. Hiramoto, a *Nisei:* "Dad got this place in 1915, about $8,000 for the whole thing, 30 acres. Later he expanded just before the war, that was about 1938 *kana?* Somewhere around there. Dad used to speculate, like with other vineyards, he used to loan money to the Otani family and bought land in Selma and all that... he buys and sells it, buys and sell it.

"Dad was a good speculator. If he had extra, a few cash, well, he liked to speculate. And he made good of his investments, sometimes he lost quite a bit but he didn't gamble in Chinese dens like a lot of other *Issei.* A lot of *Issei* were good gamblers but dad didn't gamble. No, he was a speculator."

Mr. R. Matsubara, a *Kibei:* "Well, 1919 my father owned land in Parlier, 60 acres. He sold the place in 1920 I think. That time ranch prices went way high, you know, right after the war. Price went up you know. Raisin prices 15-18 cents a pound so he could get pretty good price on ranch so he sold it and bought another 60 acre ranch in Sanger. He bought 20 acres young thompson grapes, one year old... rest all low land, he thought he could develop it and plant everything and trying to make a more money. But, ah... well, that time, 1922-23, raisin prices good and you know he spent lot money on ranch and same time he and Japanese friend get together and build Del Rey building for town business."

Outsiders often associate a pleasant image with "taking over the farm," a family tradition passed on, a legacy inherited. But it didn't always happen that way, one farmer called it one generation "giving in" to the next.

Mr. G. Ohata, a *Nisei:* "You hear stories about when they transferred a farm to the son and the son kicked out the parents. There was all that kind of story before with *Issei* and *Nisei*, it actually happened. Some of the people, some *Issei*, they got kicked out and so they hanged themselves. I know that doesn't sound good, it didn't happen here but in other places... I knew of one case in Dinuba... That's why a lot of *Issei* won't sign over the farm to their children, no matter how much they all get along. These stories the *Issei* all heard about and remember."

Farming was always dirty, hard work and the goal of many was to "get out of the fields." But family circumstances and a sense of obligation, part of the Japanese and rural cultures fusing together, these resulted in altered life plans and ambitions.

Mr. G. Fukuda, a *Nisei:* "I went to refrigeration school one year. At the same time I got experience in doing, servicing refrigeration units. That's what I was going to do in LA, I was ready to go to LA.

"I was ready to go there and I says to my dad, 'Well, I'm going to LA you know.'

"He said, 'No, you better stay...' So I had to stay. My father was dying and he wanted me to come home. He stopped me and said, 'You better farm... I'm getting too old and if you don't stay here, I'm afraid we might loose the ranch.'

"So I got stuck here. Right here."

"Farming was the only damn thing left," said Mr. N Hiramoto, a *Nisei*. He then talked about the Depression and life after World War II. "I had all kind of dreams, all kind. But dreams sometime don't come true."

Farming, while a dream of many, was often the inherited dream of others, the "only damn thing left." Taking over a farm meant taking over the family, caring for aging *Issei* parents who only knew of farm work. Many *Nisei* inherited a burden to remain out in the country, in the fields.

All farmers carry a special sense of history, a history tied to their lands. A careful observer can see these histories as they drive through the countryside, each block of orchard or vines tells a story of decisions to plant and grow. The flat parcels tell of a dream to level and scrape rolling lands for irrigation; the ripping out of older vines and trees manifest a change, perhaps a new owner, or poor and frustrating harvests and disappointing prices. And with a little knowledge of the families you often can see certain relationships, a split in a family partnership with the dividing of a block of land, or the economic financial troubles of a farmer and the growth of weeds and pests on his once clean fields. It reminds me of traveling in Japan and studying the odd shapes and sizes of the rice paddies, generations of family histories told by the irregular borders and twisted boundaries.

To develop a place, improve it, transform it, a never ending struggle, a challenge each farmer tackles in his own way. Some want to just make a living off of it, keep it from dying. For others it consumes their entire life, clearing fields, replanting dead vines, and always, always there was the *abunai kusa*.

Mr. J. Hata, a *Nisei:* "Well, we were tired back then, before the war. Hell, I don't know how many times we were moving one place to another. 'Shit,' I said, 'hell, you get one place settled and any house or little shack or whatever and then you move on to another.' It's so I got tired of moving and so I settled down.

"This place? This real estate guy came around and say, 'Hey, interested in this place?' or something like that, he just passed by while we were working right there in fields.

"We said, 'Shit man, this place run down, full of Johnson grass... yea, what a place man...'

"Well, we bought the place. Had to put in a lot of man hours in this place. Funny, end up buying the place where we had worked."

Unless you've irrigated a field you'll never know the true lay of the land. Everyone knows that water runs to the lowest spot, it will not run uphill. That may not sound important but if you farm you damned-well-better remember it. That's why farmers around here talk about their "hills."

"Hill?" a visitor once asked, "What hills? This valley is flat, not even rolling, but flat."

There are hills here, farms that have a high rise in the center of a field that gradually slopes downwards to the edges. That's why the farmer has to water from the center of his farm you see, water runs down hill and if that high spot is to get any moisture, the water has to start at the highest point and then flow down to collect in the low areas. That's why you can distinguish an older vineyard, they all have an irrigation line or ditch running along the "divide," the highest points so they can water on both sides. And older homes were always built on the highest parts of the farm, not because of the view from there but because that land was the highest and hardest to irrigate. Remember, water does not run uphill. Even today, after years of development and scraping and leveling, farmers still talk about their "hills" on their farms.

He sat with his hands up, gesturing with his stories, adding movement to each phrase and scene. His 70 year old hands were old and crusty, callused and fingernails split, dry and gnarled and twisted dry, some couldn't stand looking at them without goose bumps breaking out on their backs and arms. He told me about the farm lands around here and especially about Del Rey and "the hills."

"The hills" were the natural, gently rolling character of the land. From the roadside you don't see them as hills, these were slight undulations, ever-so-slight rises in the land. They were "hills" he explained because you just can't water them, "the damn water runs off the rises and floods the low spots."

"Japanese," he explained, "made Del Rey good, like what it's today." He told me about the Fresno scraper, that marvelous invention that a team of horses could pull and allowed a farmer to shift his dirt, pulling it from the rises to the low spots and thereby overcome "the hills.

His two hands came into the picture again. He told me how Japanese leveled these farmlands, his hands moving up and down and sideways, a wave was drawn in the air, his hands outlining "the hills" of Del Rey, the rises and dips.

"Japanese made it good," he said and his hands leveled and drew a straight line in the air, the smooth lands for irrigating. "With our backs, we Japanese made farms level." His hands swing flat before me from left to right, his shoulders crouched like an orchestra conductor communicating to his musicians. "The land made damn good and level."

Farms and Evacuation

The history of a lot of farms and farmers died with the war. Relocation, evacuation, imprisonment, whatever you felt described it, Executive Order 9066 commanded all Japanese Americans to leave the West Coast and be herded into desolate camps inland.

Farms and farmers died because dreams ended. A *Nisei* explained: "Damn war came just wrong time, whole family ready to start really working, peak earning, just wrong time." He meant that his family, the four brothers were now of age, out of high school and could work full days with full pay. Their peak earning years were beginning, the prime time to make a move on some land, the family working as a unit to make that leap.

"And I'm not alone," he added. "Think of it. All those families coming into their own. A generation about same age all at their peak."

Thousands of *Nisei* were entering the work force and beginning to dream like an adult and save for their own farms. But the war came and plans were crushed, a plague swept through households and the dreaming stopped.

You can divide the farm families into two camps when Pearl Harbor occurred, those who owned land and those who didn't. For those who did, the evacuation meant either selling out at a desperation sale or trying to hang on and cut deals with others to take care of the land. Although they may have owned the land, not all had it completely paid off. Their camp years were spent trusting someone else, hoping not only they'd take care of the land but make the necessary payments to banks.

There's a story of one family in the Sanger river bottom area, they had entrusted a bank to lease the land, to make payments and contact him in camp. But something happened during the war, payments weren't made, the account became delinquent along with property taxes and the farm was auctioned. This was the story and whether it actually happened is not of importance, the fact is people believe it happened.

For others, their trust was met by honest, good hearted neighbors and individuals. One farmer, K. Alber, took care of his Japanese neighbor's farm, raised and harvested the crops, kept a small percentage for himself and diligently sent the profits to the Japanese owner in camp. The Japanese greatly respected him for that, and when he died, his family couldn't understand why so many Japanese attended his funeral.

Another farmer, Mr. N. Hiramoto, a *Nisei* who had left for the East Coast to escape the relocation camps, explained: "We rented our place to Grower's Farm Company, some red-necks in Sanger. But they took care of the place, I have to admit that, they took care of it. One of 'em, Thomas was his name, he even came clear out to Pennslyvania to see me. He was out on a trip and I remember he called me and we talked for an hour."

Mr. T. Kimashiga, a *Nisei:* "You couldn't trust anyone, they'd take care of your place all right, keep all the profits and tell you that you didn't make nothing from the crops. You know we left in August and had a whole raisin crop on the vines, didn't have to do a thing except harvest and it was all their's. Didn't make a cent off of that, not a cent. Damn renter kept it all, imagine a whole crop a month away from harvest, all paid for, like money just hanging on the vines."

Mr. T. Inouye, a *Nisei:* "You gotta look on the bright side I guess. Our family, we were lucky. At least we hadn't put down all we had for a down payment on a place. Then we would have lost it all with the war."

The majority of Japanese Americans didn't own land, they faced evacuation with a different perspective. For them, the only thing worse than having your dreams crushed was to stop dreaming. These people witnessed the forced sale of farms, families desperately trying to sell a place and recoup the down payment they had made. Others grew confused and perplexed over the uncertainty of the future; even though the government had decreed that "no land of any Japanese was being forced to be sold," the clouded reality of evacuation loomed closer and closer.

The confusion and uncertainty exploded into anger for many. Mrs. V. Iida, a *Nisei*, related the story that when the final evacuation orders were posted, her father had talked with the family he had worked for years under, and asked if he could store some of their belongings in their barn. "They told us 'no.' That's all. And when my brother found out he got angry. He really tore into them. He yelled at the farmer, accusing him that he had used dad, used dad for the best years of his life and now was treating us like this. I remember him telling us from now on to never, never, never trust anyone and just look out for yourself."

The war, relocation and resettlement from 1942-46 altered the make up of the farm family and community. The *Issei* were trapped, stripped of their homes and honor, many had lost face and were forced into a dependent role and taken care of by their children. The return home following the war meant even more dependence, often too old for demands of hard physical farm work, they could only do simple, light work found for them by others. Some *Issei* men were crushed by this "begging" for work, it was shameful for them.

Many *Nisei* never returned to the valley and farming. When the movement of Japanese Americans to the east of the Mississippi was allowed, many Japanese Americans and especially *Nisei* resettled in new communities in the Midwest and East Coast. Without a farm to draw them back to California, why should they return?

Mr. J. Yamato, a *Nisei:* "Oh, I didn't want to come back, no, not on your life. See, my folks asked me to come back but I answered, 'come back to what?'

"But they just kept saying, 'Come back, come back.'"

"Well, I don't know, it was confusing. My mom was saying at the same time, 'we don't gamble, we go back but we don't gamble with buying any place. Look what happened, they take it away so we don't buy a farm... but we go back.'

"Now shit, does that make any sense? We go back, go back to what?"

A *Nisei* told the story of his return home, his home coming. He had just been released from the army, dropped off in New York and rode a train home, back to Fresno. He explained, "Well, when I get home, boy, I was gonna rest and sleep and take a easy for a while. Just got out of the service you know. Gonna rest and no body tell me when to get up, no more orders. Just take a easy for a while."

He continued and explained that on the first day back, during the first afternoon nap, his *Issei* mother came to him. She woke him and asked him what was he going to do? The family couldn't live like they were, where they were, what was he going to do? The family had been living in an old grocery store, a family friend's store who was going to soon open it back up. This was the first year after the war. The family, an *Issei* couple and their youngest child, a girl in her late teens, they had stayed in camp as long as they could. When they had to leave they didn't know where to go. All their children except one had already left, two in the service, the others out East where they had allowed Japanese to relocate a few months earlier. The *Issei* couple had no place else to go home to, so they returned to Fresno with no idea of where to stay, with no work they could do.

"So mom woke me up, that first day. Can you believe that? My first day back and she asked me 'what we going to do?' Hell, what a mess, pop was too old to work and mom was old too. And living in an old grocery store and cooking with a fire on an old steel drum. Boy, I thought I shouldn't never come home."

He then described about how he hustled for work in the next few weeks, found an old garage out on a ranch they could move into, rent free in exchange for field work. He found a simple, "piece work" job for his dad and mom and got a house cleaning job for his sister, the youngest sibling. "It was a live-in cleaning job, one less mouth for us to feed and at least she could get good food there..."

For families without land, without homes, taking over meant something else, something more. The *Nisei* ended his story with, "Can you believe that? The first day home and mom asked me 'what we gonna do?' Can you believe that, the first day... Hell, if I knew that, I would've taken a few more days off coming across country."

Once again, the work of building a farm began. For those who had farms, four years of lost income had to be regained, working the land back into maximum production. Yet for the majority who were landless, they had to start over, land claims renewed.

He called it "the hill," a ten acre block on his newly purchased farm, one quarter of his land. He was a 60 year old *Nisei* and "the hill" was a rise in his land, a mound of dirt and hidden layer of hard pan a few feet beneath it. The vines on that patch of land were weak and frail, root systems stunted by the hard pan and poor drainage. But it was "the hill" and its hard pan that made the farm cheaper, within reach of his means.

You may not find hard pan among the rock charts of geology. Hard pan is a compacted, rock-like layer of clay and minerals, impenetrable by roots, more like rock than anything else. Farmers swear hard pan was invented to break their backs and to protect "the hills" of the San Joaquin valley from vineyards and orchards, nature's revenge against man's tillage. In the Northeast, farmers made fences out of field stones, in Del Rey they used hardpan.

His "hill" was solid hard pan layer with a thin but rich skin of topsoil. The problem was twofold, to level "the hill," to make a flat plateau for irrigating and to get rid of the hard pan. So he had a pair of giant Caterpillar tractors rumble across his land, they ripped out the meager vines and tossed them aside and then attacked the hard pan. Man verses rock and the rocks won. "The hill" was partially leveled, flattened and ripped but it teamed with huge blocks of hard pan, like a pot of chili teaming with beans, more beans than beef, more hard pan than soil.

So he explained how he spent his fall, winter, spring and summer, clearing his field, one by one, lifting the chunks of rock, lugging and tossing them on to his old flatbed truck, day after day, truckload after truckload, one by one emptying his field and trucks in what they euphemistically called land fills out in remote areas of the county.

Some of the hard pan was stubborn, he explained, huge plates of rock, thousands of pounds lodged beneath other chunks. His main weapons: a strong back, a fierce hunger to farm "that hill," and dynamite.

His wife confessed how she wasn't fond of the dynamite, with each explosion she shook a little, partly out of the blasting noise, more out of a fear for her husband. The dynamite blew apart the plates into a sea of smaller pieces that one could lift and drag to a wagon or truck. Day after day, truck load after truck load.

He lost a year of planting. He cleared the land first, refusing to plant vines in rocky soil. Once all the surface rocks were cleared he called back the Caterpillar and ripped the earth again, a huge shank slicing the land, tearing at hidden layers of hard pan, breaking the rock's domain. His formerly clean field disappeared. New chunks of hard pan rose and blanketed the land, popping up in the earth as if they floated on water, surfacing in the wake of the Caterpillar. The mission began again, lugging and tossing, but he used less dynamite, the rocks grew smaller, averaging only a few pounds each. And he went through a lot fewer pairs of gloves this second round, a sense of progress was felt.

Now a healthy, strong vineyard stands on "the hill." The vines are vigorous, the roots penetrating and secure. Occasionally while disking or cultivating, a chunk of hard pan surfaces, he stops the tractor and carries the rock to the end of the row where a small collection stands. "They seem to keep growing," he explained. "But so do the vines. So do the vines."

"You can't even give the damn place away," a *Nisei* farmer lamented. The other farmers nodded their heads, they too knew of the legal realities of passing on a family farm.

He explained that first, you had to work with your lawyer and accountant, laws and taxes had long ago entered into farming.

Law: if you gave your farm to your children, it'll be taxed as a gift from you to them, subject to gift taxation. If not now, perhaps later with probate you would be taxed. Horror stories circulated about the breaking up a farm to pay taxes.

Law: even if you sell your farm, it has to be near market price, otherwise it could be viewed as a gift and taxed accordingly.

Law: if you sold your farm at market price and your child was one of the buyers, you couldn't just loan them the money interest free, the loan had to have a specified near-market-level interest rate. "Funny," a farmer said, "I could loan a complete stranger money with any old interest but my own son has to pay a higher amount, something about "arm's length relationship." Hell, it's my own blood and they end up bleeding me."

Children don't simply get the family farm. They buy it.

Mr. N. Hiramoto, a *Nisei:* "My goal in life... I'm getting old... I'm ready to conk off any moment... I tell you, you know what I'd like to do? This hard earned money that I made, well I stuck everything back into the farm... and you know it's just hard to give it up. But what can I do? Rather than selling this place I might as well give it to my sons. But my

Taking a bath, 1920's, from a family album. A basin for picking grapes and farm chores doubled as a bathtub, a special affinity shared between grapes and farm kids, even at bath time.

kids... ah, forget them, they'd rather do something else. Forget it. That's their attitude, they've been other places and know better. But I really don't know. I can't work much. At my age now that I have to work until morning and by afternoon, I'm all conked out. Somehow, some way I get along but I'm getting old you know."

Mr. R. Matsubara, a *Kibei:* "Well, no, I felt my son would get a white collar job. I'll probably have to sell the place. To me, I'm not that sentimental. Doesn't bother me. The farm? Well, yea, I guess it has been a struggle but you know it's been good to me, really good to me."

Mrs. F. Matsubara, a *Nisei* and wife of Mr. R. Matsubara: "It has been good. It really was, financially too because we had good years. We didn't get rich but it was good while we were raising the children... We feel very lucky. Everything really went well. The first few years were a struggle but I can't believe it myself, we picked all those grapes ourselves. I felt so sorry for my husband, he was so young but had to work so hard. I just can't believe it..."

People seemed genuinely happy to hear he was farming. "So I hear you're going to take over, how lucky for your father," people said to him.

But he wasn't so sure his dad felt lucky. Yes, he was going to farm the family place, to buy the land and continue the operation. Yes, the father could now spend his time walking through their fields, keeping an eye on things and knowing the place wouldn't go to hell, he hoped.

But the father knew how badly the son had been scarred, especially after three years of rains at the wrong time and poor market prices and a depression in agriculture. The father wasn't sure he'd ever want to push this on anyone. At one time he thought he'd like his son to take over but he wasn't so sure now. And now his son was starting his own family.

The son joked: "Hopefully we'll have a girl, at least she won't even consider taking over this farm. And if she does, I'll really know I failed."

They both chuckled to themselves.

CHAPTER 18

FARM WORK AND FAMILY OPERATIONS

Farm Work

> "Your Grandpa's generation farmed with their backs,
> and your Dad's farmed with their equipment.
> But you, the new, young generation,
> You have to learn to farm with your heads."
>
> Radio Ad for Agribusiness Computers

The times and work have changed and the business of farming, the bookkeeping and accounting, the pricing and market structure, the pesticides and fertilizer strategies, all these have taken precedence over the shoveling and clearing and walking your fields.

"You gotta spend just as much time inside, in the office," lamented a *Nisei* farm wife, a member of a generation that still clung to the old work ethic where true work is accomplished only with your hands and a lot of sweat and time. The days of a simple and pure yeoman's life of tilling the soil from sunup to sundown has gone, passed into oblivion.

But a simple truth remains, those that hate farm work, whether it's inside or outside, they have left and continue to leave the land. And those that stayed, despite the bitching and doom and gloom forecasts, they stay and work the land with their backs, their equipment, and their heads.

Mr. N. Hiramoto, a *Nisei*: "When I was a kid we had to work 'cuz about four or five guys wanted my job. See... in them days actually we didn't work as much as we do today. All right if we take a horse, we take a plow, sometimes we take a 3-10 plow or a 3-8 plow and use about three, four horses and make one round, then we take a single plow and plow right next to the vines and then we take a French plow and you gotta have a wheel on it and we gotta move around there and then we irrigate under the vine and that'll be around May of the year. And then we plow back with a single plow then we irrigate that part and that was it, that's all, end of the season. See, not much work. See, all the work we had to do?

"The water level in the ground was, what is it... 18 feet and some ponds full of water so we didn't have to irrigate. And then we only sulfured once or twice at the most. Just before the fourth of July we take a vineyard truck and Dad drives, my brother on one end and I on the other with a knapsack with sulfur and we give just one little 'puff.' No sulfur machines. Put about 10 pounds and just give a little shake until sulfur comes out and lands on the vine and that's was it. Two rows on one side, a knapsack... some sulfur on you but not as bad as the machines today. Machines worse and makes fine dust and goes row to row. But this way, just on top of the vine."

Mr. J. Hata and his wife, both *Nisei*, reminisced about the early days of work. He laughed a lot, chuckling to himself and to the observer, you weren't quite sure what that laugh meant.

"When I was just a teenager I guess... workin' behind a team of horses," he said and grinned. "Cultivating, I was too..."

"Didn't you even have to harness the horse and everything?" she injected and chuckled too.

"Yea, see... I have to get some boxes you know... couple of boxes and I lucky the horses pretty tame..." he said.

"He was short and had to stand on something to put the harness on," she interrupted while he was still talking. "Japanese menfolk not that big and you know how big horses are."

"Yea," he said, "you might say I had to throw the harness on. Yea... but they pretty tame. I kind'a remember that." He smiled. "Think about all that."

They both smiled without looking at each other and just stared outwards.

Mrs. V. Ishikawa, a *Nisei:* "My dad was a farm laborer. He just worked on the ranch. He wasn't a manager or anything. They didn't used to do things like that those days and that farm wasn't that big. They might have had a total of 100 acres. I remember there were muscats, thompson and sultana but there were no fruit trees, those days there wasn't much trees.

"My sister later married a vegetable grower and just because she was married to them they made me and my girl friend go pick string beans and we were so mad. Mosquitoes chewed us up and what I was mad about was mostly the Japanese style, my father wouldn't let me take the pay and they bought me a pair of girl scout shoes. That was all I got. I was so mad."

He was an *Issei* in his 70's and his wife was a *Nisei*, also in her 70's. They're retired now, sold the ranch and live in town. These were quiet people, their actions speaking the clearest. In the back yard a beautiful garden could be seen, meticulously kept, weed-free and raked. You sense they've worked all their lives with plants and the earth. If you studied their hands you could see the callous and rough palms, the years of work manifested in rough, old hands, gentle enough for delicate *bonsai* training and pruning, yet layers and layers of calluses, symbols of the years of farm work.

What kind of feeling did you have about working on the farm?

"We didn't think too much about it. Oh, we had to work hard, make a living you know. And get kids educated," he said.

That was your main goal, to get your children educated?

"Yea..." They both nodded.

Did the kids work out in the fields too?

"Oh yea, they helped quite a bit," he answered.

"We always thought the children should do something," she added.

Did they complain a lot?

"Oh yea. All kind of excuses... we heard them all," she said and they both laughed. "But they helped us a lot."

Did you ever think you might not survive in farming?

"I didn't think that. I just thought we were going to make it. We just had to," she said.

"We had to make it or otherwise we gonna starve," he said and again, both of them laughed.

"We did a lot of the work ourselves," she added. "We didn't hire like they do today. We started from daylight to sundown, we'd be working. We really worked hard."

Mrs. L. Nakamoto, a *Nisei:* "They, the people our family worked for, they always had work to do. My mother helped with whatever she could help, like tying vines... so they all counted on us to come help like after school and then, you see, that would be extra work done. My dad got paid by the hour for working then my mother worked by piecework, with so many acres, naturally the whole family got involved and more could help and we had to go out and help.

"I used to think, when we used to pick grapes, there was a muscat patch right by that Danish Lutheran Church and even on Sundays we had to pick grapes because, you know, when the grapes are ready to pick, it's ready for work. And so we were picking and I used to think, 'I know, I gonna marry a preacher and then I won't have to work on Sundays.' I heard the church bell ringing and I thought, 'Boy, I'm not going to ever marry a farmer.'

"But I married one anyway and right after that my girl friend in LA said, 'Can't you get your husband to do something else so you can move to LA too?'

"I said, 'I can't, he loves farming.' I know he does because when he's on that tractor I can hear him whistle and I know he's happy. He's really happy. So I could tell I know he really liked it. He always planned on farming, he had farming on his brain. "And so I shocked myself when he came back from the army and I said, 'Are you sure you going to be a farmer?" He said, 'I like it, I like it.' And so I said, 'Well, if you like it and then I kind a resign myself to it.' You know though, but I could never say that I enjoy working in farming. I tried not to, but I sort of begrudgingly helped."

Most folks have heard of the story or one like it: fact or fiction, it doesn't matter now because people believe it happened, the myth becomes a reality. The story has a type of fantasy about it, where good work is rewarded, virtue conquers, and endings end happily. The characters: a hard working young kid from a poor family, maybe a landless, poverty family in Japan who send their son off in hopes of a better life in America. And a childless Japanese American couple, a farm couple, kind and gentle yet denied children. And a rich, fertile farm land, prime land begging for attention and with work it will reward its tiller.

The story was told that this one family never had children, they owned a good place, a level, rich land and heavy producer of sweet fruit. But they didn't have any children and thus no future; the farm would end with them. So they "adopted" a son from another family, from a shirttail relative, they took in a landless son. And in return he worked hard, built up the place and always, always "took care of the folks as if they were his own." The farm remained in the family, the old folks were taken care of and the hard work of the son was rewarded.

Fact or fiction, it didn't matter. It was comforting to think it just may have happened.

YMBA, Young Men's Buddhist Association fund raiser, 1941. Can you imagine pruning vines as a fund raiser? It was one way of earning money for the club and their quick hands made good money. Besides, according to one of these *Nisei* men, "You could bull shit a lot while working." (Courtesy Jim Harada)

"No question Japanese work hard," said Mr. T. Inouye, a *Nisei*. "But they work hard in the fields. I can't figure out why they didn't do that inside, with a business. With a raisin plant or packing operation for *Nihonjin* [Japanese].

There are no Japanese American-owned raisin plants. There are Japanese American fruit packing plants, but they began as a single family's operation and have expanded; but raisins are a different story. A lot of farmers wonder why there wasn't a Japanese cooperative formed, why Japanese didn't pool their resources and work together. "I guess they're too damn independent," Mr. T. Inouye commented.

Folks often speculate about the reasons for Japanese not owning and expanding sooner into the processing side of farming. Some think it was because Alien Land Laws prevented the *Issei* from owning land. Others say it was the Depression and loss of farms and finances of the war and relocation. Still another faction believes there was never enough financial backing in the community, especially after relocation. A few admit it may have been something emotional, a fear of gambling and risks or the shell-shock repercussions of the war and relocation, scars that cut deeply and left a constant threat in the future. An *Issei Obaasan* [grandmother] once warned her son, "Don't go and buy land, we don't know what will happen in the future, anytime the government might take it away!"

No one knows exactly why or in this case, why not. The tendency is to study and examine why something happened and forget about the "why didn't's." It's a history ignored all too often.

When we were kids, we looked forward to summer vacation. Vacation meant a break from school but not from work. The peaches, nectarines, plums and grapes ripened each summer and the whole family would work, harvesting our fruits and working in the fields.

We were expected to work and didn't know any better. No doubt we complained but all of us knew there wasn't much choice: the work had to be done and we were a family operation. When I was very young, I thought everyone worked during the summer and only when I was older, near teen age did I realize that some kids actually had nothing to do for the whole summer. "How bored they must be" I used to think.

Even the kids worked and operated much of the equipment, such as driving tractors and forklifts. During the 50's and 60's, farming was in a transition, much of the work was still done by hand but with the help of equipment. For example, to spread fertilizer in the orchards, the father used to hook up a wagon to the tractor. He loaded it with sacks of dry fertilizer and two of them, perhaps an older child and himself would sit on each side of the wagon with a coffee cup in their hands. As a younger child drove the tractor, the father and his helper would dip their cup into the fertilizer and toss it next to each tree where the root system was dense. At the end of the row the father would stop and check how much fertilizer remained in the bag, calculated if they should fill up their cups with more or a little less in order to evenly spread the fertilizer to each tree.

Today they have a machine that does the whole operation, one man operation. You sometimes wondered though if that displaced thousands of farm kids each summer.

"While working in the fields I used to think about sci-fi, to think about something else other than the heat and dust and sweat," a *Sansei* explained.

Science fiction would "get him through the day, through the vine row, through the season," he continued. He then explained and described all the wild, imaginative stores he invented, some tied to his work such as each vine becoming an alien monster and he had to "cut out all the poisonous tentacles [the grape canes]," otherwise the creature would conquer the universe. Other tales were as far removed from the work as possible.

"You had to think about something," he repeated, "you just couldn't just work, you had to do something."

The work of farmers was to supply raw materials to the agribusiness industry. Raising and harvesting a crop was only the first step in the operation, farmers delivered their crops to processors who packaged the produce and then it was marketed. Some farmers had their own packing and marketing operations, but most were only the suppliers. That put them in an awkward situation: they had to accept the packing charges and the market prices. It seemed like a crazy position to be in, always at the mercy of not only the weather but also business people and market cycles.

Mr. G. Fujita, a *Nisei:* "The biggest change in farming during my life wasn't the equipment but with the fruit packing companies. Before we didn't take our fruit to these places because there's too many *chokujin*, you know, people who cheat you and don't give the right price. You know they're selling it but they won't give you the price.

"So *Nisei* farmers started looking for places, outlets and we found a few places to sell our fruits, like Sunnyside Marketing and in Reedley they organized their own co-op and selling it themselves, and in Sanger they established Blue Anchor. We started looking for those outlets. And those other packing houses couldn't get the business so they started getting more honest.

"So now they're honest. So we quit packing ourselves and now we're taking it to the packing house. For a while they were just ripping us off. Now we take it to the packing house and they get us the right price. You know if something goes wrong they'll come back and tell you what's wrong, you know. If they think you're going to get red ink why they'll tell you to stop picking. Before they didn't do that at all, you know they gave the people red ink anytime they wanted to. They kept the fruit a long time before selling it and tell you they have to go dump it and all that business.

"I think the *Nisei* got educated."

Mr. G. Sato, a *Nisei:* "Oh, there were a lot of hardship, a lot of them, especially when you're farming. I remember one year we had a frost in

May, everybody got hurt you know, especially around where we were at, just wiped everything out. You know one year's all shot, you know. There's nothing coming in, you just have to have something to work but there's nothing.

"Then after you get the grapes picked and got them on the trays you know what happens: rain. Oh, we had about two years of that you know. It's a struggle. I mean at times everybody struggled. And when you have some of those mishaps, like I say when you're farming you got two strikes against you before you even start.

"I learned a lesson. I wanted my children to do something else beside farm. Farming wasn't the thing to do. It's pretty hard."

Mr. G. Suzuki, a 30 year old *Sansei* left the valley and farming for a career in a large urban area. He recalled his feelings and memories about his growing up on a farm and working.

"Let's see, there were a whole bunch of bad times on the farm...

"But probably the only one I really remember was not getting paid what I thought I was worth. I think I was about seven years old and they wanted to pay me only a half cent a box for stamping a box or something like that. And then I thought that, well, I should get at least a dollar a box for stamping boxes, so I got pissed off and took off.

"I came back the next day. It was more 'let's get back to work, we gotta go' and I just went.

"On the farm I worked as a family slave. I did anything that had to be done on the farm, picking, packing, box boy... My pay? Slave laborer. Starting out with peanuts to just keep me in there, working up to big bucks, a whole $4.50 an hour at the end."

Mr. S. Kiyomatsu, a *Sansei:* "My farm work was to do the little jobs, getting things prepared for the bigger people so they wouldn't have to hassle things. Eventually these jobs got expanded as the older ones got older and went away. Then my job started being to take over their jobs, doing the heavier work.

"There was a lot of competition. It got to the point where I finally started getting strong enough to do a lot of the loading of trucks and things like that. It got to the point where one of my uncles thought he was real strong and always tried to push us and beat us in loading up the trucks. It got to be almost like a joke. There were a lot of broken boxes from not being clamped down correctly while loading the truck and boxes tipping over off the truck. We raced at the beginning and he won just because I was smaller and it got to the point where I got to be a lot bigger and

Passing out wooden trays for raisin harvesting, 1938. They didn't take a lot of photographs of their work. "Why would we want to remember all that sweat and hard labor?" stated one farmer. (Courtesy Steve Morishita)

stronger so there was no competition after that, but he still wanted to race and try and do that.

"No, I never wanted to be a farmer. It was just too much work.

"It's a little sad basically that since all the kids are leaving the farm and that the community is starting to dwindle. It's going to be some tough times in the future depending on how many people are really left in the community. Age-wise, it's probably gotten older rather than younger as far as the median age is, just because all the kids have left and that leaves just the older parents.

"As far as the future... I'm not sure if the kids will be coming back because the future isn't on the farm. The future is more in the cities and situations where they would go into professional ranks."

Family Operations

Like any small family enterprise, family members were woven into the daily operation. Few children escaped farm work, most were raised with it as a given: "we didn't know better," they later would confess. And you also married into a family farm, the land and extended family came with the wedding and your spouse. The meaning of family became inseparable from the farm operation, life was planned around summer harvests, winter pruning and daily chores, a family rhythm that became fused with the land, crops and cycles of nature.

Mrs. D. Murashima, a *Nisei:* "Oh yes, as a child we picked grapes, tied vines. And that was piece work so naturally... you didn't have to keep up with the adults, you just did what you can.

"And we worked as a family. We take one row and all of us would pick in there. That's how I did it... naa... that's how we did it.

"Actually we weren't paid. You know our parents got the money. But then they buy us things so, you know... in those days it was different than it was today. You pay a kid now...ha,ha,ha... But in those days, why, you just worked, that's part of your duty. You work along with the parents. We really didn't work for ourselves, we really worked for our parents.

"We were competitive. We were competitive in the sense there was this one other family... they were so fast... but we couldn't keep up with them. They came at the crack of dawn and stayed until the sun went clear down to pick grapes. But we could never do that, never do that. But they were really, really gung ho... Strong I guess."

Mrs. V. Ishikawa, a *Nisei:* "My sister's and my birthdays fall in September. Right when the grapes are in season, so we hardly ever had a birthday party. But I remember one year, they finished the grapes a little earlier so when we came home from school to help out, they were fixing up a feast for our birthday, at least that's what they told us. I can't remember how old I was but imagine, they were fixing us a big feast!

"Speaking about food, I remember Thanksgiving. Dad would always fix us a Thanksgiving turkey. He always made a turkey for us, even though there was only our family, all of the cousins and aunts and uncles were still in Japan. We ate like pigs, Dad would tell my brother to eat, eat because Dad had been deprived of food at one time and with farming you never know how rough it might come, Dad'd say, 'So eat, eat.' I remember him saying that, 'eat."

Mrs. D. Yanagi, a *Nisei:* "I got married to a farm and three brothers, all partners. They were vegetable growers. The whole place was vegetables because they were once vegetable growers in west Fresno before all three came here, truck gardening I guess that's what you call it. There were chili peppers, eggplant, cabbage, I guess it was seasonal. In the fall there was spinach and what else was there? I think there was squash too. Oh, string beans too.

"This was a different type of life. Because in the old days the 'vegetarians' worked until the sun went down. The three brothers and their wives, all of us and you know how long the sun is up in the summer time. So you have dinner at 9:00 or whatever time.

"Hard work, that's the old style. Like the Mitsune family, they always ate late. OK, that's from the old school of thought. OK, we did that too. Until we went to camp and then... see, some good came out of going to camp - ha, ha - when we came back we always ate early. It became five or six o'clock at the latest but usually it was sort of like a cutting off time.

"But all of us did work late, there's always more work."

He was a single man, the story began, a bachelor who journeyed from Japan to buy land here in America. He succeeded in his work, he formed his own corporation and purchased land to evade the restrictions of the Alien Land Law that prevented *Issei* from owning land.

For years, even after "getting his own place," the bachelor farmer lived with a neighboring Japanese family in a separate little shack behind their main house. They were all from the same *ken* (province) in Japan and they were all Christians rather than Buddhists.

When the family's oldest son turned 18 and eligible to own land as an American born citizen, the bachelor *Issei* turned over the farm to the boy. They took care of each other, what ever was the bachelor's was also the family's. "They were both lucky" I was told.

Ken Anderson, a Del Rey farmer, related a story about his grandfather. The Anderson family had established themselves as major landowners/farmers in the county. Grandfather Anderson "adopted" and took in an *Issei* bachelor and gave him a "free hand at running the place, including the family."

This *Issei* was treated like part of the family, he was both a farm foreman and a male nanny, raising the crops and kids along side the grandfather. He even yelled like the grandfather, bitched about the weather and "took the strap" to the kids for discipline. In one family photograph, the *Issei* stood next to the grandfather, both dressed exactly the same, faded overalls, wrinkled work shirts and beat up boots.

"Swedes tan well," said Ken Anderson, "Grandpa looked so dark, just like a twin to the Japanese bachelor."

Both men aged together but when he was in his 60's, the *Issei* died. The Anderson grandfather had often heard the Japanese bachelor express one final wish, to return to Japan. So as a final act of friendship, the grandfather sent the body of the *Issei* "back to Japan for a proper burial."

Not all family operations continued as planned, many dreams never materialized and farms were lost due to family circumstances. Futures were altered, "what might have been" became a haunting echo in most families' histories.

Mrs. V. Ishikawa, a *Nisei:* "I remember my dad saying that they kept trying to save to get a place of their own. But he never had enough money. First he thought he saved a little bit, then when I was young we were riding with the neighbors and got in a terrible accident. My dad must not have had any insurance or nothing and my brother was in the hospital for almost a year. My brother broke a leg and it didn't set right and they kept trying and had to do it over...I remember my folks being so upset, it took so many operations.

"It took all their savings. That's the story my father told me. And it's probably true, it probably wasn't a whole lot of money but when the accident came it kind of wiped him out and set him back.

"Then my mother got sick... she had a first stroke and she got so sick that... she had never been back to Japan since she married my dad and came from Hawaii to the US and she always wanted to go back to Japan. A grandmother raised her and she wanted to go to her grave. You know Japanese believe in going to the cemetery, they walk around it three times or they have some kind of superstition. And she was hell bound to do that and she wanted to go.

"So she told my dad when she sort of got better that she had to go to Japan, she was gonna go. She demanded that she go back. That took a lot of money, it wasn't a lot in those days but it was a lot for them. It took all their savings, cleaned them up. Dad said he just didn't get anywhere after that, that's all."

Developing a farm went beyond the physical demands. Family relationships necessarily became involved. You don't hear a lot about the arguments within families, you just see the results in their farms.

"I know they were running a big farm and they lost it," said Mrs. Asakawa, a *Nisei*. She sat next to her husband, both in their seventies, both retired from their farm. "They had a big place, and something must have happened... This was way before the war."

"Well... I don't know if I should say this...," he hesitated, his silence becoming part of the story. "This older brother...," he began slowly, "when he made money, he send it to Japan and deposit it in Japan. And the younger brother... he don't like to do that so later they argue and separate.

Younger brother bought another ranch. And the other brother, without help he begin to lose the place a little each year."

Neither volunteered more information as if it wasn't right to talk about another family's matters. A silence returned as their concluding remarks.

You don't hear a lot about arguments within families but you see the results. The silence becomes an appropriate concluding remark.

I knew of other stories, of a brother who married a *hakujin* (Caucasian) and even though he owned half of the farm, he left the area, giving up his claim to his land. "He didn't want trouble," I was told.

Or another story of a Buddhist becoming a Christian and the split within a family, a problem with farm operations between the two factions, resulting in a division of the property and of the family.

These stories have more to them, more meanings and history but folks don't like talking about them. Perhaps it's because no family is immune to such problems, and out of respect and superstition it's not right to talk about other families.

When I was growing up, each summer our shed was transformed into a miniature factory. A "packing operation" where the fresh peaches and nectarines and plums were sorted and packed into boxes for shipment to stores.

We had an average sized operation. Once I added it up, 20,000 boxes a season, a staggering number to us kids as we envisioned each box that we had handled, lifted, stacked and the season that began in early June and ran through to late August, five or six days a week. We weren't alone though, there were a lot of Japanese American family packing operations, part of that integration of work and family.

Dad had planted a half dozen different varieties of fruit, each only a few acres, each ripening throughout the season. The staggered ripening kept us working week after week, disrupted only if a hot spell accelerated the ripening of one variety and caused a welcomed overlapping of fruit.

The family provided the labor force for all the shed work. Family meant not only my brother, sister and mom, but also uncles, cousins and grandmother. Despite all the work, summer meant a glorious time for us kids, the cousins came to live with us, we had friends and playmates everyday. I grew up thinking everyone spent their summer working with family.

My dad started early each morning with a small crew of Mexicans first picking the fruit and selecting only the ripe ones, leaving the rest to color up for a few days before their next round. Today they use large bins to pick and haul fruit, four by four by three feet deep, but when I was young we used lugs, flat boxes about a foot deep and swamped onto wagons and hauled to the shed.

We all had our own jobs, a division of labor based on physical ability and hierarchy determined by age. The heavy jobs of lifting boxes were handled by the males, the sorting and packing of fruit from the lugs was done by the women, and the degree of responsibility matched to our ages. My older brother had a lot to worry about, adding up the box count at the end of the day, loading the truck with a hand cart. I was the youngest and my job was simply to make sure the packers had enough empty boxes at their stations.

With the older cousins around we heard the latest radio hits and memorized the top forty played every Wednesday evening on the radio. Personalities also unveiled themselves, the lazy family members were the last ones out in the morning and took the longest lunch breaks (we ate in a half hour), or the ones who liked to talk and had stories they'd tell us kids, half of them untrue but we were a captive and naive audience, or the complainers whose whining didn't help you get through a ten hour day in summer's heat. We were like a family tribe working together, a gamut of personalities and attitudes and work ethics, all with the simple goal of packing the best fruit each harvest.

The fruit industry has changed a lot since then, much more technology has been introduced and fruit quality standardized. For example, today there's electronic sorters and sizers, miles of conveyer belts and electronic scales and cardboard boxes. No more of our eyeball sizing methods or simple metal rollers and wooden boxes that when given a proper push, would roll the entire length of the shed because we had tilted the rollers to match a cousin's arm muscles. A long time ago they invented machines to clean and "defuzz" peaches yet I can still fondly recall my grandmother's job: with a feather duster she cleaned up each box of peaches, "defuzzing" them with her rough old callous hands that clutched a duster, personally scrutinizing each box like a government inspector. She also kept an eye and ear out for "rattle packs," boxes of fruit that held an assorted mixture of sizes, a poor packing job with fruit loose and rolling around inside, rattling when moved and sent down the roller.

I can't call them the "good old days" because they weren't. The work was long and hot and tough, it made us all want to leave the farm, to get out of the fields and to inside jobs with air conditioned offices and desks and cushioned chairs. And despite the labor savings with family, our farm income was sad, we were shielded from the economics of our operations but I could picture Dad coming in from the fields late in the evening, beat and exhausted and silent. There were years where we lost money, a disaster very few can understand because we think of losing money like gambling but it's more like this: you work an entire year and your boss comes up to you and informs you that you owe him money for all your labor.

Yet there's a quality about the whole experience that clings to all of us, we were family then, with a special sense of family attached to our memories. There's something different when you have to work side by side with family, we are exposed to the best and worst in all of us.

Raisins are a peculiar product, harvest time seems to lend itself to family, perhaps it's because raisins are still made about the same way they have been made for decades, for generations. There's not a whole lot of difference between 1900 and 1980, you still pick the grapes in late August or early September, lay them out on trays that lie directly on the ground, and wait and wait and pray for no rain for around 20 days or until the sun has dried the grapes into dark, sweet raisins. Basically, it is the same archaic way my grandparents worked with raisins and my parents and probably will be with my children: one of those few practices no one has found a better way to do.

Raisin harvests have always involved family in one way or another. Local rural schools used to delay the start of September classes to allow families, both farmers' and farm workers' families, to help pick grapes. Our family used to pick together, dad and mom armed with their knives slashing away at the hanging bunches, us kids crawling around on our knees, laying out the trays (there has been one major change with raisins, the trays used to be all wood, about two by three feet long, but now most everyone uses paper trays), then the folks would dump their grapes out of their pans onto the trays and we kids would spread it out. Today I watch the Mexican families doing this annual ritual, the parents picking away and the kids, just like we were, crawling around, spreading the grapes, complaining about the dirt and dust and heat and spending the afternoon napping under a vine.

But raisins don't instantly become raisins after picking. You wait, green grapes turn pale, wither and a light purple hue remains as each berry dehydrates. You wait, the top side dries quickly so you must turn each tray, you and a partner, a husband and wife, a brother and sister, one on each end of the tray, bending over, empty tray on top. With good timing and a quick flip, the entire tray is turned over, the top now on the bottom, the underside green grapes exposed to the sun and heat, soon to dry. The good teams work fast and smooth, you can hear their teamwork, a steady rhythm unbroken and true.   Bad teams are sloppy, raisins flying everywhere, trays crumpled and twisted, and piles formed instead of even layers.

A few sunny days later the raisins arrive, turned dark and meaty, the sun a cheap dehydrator. Then the rolling begins, trays rolled like a cigarette or with a few flips a "biscuit" roll is made, the raisins safely wrapped inside.

Then teams begin the "boxing." Children drive tractors that pull wagons between the rows, the parents pick the raisin "biscuits" and dump them into boxes or bins, containers for transportation from farm to processing plants like Sun Maid raisins or Del Rey Pack. Trailing the wagon is a second child, collecting the used paper trays and burning them in small piles.

Raisins and family, perhaps the relationship is best seen in critical moments, like an advancing storm bringing disastrous rains or scorching heat that bakes and overdries raisins into "beans." In these times families wage miniature battles, rolling up trays before they got wet or cooked, trying to protect a year's labor in a few hours, everyone crawling around and working with tray after tray, 1000 trays to an acre, 40,000 trays to an average farm. You can call it a type of bonding, family working side by side, feeling a panic and pain as clouds gather overhead, knowing that a harvest can be salvaged. They also know that you may be rolling too early and will have to unroll all 40,000 trays no matter if it rains or not.

Raisins and family, a time of sharing.

Most of the *Sansei* have left the farm, many say the family farm is dying, to be replaced by corporations. They may be right but you have to think that somehow, in some way, the family will survive on the land, perhaps in a different way than before, but with some type of sensibility that accompanies family and farm lands.

Mr. L. Murashima, a *Sansei:* "When we were kids, the kids thought we weren't being paid enough. And then the parents would come back with that line, 'We're paying for everything you eat.'

Raisin harvests, 1930's. Tractors began to replace horses in the fields, but some things never changed. Raisins were "boxed" into wooden crates, stored undercover until delivery to the processing plant like Sun Maid Raisins. Old "picks" were small crates that could be hand carried and would hold about 40 pounds of raisins. They were replaced with the advent of electric hoists and "sweat boxes" which held about 250 pounds. Today forklifts are used to load "bins" which hold about a half ton each.

Yet the way raisins are made, simply by using the sun, has defied time and progress. The process remains the same as generations before, possibly the biggest change has been the size of the boxes. (Courtesy James Yamamoto)

"At first for me there was pressure the first year to come back summers from college. But after that they realized I couldn't do that for the rest of my life. I didn't think there was a whole lot of pressure.

"My older cousins, I don't know, they just took off. They don't even come back for fruit. They just kinda living their own life.

"With me personally, I guess, deep down inside I still had that devotion to the point even if other kids did things, like summer camp, I didn't even ask if I could go. Because I felt that obligation that I was needed to help.

"There's a feeling of obligation to the farm and community here. It's still there and will probably exist for a while and again I have an obligation to repay them in some way, whatever way that I'm able to do it. I'd still like to put together an information bank for small farmers, just because I see them not having the knowledge and resources to do things on their own because in a lot of senses they're too busy with the farm itself to expand out into other things."

Mr. S. Mitsui, a *Sansei:* "It was important to have family on the farm, especially in our situation where family was the main work force. We were the technical help, we were the peons, we were everything so it was important for family to be as a unit.

"Now it isn't as much as important but I think in order for the family working to go on, I think you have to pull together at some point either through reunions, Christmas time, Thanksgiving, or working together on the farm. I think I tend to prefer working together on the farm because it's the only time I have a chance to really talk to my father and mother because at these social gatherings we have nothing but pleasantries, we don't talk about the old times, we don't talk about the things that they've experienced. It's much easier to ask those types of questions in the tedium after eight hours of work than it is sitting around a table.

"I come home raisin harvest time, I do it as much for myself as I do it for them. 'Cuz I think it's the only way that I can get close enough to my own father, in particular, because he's not one who talks a lot."

The old, retired *Issei* was alone, he had outlived his wife and remained alone in their home. He refused to live with his children and their individual families, not wanting to burden anyone. But most every night, especially during raisin harvest when the grapes lay outside, exposed to the elements, he would phone each of his four sons to ask "how's it going?" He still wanted to be involved with the farming operations, even if physically he was too old to help. But he would lend his moral support and thoughts, ending each conversation each night with, "don't work too hard son."

One of the sons explained that his dad really didn't mean that about "working too hard," because if he could, the father would work hard, just as he had always done and still did, even if it were only via phone calls and added concern and worry. Yet the sons didn't mind the phone calls, they felt it was "important when you're old to keep your mind still thinking."

Still thinking about the land and family, the family operation.

CHAPTER 19

NATURAL DISASTERS AND SEPTEMBER RAINS

Natural Disasters

Spring frosts and September rains. Natural disasters you learn to live with if you're farming.

Japanese American raisin farmers will remember the spring of '21, the rains of '36 and '46, the killer frost of '72 and the thundershowers on innocent raisins in '76, '78, and '82. A veteran of these wars can glance at a chart of raisin prices and quickly recall the pain and struggle of each of those years where nature chose to teach farmers a lesson in humility. That's what it's like to stand outside, watching sheets of rain pour from the sky and witnessing an entire year of work begin to ooze with rot and mold. "Did I do something wrong and you're punishing me?" their voices cry out as they peer up into the skies. Farmers will never, never forget how fragile their livelihood is, how insignificant they are in comparison to what nature can unleash in a mere 15 minutes.

Disasters have a way of bringing out a lot of human qualities in all of us: strength, frustration, disillusionment, anger, depression, human emotions are exposed, a drama unravels. Nature teaches us a good lesson about the real powers in the world, shattering that delicate bubble within which we live; we deceive ourselves by believing we can control the ripening of grapes, and the coloring of peaches. There's a Buddhist saying that farmers have a clear and succinct understanding of human relationships: farmers all know too well of their fragile existence here on this world.

Yet with all disasters there's some who benefit, a lucky few who reap a reward from another's catastrophe. They will have escaped a frost or rain and delivered a "load of gold" during harvest, with prices having rocketed upwards with a short supply. They deliver their produce with a little humility mixed with a lot of smiling and occasional laugh that slips out.

Even with a disaster, most farmers remain hopeful and few concede to defeat. A part of their psyche still believes they can salvage this year's crop or look forward to next year with even more determination. A streak of blind faith guides them onwards, "maybe there's something we can do" you'll hear as farmers scratch their heads and try to figure out a way of saving some of their harvest and recover a type of self respect. Staunch business folk will never understand this irrational behavior as the losses mount and farm debts swell. They can't understand from where that optimism emerges, the source of a farmer's attitude that "next year will be different" when all of the numbers and records and dollar signs compute "something else." But it's that "something else" that makes a farmer continue and rely on his greatest ally: hope.

The frost scare comes in late March and early April, just when delicate shoots begin pushing out of vine canes, bright green and clean, and within each shoot hides the flower clusters that will swell to juicy grapes within six months. The countryside has a thin blanket of green that grows daily, pushing outwards and reaching toward the warm sunlight. But with an early morning frost, a blast from a northern front that brings temperatures in the high 20's, fragile buds will literally burn off. After a few days, fields look as if a blow torch visited the vineyards, the brown-black remains of dead tissue dangle on the vines, the shoot will grow back but absent will be the all important flower clusters and a year's crop.

"In old times," a *Nisei* farmer explained, "we used to use old tires for frost." He continued to describe the method, crude yet effective. He said that around the perimeter of a field, the farmer would toss old tires, maybe a dozen or so a few rows apart, about 30 feet. Then he'd spend the night watching the thermometer and feeling the air. With dry, still air the temperature plummets, it can drop ten degrees in a few hours. If the wind stops anytime past midnight and the dry air begins to settle, a wave of frost may visit the fields.

"That's where the tires come in," he explained, "they'll burn for hours, throwing off that stinky smoke for hours." So farmers used to take some gas and at two o'clock in the morning they'd ignite the tires. Not for their heat but for their clouds of smoke. The billows would hover over the vineyards, hugging the earth and vines and provide a protective layer, a thin blanket of warmth just enough to prevent frost from settling on the ground.

Frost is like an invisible glacier, a mass of cold collecting in low spots and spreading along the lowest contours of the land, like a glacier etching a path between mountain tops. So smoke may generate a minute amount of warmth and block the advancing frost, it may split and go around the protected field or bounce right over it.

"Old tires worked pretty damn good," he said. "Stunk up the place but they worked." Of course they don't use old tires anymore. Electric pumps now deliver warm pump water from deep within the earth to the vineyards and with air pollution regulations, those old, stinking tires can't be used anymore, a victory for the frost.

SEPTEMBER RAINS

I heard the soft rhythms of a September morning rain and looked out the window: "damn". Eighty acres of grapes lay unprotected on the ground. They needed another week of sun to dry into raisins. I turned, hesitated, and said: "Dad, you know it's..."

"I already know," he said.

Puddles began to appear in the rows. Fed by clouds, they slowly advanced towards the grape trays. Raisins can withstand a light rain with minimal damage. But with long, constant showers, a year's work begins to rot: the stench would soon fill the countryside.

"How bad do you think they are?" I asked.

"We'll see when it stops raining," Dad answered.

It had rained more than an inch. The paper trays seemed to melt, saturated with water. The lower third of each tray became submerged. Loose grapes floated in the pools they had formed.

I grew restless, hating the noise of rain. "What we going to do?" I asked Dad.

"What can we do?" he answered.

Dad occasionally glanced outside, pretending to look for the newspaper or mail. He spoke little, saying nothing about the harvest laying outside. He spent the day reading old issues of Popular Mechanics and some farm magazines. The newspaper had been accidentally thrown into a puddle. "Son of a bitch," he said, returning with the drenched sheets, "at least I want my paper dry."

Dad was once a migrant farm worker. "After the war and the damn relocation camps, we had to live out of a garage, shared it with another family too. Had to hustle for any work," he told me. "Then I got this

"Eighty acres of grapes lay unprotected on the ground. They could have become raisins but now... a year's work would soon begin to rot. Raisins can withstand a light rain but with long, constant showers... the stench would soon fill the countryside."

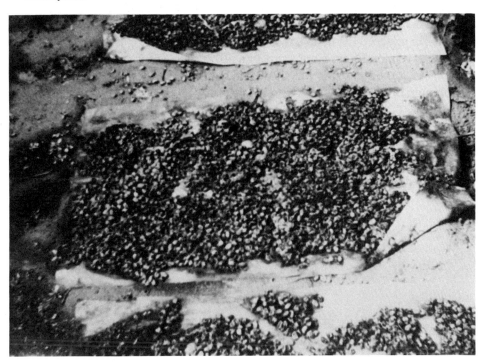

bright idea to gamble and get my own place. Why should I break myself working for somebody else?" That was thirty years ago. Now, Dad was over 50 but still retained his farmer's tan: a dark face and neck, with arms tanned until just above the elbows and rolled shirt sleeves. In the last few years, Dad had begun to slow down. On winter mornings he stayed inside an extra hour or two before going out to prune. He also began to teach me more of the important work like spraying and irrigating. We talked more these days, about farming and politics or football and baseball.

The rains continued. Dad wrestled with the soaked newspaper, peeling apart each page and spreading them over chairs to dry.

Two years before, in 1976, it had rained like this. Over two inches in 24 hours. We had tried to salvage the harvest, working with each bunch, picking away the mold on each grape. For a few days, the sun appeared and the ground began to dry. We made a crude dehydrator to speed the process. Then, another storm and another inch. Dad "couldn't stand the sight" of the rot. He hooked up the tractor and in a single day disked under the entire '76 crop.

The rain ended the next day. We walked outside, dodging the deeper puddles. I wanted to hope, to try and save something. Dad bent over a tray, picked up a bunch and shook off the water. The skins of the half grapes-half raisins had already decayed into a yellowish-brown. As he ran his hand over the bunch, the skins broke and the meat of the grapes oozed onto his fingers.

He replaced the bunch, rose and said: "I'm not going to spend the next couple of months crawling around on my knees. Not for this crap".

He turned towards the shed, grabbed his shovel and left for a walk through his fields.

CHAPTER 20

SPIRITS IN HARVEST: FRUIT LABELS
AND FARM WOMEN

Fruit Labels and Japanese American Family Farms

"Aki-*san*, Arty-K, GHI, Carol's and Henry's Choice." These are some of the fruit labels you may have seen in the produce section of your local grocery store. But there's more than meets the eyes with these labels, a history of a family farm is told through these labels, a legacy lives within each label.

Fruit labels carry meaning beyond the commercial and agribusiness dimension, they represent an act of expression, born from the farmer's creativity and a dream of establishing a family farm. Labels symbolize a living tradition, reaching back to the history of Japanese in California agriculture and at the same time tells of the emergence of a new Japanese American family farm community.

The story begins with the *Issei* who immigrated in the late 1800's and early 1900's, attracted by stories of quick wealth and prosperity. Instead they became farm workers, laboring in the fields for cheap wages, clinging to dreams of success and wealth. Many were from agricultural backgrounds, second and third sons who, by tradition, were not destined to inherit the family rice farm in Japan.

But hopes of land ownership were shattered by the economic hardships of the Great Depression, by Alien Land Laws which barred Asian immigrants from property ownership, and by the tragedy of World War II evacuation and relocation. By 1942, few families had obtained land and for many, their fifty years of work and struggle would be erased within a few months by the war hysteria and racism.

As Japanese Americans trickled back from the relocation camps many returned to their home communities, re-populating Fresno and the surrounding towns. Some sought to regain property, others returned simply because they had no other place to go. Agriculture was "the only damn thing we knew of and where the work that no one else wanted was," said a *Nisei*. Again they became farm workers, toiling with the crops, enduring the seasons.

Slowly, some obtained land and began to farm for themselves, they followed the pattern of first renting land while still working for wages, then renting only, and eventually purchasing farms of their own.

This was often carried out as a family affair. One *Nisei* farmer recalled: "Everyone had to work, my folks, my wife, me. Everyone had to do their share for ends to meet."

The extended family played a pivotal role, partnerships between brothers surfaced, either from bonds of land ownership obtained before the war or a combining of productive efforts when two or three brothers joined together. Families often worked together under the *Issei* parents who needed and expected the support of their children and family.

Gradually dreams were realized: family farms were established and deeds were filed with the county recorders' offices. Even these deeds mirrored the variety of family arrangements, some recorded under the *Issei* parents' names, others in partnerships between brothers or sometimes brothers-in- law, some farms were "married into" as a son-less family brought a male into the family operation.

The bond of family had traveled with Japanese Americans and continued as a vital part of their experience. A sense of family was reaffirmed and the values of hard work and discipline were rewarded. The family farm translated into economic success and prosperity.

Within this setting, families created their own fruit labels for their produce.

In the world of agribusiness, a fruit label provided an identity. Reputations were developed based on a consistent quality of fruit and at the wholesale marketplace where buyers judged fruit lots through inspection and reports from retailers. Prices were set by a demand for one label over another. A farmer's label became a marriage of a name with a level of quality, this combination commanding a top price and strong demand with superior quality or the opposite, a bad reputation, poor track record and lower prices with poor quality. The selection of a label became an important choice: the name would travel with the produce, a symbol of its quality.

From the array of potential names, Japanese Americans often chose their family name for their fruit labels. Many labels were simply printed with the family name, such as "Mizuno" or "Kimura." Other labels were shortened forms of the family name: "Kash" was the shortened label name for Kashiki. Initials of family members were also utilized, for example "Arty K" stood for R.T. Kimoto.

In these fruit labels, the family was recognized and acknowledged as central to the operation. Behind each label stood a family farm, the label a signature of a particular farmer and his family. Meanings then were carried beyond the economic realm. The emotions of family honor and pride played a vital role: the label stood as a symbol of the family name and maintenance of quality reputations.

For example, Harry Morishita, a *Nisei*, explained: "My label? It's from the initials of us three brothers. G is for George, H for Harry and I for Irving. GHI. We three had gotten back together after the war and began farming again. We had pretty good quality so we decided to use our own brand name. We chose our names because this is a family place. We tried to have our name mean quality fruit."

Henry Mayeda, another *Nisei* farmer, described his label: "I wanted the whole family in the label, so I chose 'Carol's and Henry's Choice.' Carol is my daughter and Henry my son. At the bottom of the label reads 'H and K Mayeda', for me and my wife. That way, all four of us are on there. The family, we've worked hard over the years and a label, well it was just something we had to do."

Even in cases where no label was ever created, stories about dreams and labels existed. "We always wanted our own label," said a *Nisei* farmer. "Had talked about it and it would have been the family name. We talked about it for a long time, something we'd work for, sort of like a dream." As if tradition, the family name was selected from the huge variety of other potential names.

Today Japanese American farm families are being recast as the older *Nisei* generation bows to the young *Sansei*. At the same time, agribusiness, the economics of farming, now occupies a major position in the minds of farmers. As a result of this, a new type of family farm emerges, one that dispels the myth of the dying family farm: a restructured family operation with modified agrarian dreams in juxtaposition with agribusiness.

Amidst this, new fruit labels are created, acting as a vehicle that symbolically transfers the family dream from one generation to another.

Family farms, family labels.

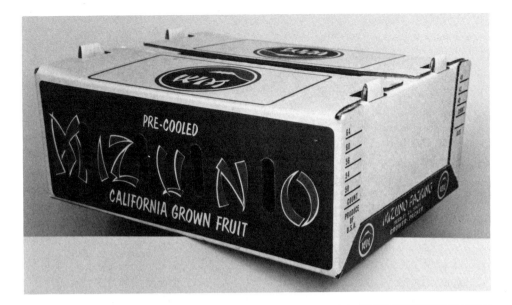

Fruit labels and the magic in a name.

Labels symbolize the maintenance of the Japanese American family farm, a package of traditions and culture inherited by the next generation.

For example, Pat and Donna Chiamori, both *Sansei*, explained their label: "When we began packing our own fruit a few years ago, we naturally needed our own label. We ended up with 'Aki- *san*.' At first we wanted to use our daughter's names in the label but couldn't think of anything. Then we thought of Pat's parents who had started the farm before the war. Pat's father's name was Akira. We chose his name for the 'Aki' part of the label. A lot of people think the *san* in the label is because of the Japanese, you know, how it goes with people's names like Tanaka-*san*. Well, it's not. What we did was to have our three daughters stand for the *san*. *San*, that's three in Japanese, *ichi, ni, san* [one, two, three]. So the *san* is for our children while 'Aki' is for their grandfather. You'd say this is a family farm with a real family label."

In recent years many Japanese American family farms have completed the transition from *Nisei* to *Sansei* generations. Labels symbolize this development, the spirit of a family farm captured and a legacy inherited: the family remains bound to the land.

The new fruit labels point to an important adjustment being made. A synthesis of the enterprising, agribusiness outlook and the agrarian dream of a family farm has been achieved.

Fruit labels act as a metaphor of development, a new spirit in the annual summer harvest and a new harvest of family and community traditions.

JAPANESE AMERICAN FARM WOMEN

> "... that's a powerful woman there..."
>
> A *Kibei* farmer describing his wife.

They were farm women: wives and mothers, workers and farmers. A *Kibei* farmer once said, "I never thought of women as being different. We all worked side by side all day, did everything together. No, not that different."

She was an 80 year old *Issei* farm woman with ancient, frail legs that shuffled through garden weeds. Her four foot, eight inch frame was slouched forwards as if she walked against the wind, plodding along the earthen trail. Despite her age she still lugged buckets of fruit and from her garden and into the kitchen, a strength transfused from the years of farm work.

When she was younger she used to tease the kids by showing her bulging biceps and tell them, "There's an egg underneath the skin."

The children would laugh and scream and whisper to each other, "You touch it, you touch it." Eventually one would bravely reach out and tap her muscle and giggle and nod to the others that there was an egg in there, followed by a chorus of more laughs and screams.

She came to California as a farm wife and farm worker in 1918. The long years of work were manifested in her hands, roughened with calluses, cracks that had broken into sores in her hardened, dry fingertips, and fingernails that had yellowed, flattened and split. Yet these were the same hands that became filled with a warmth as she massaged her grandchildren's backs. The kids called it "to *momo*" and one of the few Japanese phrases they knew was, "*Baachan* [Grandma], *momo, momo. Baachan, momo* us."

She never learned English and that massage was often the extent of their communication. With her hand, old crusty hands, she'd generate a friction, a gentle warm touch on their skin.

She was a farm woman, no less a pioneer than her husband, just as able a farmer beside the other *Issei* and *Nisei* men. She, along with thousands of other *Issei* and *Nisei* women, shared in the adventure and pain and sweat of working the land with their hands and backs, and at the same time raising families and grandchildren and talking with those old crusty hands.

The *Kibei* husband and the *Nisei* wife sat across the table. Both had retired and now lived in town, a quiet suburban development with a backyard full of *bonsai* and plants, part of the farm they didn't leave behind. They reflected on the "olden days," the years of farm work, the aches and pains now behind them.

"I didn't think about the farm work too much," said the *Nisei* woman. "I had an uncle and aunt in Oakland, she did some house cleaning and thought it would be good for me too, better than out in the fields. But even after we were married, I stayed out and worked on the farm."

"Yes, it was hard work. Oh, how about raisin time... I helped carry those sweat boxes, full of raisins. We had to load them onto the truck and we didn't have equipment in those days. Those wood boxes must have weighed over 150 pounds... I'd carry one side, he [the husband] carried the other. It was hard work but working together for our own place, you didn't think about it. But those sweat boxes, oh now... I can't believe I did it."

After a few seconds her *Kibei* husband added with a smile, "She worked... that's a powerful woman there."

Everyone grins and smiles.

Mrs. D. Murashima, a *Nisei:* "My mom dreamed, she even had her eye on this one ranch. She'd say, 'Maybe one day we'd own this place.'

"I think mom was strong, that's what I think. You know everything went through my mother. I don't know if you do that too, tell your mom something to ask dad. OK, I think that's from the Japanese thing... I kind'a think so 'cuz we did that, everything we did went through mother. We didn't ask dad directly. Dad was never much of a talker, everything was mom."

Life was difficult. Not everyone was completely content and country life, especially the social life, it's not exactly the same as life in the city.

Mr. R. Matsubara, a *Kibei:* "Well, some didn't stay you know. Some women surprised...their picture bride husband... the men used somebody else's picture, young guy... those kind of pictures. And he working for a *hakujin* [Caucasian] man or something and take a picture of big house in the back, people think big shot or something. Wife come along and just nothing you know, live in a small shack.

"Most women complained. Ha... they arrive and think he good looking and he rich but not you know... She think he a young man and he just an old man ... use someone else's picture... An, a mess."

Mrs. L. Nakamoto, a *Nisei:* "First we women had baby showers for each other. Just the women, all of us farm wives, getting together. We ladies didn't go out much in those days 'cuz we're out in the country and there's children. But if you had a baby shower the women got to go out to dinner. So we all had our babies and the ladies kind of enjoyed it, the dinner. Someone once asked how come the men didn't go with us and we said, 'Well, if there's a child at home, both parents can't go. Besides, this was our baby shower.'

"So then we ran out of baby showers, we all had all of our babies, and someone said, 'Let's celebrate the 25th anniversary.' We felt 'what a good idea,' we could still get out, not stay on the farm all the time.

"The funniest thing was when we first thought of it several in the community had already passed their 25th so we combined them and went out to that first dinner, just the ladies. That's how it started up, just the ladies getting to go out to dinner.

"Then a few years later and after a few more anniversaries, we went to one restaurant and the waitress saw all of us having a good time and wanted to know and asked, 'What are you ladies celebrating?'

"We said, '25th anniversary.'

"Then the waitress said... 'Where's the husbands?'

"We all got to thinking that maybe we should invite the men. By then the kids were older and able to leave them home alone and we, the men too, we all began going to dinner, all of us."

New voices are scattered through the countryside, a new generation of farm women. Few of them work out in the fields like their predecessors, but neither do the men work like the *Issei*.

Some *Sansei* women have remained in the countryside, they married farmers or stayed or came back home to take care of aging parents and help with the farm operation. They have new jobs and roles to fill, bookkeepers and financial planners in addition to being mothers and keepers of the home. "I do all the outside work, he handles all the inside," a *Sansei* male said. "We each do what we do best."

And some *Nihon* (Japan) wives had settled the land, just like the *Issei*, young men have returned to Japan and marry. "Find a country girl back in Japan," they were instructed. "One that will be happy out in the *inaka* (countryside)."

The two biggest changes though are the new faces and new types of work farm women do. New faces because there's more interracial farm families, and for the most part the Japanese American community readily accepts such a change. The older generation enjoys these new faces, a reality necessary for the community to remain alive, and the potential birth of a new generation, often out weighing the old racial/cultural biases.

The new work is the off farm income, often in the medical or educational arenas, a necessity and requirement for many families. Farming has changed, it's difficult to survive on a small 20 acre place, so the wife goes and works and the husband stays home and farms. There's a lot of years where she makes more than the husband, but not much is said about it; some things don't change.

These new voices blend two worlds, the rural and the Japanese. There's not a longing for the old days, the times of struggle and traditional male and female roles. Sometimes it seems the ones who have the worst trouble with these changes surrounding the farm family and rural community are those that have left. They're the ones who return for a visit and comment how much has changed, almost as a lament for the past. But those that are here, they have chosen this life, perhaps no differently than the *Issei* women who left Japan and dreamed of a future in the *inaka* of America.

Mrs. T. Tanaka, an *Issei*, told of a way of accepting, even welcoming the changes: "The people now have it easy compared to us. We all worried about saving money to pay taxes each year. The younger generation have a much better standard of living than we ever did. I used to use the scrub board to do my heavy laundry for my family. All I have to do now is put it in and push the button!

"Now each time I take clean clothes from the dryer after having washed in the automatic washer, I say, 'Thank you.' I feel grateful when I compare laundering to the olden days."

CHAPTER 21

NEW FARMS AND EMPTY HARVESTS

New Farms

The 1980's demark a major shift in the life and rhythms of rural America and especially for Japanese Americans. Like the waves of history before them, each era in American agriculture must cope with new circumstances and for Japanese Americans, an entire generation must face a new and partially unexpected situation: things have changed and farming is not an alternative for this next, youthful generation.

Mrs. V. Iida, a *Nisei:* "I thought he [the *Sansei* son] would farm. When he was young we taught him to prune, to drive tractor. But even then he said, 'I'm not going to farm.'

"We told him he's got to learn anyway, even with some other work or profession, you have to know farm work. Even to teach someone else how to prune, some worker on how to do the work.

"So as soon as they were old enough we had them work. The joke was that as soon as their legs were long enough to reach the tractor clutch pedal, they began work. It was cute to see the older kids measure the younger ones... by sitting them on the tractor to see how much longer they had to wait before someone else had to work.

"But he's not going to farm. And no, I'm not too disappointed. I figure he has his own life, and it's not my responsibility.

"I guess we'll sell this place. It's been good to us though."

Mr. J. Hata, a *Nisei:* "I guess so, I might retire, find a sharecropper. Maybe one of my daughters will find a sucker to take over. The future is up to the young folks, their kind. Many of us old folks might just give up, hard to say..."

Mr. G. Fujita, a *Nisei:* "The future? Hard to say. Because most of the kids not going back into farming you know. There's something else, very few families have a boy or somebody to take over. So I really don't know how it'll come out.

"My son says he wants to look after the place. He's a doctor in town. We have the land in a trust, it'll go down to him. So I want to take out all the trees and put in vines so he could lease it out and somebody rent it. Nobody wants all trees, year like this aren't going to make nothing.

"He always said he'd like to look after the farm. Make me happy? I guess. I don't care one way or another. After I go I don't care what they do with it... Well, because, what can I do after I die?

"I stay here though until they carry me off to the rest home."

Mrs. D. Murashima, a *Nisei*: "That's a big question, look at those families, no children to take over. You don't know what is going to happen. If no one's going to do it, you're going to have to sell it. But we're lucky when our kids will do it. We are, because it's nice to carry on. You can't make anybody carry on. Parents couldn't make their children to come back, they would fight it more than ever. You can't make anybody farm.

"We're lucky our son is coming back. He says, 'Now I'm not going to sit behind a desk.'

"I says, 'Well, it's not cut out for everybody, you do what you like best.'

"He said, 'Boy, I'd rather be out there on the tractor, I'm happy when I'm out there."

Mr. G. Takahashi, a *Sansei*: "In the beginning it was a total family operation and then as family members left, they had no choice but to start hiring outside people until now, it's almost all outside people doing most of the hard labor. Sometimes they hired family friends but it got to be mostly Mexicans or Filipino workers.

"Little sad in that because all the kids are basically leaving the farm that it's started to dwindle and it's going to be sure tough times in the future depending on how many people are really left in the community. Age wise, it's gotten older rather than younger because all the kids have left and leaving the parents. I'm not sure if the kids will be coming back, the future isn't on the farms. The future is more in the cities and situations where they could go into the professional ranks.

"Basically the farm's got no choice but to change. There's too much competition from big farmers and before, when the kids were around to help out on the farm all the time, it made costs easier. But now with the kids leaving they have to compete and pay real wages, it's almost impossible for a real small farm to survive.

"The younger kids are using new techniques and expanding the farm and hopefully becoming even more efficient but the big thing is that it has to be a business now rather than a family kind of thing.

"My brother is farming and he's found something that he enjoys. Sometimes I almost feel it was dumped on him because none of the other kids wanted to farm at all. He really didn't know what he wanted to do and I think there was a lot of pressure on him as far as trying to compete with the older ones which he couldn't do and he just went off on his own direction that he felt comfortable with. He'll probably make a real good farmer, ha."

Mr. S. Okamura, a *Sansei:* "I think the farm will pretty much stay the way it is, it might change in size so long as my older brother is healthy and willing to work. I think it's going through many changes now, from my father's hands to my brother's, a pretty drastic change.

"Why? Because my brother has a masters in plant science. His view on farming is really different than my father's who's very traditional, plays it by the seat of his pants while my brother got all his text books, whatever he needs as references to try and improve things. My brother also is a plant biologist so he looks at things differently than my father.

"It has been different because we still are a family farm, my brother needs the expertise of my parents because they're the best labor force that he could possibly have access to. Nobody from his point of view could prune better than my father.

"The future? It depends on prices on the farm, the crop prices. I think people who buy new land and are able to maintain their ranch payments without having to rely on outside sources have a chance... if not then you'll probably see more corporations being formed and this land being bought'n up. But if that doesn't happen and crop prices get down lower again, the land prices will come back down and then you might see problems. But maybe then people from the city will be moving out to the country a little bit more. You might have more family farms tied together with outside income. That would be sort of nice.

"In order for a person to grow and maybe appreciate what he's had in the past he has to have other things to compare with and other experiences. So it's good to have gone away from it, to look back as an outsider and then come back to be immersed into it, sort of nice too.

"It would be nice to come back. In fact now I think more and more of it than 5 or 6 years ago. I enjoy the farm. I enjoy coming out. I think working all day and sweating and all that is really nice. Yet... it would be hard... especially for my family. All of us farmer's kids would like to come back to the farm, we have this idea we could improve it just a little like for the next generation, a little better than the one before."

The number of Japanese American family farms is shrinking. As *Sansei* were educated, their professional interests pulled them further away from the land. In some cases land was sold or with others it was leased to others. However, a scattering of Japanese American family farms remains, different but still on the land.

Today an "American Gothic" of a Japanese American farm couple may look like this:

-a tractor and the latest equipment sits in the background;

-a computer keyboard replaces the pitchfork;

-and a non-Japanese wife stands next to the husband.

The landscape changes along with the economics and politics of agribusiness. Farming has become a new business, no longer are the old ways valid, the arena of competition has shifted from the field and barn to the office and marketplace. New technology and an ever changing market structure has replaced a yeoman's concern over weather and rainfall. Today, the farmer may raise plentiful produce but lose a harvest in the market.

Yet therein lies the new challenge. Just as the *Issei* and *Nisei* faced a new world, the young *Sansei* farmers stand before a different world but no one expects it to be the same. As one *Sansei* explained: "Only the city folk think it's supposed to be the same, only the city folk."

Empty Harvests: Nothing More to Dream

I picture the haunting Depression photograph by Dorothea Lange - the Dust Bowl farmer slouched behind the wheel of his old car, leaving his home in a desperate search for work. His land is gone and his farm is lost, the devastation revealed in his face: dark shadows frame his features, wrinkles cut deep into his weathered flesh. Behind his staring eyes I see the dreams of full harvests shattered; only bleak hope of the promised land in the West remain alive, flickering within.

Welcome to California and farming, 1980's.

I picture the haunting Depression photograph of the desperate farmer, behind his staring eyes lie shattered hopes, nothing more to dream...

    We are deep into the summer harvest, the annual return of searing heat, labor and sweat. For small, family farmers like myself, a depression endures, a pain persists. The 1985 market for fruits and vegetables has collapsed. Nectarines are at an all time low, peaches at a wrenching break even point.

    A general depression in agriculture holds fast, and along with thousands of other farmers in the Central Valley of California, I'm filled with deep, searching questions. But we aren't just scratching our heads, wondering what went wrong and hoping that next year will be better; like the Dust Bowl farmer, we stare out at our fields, exhausted and drained, and a chill sweeps across our backs: we are empty.

    "What more can you do?" we ask ourselves. We have cut back, practiced efficiency, become business oriented. In my peach orchard at thinning time I dropped a lot of the crop onto the ground in order to produce a larger, quality harvest. I've kept informed of the national outlook, and I anticipated a fair return this harvest - but only at the expense of other farmers and their winter freeze on the East Coast. Perhaps the freeze was an act of mercy; at least those farmers knew the fate of their harvest quickly and early.

I keep wondering what I did wrong. The answer is: nothing. I talk with other farmers and they agree, there seems to be no good reason for this year's market to slip and collapse so badly. We shake our heads and stare at the the juicy red fruit hanging on our trees-one of the better crops that we've raised in years, and the results are the same. I now know how that Dust Bowl farmer must have felt with hard times a familiar companion, a haunting shadow.

An alien feeling lies deep within me, a gnawing thought that grows and spreads. Like many small, family farmers, we have become obsolete. Certainly, in the future, researchers will study this crop year and determine what political and economic forces acted on us, and journalists will report in shorthand terms to explain our plight, overextended, highly leveraged, foreign competition. But in a word, we're obsolete.

Many believe that those of us who are failing are dumb, inefficient farmers, simple-minded folk who would have failed in any venture. But if you look around, especially at the young farmers in trouble, you may be shocked to find the high percentage with college degrees and training. I graduated from the University of California, Berkeley with honors, have a master's degree from the University of California, Davis and was a Regent's Fellow. If anything, though, I was dumb in one way: I still believed.

I believed in an obsolete work ethic-the simple idea that with hard work you will be rewarded. Yet I thought that I had learned a lesson from the last few years. You have to mix a good helping of cold, rational business thinking with that hard work. I, like many farmers, did that this past season, and the results remain the same: collapsed fruit prices.

The work ethic no longer functions as it once did. The powerful myth that so many of us believed in, the legacy of a family farm that I inherited, the dreams that drove Dust Bowl farmers West, all have collapsed, and our spiritual fiber has been left in shreds.

A vacuum now drains us, and an empty harvest fills the summer. No matter how deeply rooted our dreams may lie, not all of us can farm. But I won't cry at the funeral; rather, I fear what might replace my aging dreams. Will I slip into a Yuppie mentality based on status and material accumulation?

A fundamental change is unfolding in the Central Valley of California. Some farms will survive, but a different sort of agribusiness industry will emerge. I am just a casualty of this current battle, but, unlike the Dust Bowl farmer I don't even have the hope of promised lands to dream of. That's the underlying meaning of obsolescence; nothing more to dream.

In the summer of 1985 a belief in work and spiritual justice has been rendered useless. And, as we go under, it is more than farmers that will be bankrupt.

Futsu no hito/ordinary people.
Two kanji characters combine
to translate into the word
ordinary.
"Fu" which means "the
universal" and "tsu" which
means passing through.
Individuals with the universe
passing through, that's the
meaning of ordinary people.

FU

TSU

NO

HITO

FUTSU NO HITO/ORDINARY PEOPLE

CHAPTER 22

ORDINARY PEOPLE: CONCLUSION

This book has been about *futsu no hito*, ordinary people. We have journeyed into the minds and souls of country folk, farm families and their community. I will have succeeded if you have gained a feel of this place, an understanding of a history, culture and land, a sensibility of the people and their lives.

Yet their story goes beyond the community bounds of Del Rey for it touches the life blood of all rural communities, places with a not-so-distant past when country life dominated and within a span of a generation or two witnessed the en masse exodus to the cities. Very few of us can ignore nor deny the farm bloodline in our family and community histories.

Throughout the journey, change was an accepted part of life and accompanying that change was an equally resilient stability. People adapted to new challenges and brought with them a continuity from the past, a tradition that was remolded and reshaped into new meanings. It's like the old farmer who still thinks of Johnson grass as *abunai kusa* (dangerous grass) and because of that fact he doesn't hesitate in using both Paraquat and Roundup, two of the most potent herbicides manufactured, to keep those weeds in check.

We also witnessed the transference of culture, a heritage transmitted from one generation to another. Of course conflict existed and accommodation occurred, for example despite the geographical distances between family members, memorial services have survived as a time for family reunions. Such a family obligation was maintained although in the process a different type of tradition arose, the "proper" dates and years were hedged on and instead families grouped their services and combined the years together, thus, out-of-town *Sansei* children wouldn't need to give up too many weekends. Differences were mediated and tradition was redefined.

The immigration service certificate,
1899. Date of the Issei's arrival was
September 5, 1988 and having
passed through quarantine he was
admitted September 11, 1899.
On the back of the certificate he
translated the document's meaning:

> "From Japan
> to Seattle
> I've come,
> having passed
> inspection."

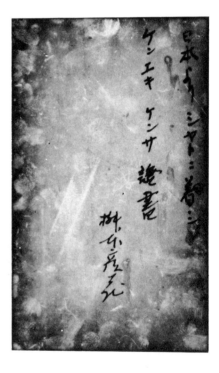

We live with ghosts or spirits around us, they are a sense of history that bonds all of us. Culture is alive and evolving, this book was simply a glimpse into this process, a collection of just a few of the hundreds of stories. The facts are not as important as the process of change and acceptance, what people believe to have happened remains vital to our understanding of a place and its history.

For we too are simply ordinary people with a universe passing by us and through us.

GLOSSARY

abunai - dangerous, perilous.

baachan - grandma, informal version of *obaasan* or grandmother.

baishakunin - matchmaker.

betsuin - used as a name for the Buddhist Church in Fresno.

buranketto - blanket, a pidgin California Japanese term.

butsudan - Buddhist altar.

futsu no hito - ordinary people.

gaman - perserverance.

gochisoo - good food.

hachimaki - headband, to tie a towel around one's head.

hakujin - Caucasian.

inaka - the country, rural area.

hana - can mean either nose or flower and also a name for a popular card game.

Issei - first generation Japanese in America.

Jiichan - grandpa, informal version of *ojiisan* or grandfather.

kanji - written characters, a complex series of strokes used as a written form of the Japanese language, originally Chinese ideographs.

Kibei - a second generation Japanese American who was born in America but journeyed to Japan for some education, often for years.

koden - donation given at a funeral.

kusa - grass.

Kyowakai - community club.

mochi - rice cake made often at the end of the year.

momo - to massage, from the verb "momu", to rub.

nenmatsutaikai - end of the year party or gathering.

Nihon - Japan.

Nihongo - Japanese language.

Nihonjin - Japanese person.

Nikkei - Japanese American.

Nisei - second generation Japanese American, born in America.

obaasan - grandmother.

obon odori - summer dance festival to honor the ancestors.

ON - duty, respect.

onsen - hot springs.

Oshogatsu - New Years Day celebration.

sake - rice whiskey.

samurai - warrior.

Sansei - third generation Japanese American.

sensei - teacher.

shaburin - to "shovel" or hoe, pidgin California Japanese for the word "shovel".

shibai - Japanese play or skit.

shoyu - soy sauce.

sushi - vinegary rice, often rolled or packed into small rolls.

tofu - soy bean curd

Yonsei - fourth generation Japanese American.

INDEX

abunai kusa (dangerous grass) 57,167,168,173,231
"adopted son" 192
Adult Buddhist Association/ABA 64,70-2
Aki Hardware 102-4
Alien Land Law 10,42,193,199,213
American Gothic 226
Armenians 6,94,95,122,125
Axis Alien registration 44
baby ("his farm") 172-3
baby shower 64,72,220
baishakunin (matchmaker) 30-2
bakape (gambling game) 19-23
Bank of Tokyo (Calif First Bank) 103-4
baptize 149,162
Bert's Del Rancho Rey 21,103-4
"blow outs" 73
boomtown 14-17
bootlegging 5,19-23
brown rice sushi 111-21
Buddha nature 145,147
Buddhism 146-58,161-3
Buddhist & Christian feud 82,150-2,201
Buddhist Sunday School 68-70,124,146-8
buranketto (blanket) boys 16
chiha (gambling game) 19-23
Chinese 6,61,116,153,166
Christmas cards 75
choba (funeral committee) 67-8
chokujin (cheaters) 195
community organizations 62-75
community picnic 66,72,82,99-107,124
community pot luck 4,72,83,118-21,160
"coolers" 29-30
corporation (farm) 176
crew bosses 9-10
cultural delivery 159-63

ABOUT THE AUTHOR

David Mas Masumoto, a *Sansei,* grew up in Del Rey, California. Throughout his life, he has written stories about the rural community, the land and its people.

Masumoto won the 1986 James Clavell National Japanese American Literary Contest and has received an award in the California Newspaper Publishers Contest. He has written numerous magazine articles and feature stories for a variety of publications including the LA Times and anthologies. A collection of his short stories, **Silent Strength**, was published in 1985 by New Currents International, Tokyo, Japan.

He has received a BA in sociology from the University of California, Berkeley and a MS in community development from University of California, Davis. He currently farms with his father on an eighty-acre peach, grape and raisin farm in Del Rey and writes.

Masumoto welcomes comments and inquiries. Write: 9336 E Lincoln, Del Rey, Ca. 93616.

Tom Uyemaruko graduated from CSU Fresno with a degree in graphic arts and continues to draw and paint. He also owns ands operates an eating establishment called Tommys in downtown Fresno. He wonders: "If I majored in fast food in college, perhaps I'd be working in art with fast food as a side line."

Glenn Hamamoto, with his wife Sherian, own and operate Sir Speedy Printing Center at 5102 N. West Ave in Fresno. Because it was a "different sort of job, a challenge," Hamamoto undertook Country Voices as a special project, a contribution to the Japanese American community.